Computer Technology for Middle School Students - KS3 (7-9)

O'Neil Duncan, PhD.

ISBN-13: 978-1503210189
ISBN-10: 1503210189

AUTHOR'S BIOGRAPHY

Dr. O'Neil Duncan is a Jamaican national and a teacher by profession. He has been in the field of computing for over 15 years. He holds a doctoral degree in Educational Leadership and Technology. Dr. O'Neil is also an author. He has one published book by Hodder Education that is used extensively in the Caribbean. His CSEC Information Technology book is highly sought after and is a favorite among Caribbean students. Dr. O'Neil is currently working on an Electronic Document Preparation and Management book. He also has an Advanced level Information Technology book available online. This Book covers both the CAPE Information Technology and Computer Science syllabus. O'Neil is also the author of the book 'Man Talk' that was published earlier this year.

Due to the lack of resources at the middle school or Key stage 3 (7-9) levels in Information Technology. Dr. Duncan has written this resource to satisfy this need. It covers all the topics that are relevant to the CSEC Information Technology and Electronic Document Preparation and Management. Both students and teachers will find this resource invaluable. O'Neil currently works at the John Gray High School and part time at the International College of the Cayman Islands as an Information Technology teacher .

Course Units

1   Keyboarding, Mouse Skills and Graphics Management

2   Computer Software

3   File Management

4   History of Computers

5   Computer Hardware - I/O Devices, Storage and the Processor

6   Research

7   Data Communication

8   Ethics

9   Problem Solving A, B, C

10   Word Processing A, B, C

11   Spreadsheets A, B

12   Database Management A, B

13   Desktop Publishing and Multimedia Management

Table of Contents

Learning Objectives

This unit is designed to help you develop the knowledge and skills so you can use a computer as efficiently as possible to perform work tasks. Upon completion, you should be able to:

- Use the keyboard and mouse to control the computer
- Manipulate text and graphics
- Use graphic tools to create or modify images consisting of patterns, figures, or logos.

Controlling the Movement of the Cursor

A cursor is a movable indicator on a computer screen identifying the point that will be affected when you perform your next task. The appearance of the cursor may differ depending on what type of task you are performing. Here are some examples as seen in "Mouse Properties" in the Windows 7 Control Panel.

Cursor Appearance	Description/Type of Task Performed
➤	<ul><li>Arrow.</li><li>Indicates where your next text input will be. Note: The arrow on your computer screen may look a little different.</li></ul>
I	**Text Cursor** Appears after you press the left button on your mouse. This indicates where your text entry will begin
⧗	**Busy** The computer is working
➤⧗	**Working in Background** The computer is doing something; if you want to remain in this application, you'll need to wait.

The Computer Keyboard

The keyboard is a typewriter-style device with keys that work as mechanical levers or electronic switches. The most often used English keyboard is the QWERTY keyboard, invented for the typewriter in 1868 by Christopher Sholes. Several different types of characters appear on individual keys, including **alphabetic**, **numeric**, **symbol**, **movement**, and **function** keys.

Types of Keys

A keyboard used with a Windows desktop computer contains the following groups of keys:

Typing [alphanumeric] keys. These keys include the same letter, number, punctuation, and symbol keys found on a traditional typewriter.

Control keys. These keys are used alone or in combination with other keys to perform certain actions. CTRL, ALT, the Windows logo key, and ESC are frequently used keys.

Function keys. Function keys are used to perform specific tasks. They are labeled as F1, F2, F3, and so on, up to F12. The way these keys are used differs from program to program.

Navigation keys. These keys are used for moving around in documents or webpages and editing text. They include the arrow keys, HOME, END, PAGE UP, PAGE DOWN, DELETE, and INSERT.

Numeric keypad. The numeric keypad is handy for entering numbers quickly. The keys are grouped together in a block like a conventional calculator or adding machine. [Note: most laptops do not have a separate numeric keypad.]

Below is an example of a typical keyboard layout for a Microsoft Windows desktop computer.

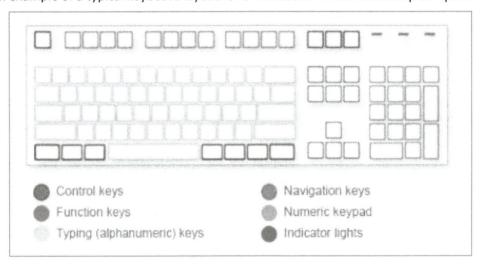

Letter Keys for Typing

The most often used letter keys are easier to reach; keys used less such as **Q, Z, or P** are found in the corners. The spacebar for entering a space as you type is centered at the bottom of the keyboard — for easy reach by either thumb. If you are typing all uppercase text, press the **Caps Lock** key, then release it when you want to return to typing in upper and lower case.

Using the Appropriate Keys to Enter Text

As you type, you press alphabetic and numeric keys and the spacebar to form words, sentences, and paragraphs. In addition to these keys, there are several other typing keys. Below are the most commonly used manipulation keys:

Press **SHIFT** in combination with a letter to type an uppercase letter.

Press **CAPS LOCK** once to type all letters as uppercase. Press CAPS LOCK again to turn this function off. Your keyboard may have a light indicating whether CAPS LOCK is on.

Press the **TAB** key to move the cursor several spaces forward. Note: You can also press the TAB key to move to the next text box on a form, such as an application for a job found on the Internet.

Press **ENTER** to move the cursor to the beginning of the next line. Note: In a Windows dialog box, press ENTER to select the highlighted button.

Press the **SPACEBAR** to move the cursor one space forward.

Press **BACKSPACE** to delete the character before the cursor, or the selected text.

Tip! Learn to touch type for efficiency. Touch typing means typing without looking at the keys, because you have memorized their locations on the keyboard. To touch type, you place your eight fingers in a horizontal row along the middle of the keyboard [the home row] and reach for other keys. You should be able to find touch typing lessons at Internet sites for free — or inexpensively.

Using Special Keys to Edit Text and Manipulate Documents

Many special keys serve important text editing and manipulation functions, saving time and effort.

Key:	Purpose/Use:
Delete	When pressed within text, deletes the letter to the left of the cursor. If pressed in a non-text area, removes one empty character space.
Insert [Ins]	Insert is a **toggle key**. Press **Insert** to switch between two modes: Insert or Overtype. In insert mode, pressing a key inserts a character at the cursor, forcing all characters past it one position further. [In Overtype mode, text typed replaces existing text. This is not used frequently.]
Num Lock	Num Lock or [⇧] is a key on the numeric keypad of most computer keyboards. It is a lock key, like Caps Lock. Once pressed, you can enter numbers from the number keys row on the main part of the keyboard. [On a desktop keyboard, pressing Num Lock isn't often necessary; instead, you can type numbers using the number keypad on the right side.]
Control [Ctrl]*	Ctrl is a modifier key; it does nothing pressed alone. Press Ctrl and then one or more keys to perform a special operation. For example, to copy a group of words you selected, press **Ctrl + C**. to paste the copied words, press **Ctrl + V**.
Alt*	Alt is a modifier key; like Ctrl, it also does nothing pressed alone. Press Alt and then one or more keys to perform special operation. For example,
Windows	The Windows logo key [also known as Windows key] is today a standard key on PC keyboards. Tapping this key produces the Windows Start menu where you can perform many operating system tasks.
Escape	The escape key is almost always located at the upper left corner of the keyboard. It is used in Microsoft software applications such as Word. Press **Escape** to cancel a current task, such as printing or spellchecking.
Function [F1 – F12]	Function keys are located on the top row of the keyboard. A function key is a key which has been programmed to cause the computer to perform a certain action. A commonly used function key is **F1**, which typically produces a help

	screen in Microsoft Office software applications.
Print Screen [Prt]	In Microsoft Windows, pressing Prt or Prt Scr ⏻ PrtScr will take an image the entire screen, which you can then paste into an application such as Microsoft Word. Or, you can edit the image before pasting it.

* Most keyboards today have duplicate sets of control and alt keys on the right of the spacebar.

Keyboard Shortcuts

A keyboard shortcut is a set of one or several keys that produces a software or operating system operation [in other words, cause an event] when triggered by the user. Often a keyboard shortcut can replace an event accessed either by clicking a menu or a button on your screen, saving you time. To use a keyboard shortcut, you must press a modifier key such as Ctrl or Alt, and then some other keys. Keyboard shortcuts vary by software application.

Tip! In many software applications such as Microsoft Word, click **Help** on the menu bar, or press the **F1** function key. In the search window, type **Keyboard Shortcuts** for a list of shortcuts available.

Keys for Cursor Movement/navigation

Most cursor movement keys that allow you to move around are located to the right of the letter keys. Press one key to produce one movement. Below are the actions of several cursor movement keys.

Press:	To Move the Cursor:
Enter	Down one line
Page Up	Up approximately one page, depending on the size of your screen and the amount of information it holds
Page Down	Down approximately one page, depending on the size of your screen and the amount of information it holds
Direction Keys	Up or down one line, or left or right one character. [Direction keys are sometimes called distance arrows.]
Home	To the beginning location in the document
And	To the ending location in the document
Spacebar	One blank space to the right

Deleting Text Using Special Keys

You're not limited to deleting a single character or word. You can also delete lines, sentences, and paragraphs at one time. Here are the basics of deleting text in an application such as Microsoft Word.

Delete a Single Character

Press **Backspace** to delete the character to the *left* of the text cursor.

Press **Delete** to delete the character to the *right* of the text cursor.

Delete a Word

Press **Ctrl + Backspace** to delete the word in to the left of the text cursor.

Press **Ctrl + Delete** to delete the word to the right of the text cursor.

Delete a Line of Text or a One-Line Sentence

- Place your text cursor immediately to the left of the line.
- Press **Shift + Down Arrow** to select the line. [The selection is highlighted.]
- Press **Delete** or **Del**.

Delete Multiple Lines, Sentences or a Paragraph

- Place your text cursor immediately to the left of the line.

- Press and hold **Shift.**

- Press **down Arrow** as many times as needed until all the lines are selected. [The selection is highlighted.]

- Press **Delete** or **Del**. After you make a deletion, any text to the right or below the character shifts to the left to close up the space.

Tip! For long periods of work at a computer keyboard, pay attention to how you sit. Below is an example of correct posture while using the computer. Notice that the arms are bent at a 90° angle and that the wrists are straight above the keyboard.

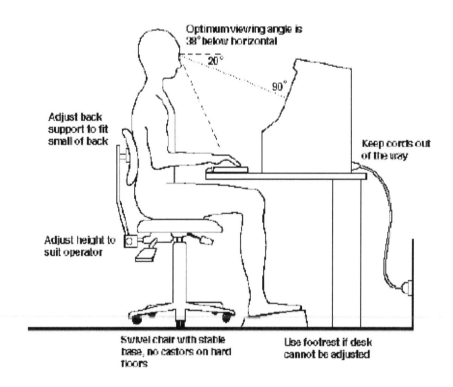

Keyboarding Skills

Please refer to the lessons in the document entitled **Keyboarding Skills Unit 1.docx** provided by your teacher.

Manipulating the Mouse

A Mouse allows you to communicate with areas, objects, or items on your computer screen. You can move objects, open them, change them, throw them away, or perform other actions, all by pointing and clicking with your mouse. A mouse typically has two buttons; a **left button** and a **right button**.

You will use the left button most often. Many mice also include a scroll wheel between the buttons to help you scroll through documents and webpages more easily. On some mice, the scroll wheel can be pressed to act as a third button.

Moving the Mouse Cursor

Your mouse is located next to your keyboard. Move the mouse up or down, or left or right; the cursor [sometimes called a mouse pointer] moves correspondingly on the screen.

Tips!

Since your hand will be on the mouse much of the time, here are some tips for using it more comfortably.

> Relax your hand as it rests on the mouse.

> Consider using a mouse pad beneath the mouse to provide more precise and avoid scratching a work surface.

> You may want to place a wrist rest, a small pad that cushions your wrist in front of the mouse.

Selecting and Dragging Items on the Desktop

You can select text. Or, you can select items, commonly called objects. To select text:

- Move your mouse just to the left of the first character of the text you want to select. [A text cursor appears at the insertion point.]

- Press the **left button**. Note: This is commonly termed **left click**.

- Press and hold the left mouse button.

- Move the mouse until the text you want is highlighted, usually in blue.

- Release the mouse button.

To select an object:

- Point to the object you want to select. The mouse cursor hovers on top of the object.

- Left click your mouse.

- Release the left mouse button. A box is placed around the object so you can work with it.

To drag the mouse while selecting:

- Press and hold the left button.
- Move the mouse without releasing the left button.
- When your selection is complete, release the left button.

Scrolling Within a Window

Bars called **Scrollbars** are automatically added to any window on your screen if there is more content than the screen can show. To scroll, point your mouse cursor on either the vertical or horizontal scrollbar, then drag up or down, or left or right. The arrow in the illustration below shows a good place to position your mouse pointer scrolling.

Manipulating Graphics

Construct an Image Using Lines and Shapes

Opening Microsoft Paint

Paint is a feature built into Microsoft Windows. It is used for creating images. To open Paint:

- Click the **Start** button .
- Click All Programs.
- Click Accessories.
- Click **Paint**.

Many of the tools you use in Paint are found in the **Ribbon**, which is near the top of the Paint window. This illustration shows the ribbon and other parts of Paint in Microsoft Windows 7.

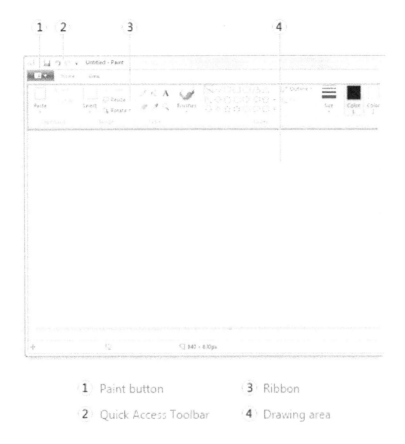

1 Paint button   3 Ribbon
2 Quick Access Toolbar   4 Drawing area

Drawing Lines

You can use several different tools to draw in Paint. The tool you use and the options you select determine how the line appears in your drawing.

The Line Tool

Use the Line tool ＼ to draw a straight line. You can choose the thickness of the line, as well as the appearance of it.

- On the **Home** tab, in the **Shapes** group, click the **Line** tool ＼.
- Click **Size**, and then click a line size, which determines the thickness of the line.
- In the **Colors** group, click **Color 1**, click a color, and then drag the pointer to draw the line.
- To draw a line that uses the Color 2 [background] color, right-click while you drag the pointer.
- [Optional] To change the line style, in the Shapes group, click Outline, and then click a line style.

Tip! To draw a horizontal line, press and hold the Shift key as you draw from one side to the other.

The Pencil Tool

Use the Pencil tool ✎ to draw thin, free-form lines or curves.

- On the **Home** tab, in the **Tools** group, click the **Pencil** tool ✎.

27

- In the **Colors** group, click **Color 1**, click a color, and then drag the pointer in the picture to draw.
- To draw using the Color 2 [background] color, right-click while you drag the pointer.

Brushes

Use the Brushes tool to draw lines that have a different appearance and texture—it's like using different artistic brushes. By using different brushes, you can draw free-form and curving lines that have different effects.

- On the **Home** tab, click the down arrow under **Brushes**.
- Click the artistic brush that you want to use.
- Click **Size**, and then click a line size, which determines the thickness of the brush stroke.
- In the **Colors** group, click **Color 1**, click a color, and then drag the pointer to paint.
- To paint using the Color 2 [background] color, right-click while you drag the pointer.

Curve Tool

Use the Curve tool to draw a smooth, curved line.

- On the **Home** tab, in the **Shapes** group, click the **Curve** tool.
- Click **Size**, and then click a line size, which determine the thickness of the line.
- In the **Colors** group, click **Color 1**, click a color, and then drag the pointer to draw the line.
- To draw a line that uses the Color 2 [background] color, right-click while you drag the pointer.
- After you have created the line, click the area in the picture where you want the arc of the curve to be, and then drag the pointer to adjust the curve.

Drawing Shapes

You can use Paint to add different shapes in a picture. The ready-made shapes range from traditional shapes—rectangles, ellipses, triangles, and arrows—to fun and unusual shapes, such as a heart, lightning bolt, or callouts [to name a few].

Draw a Ready-Made Shape

- On the **Home** tab, in the **Shapes** group, click a ready-made shape.

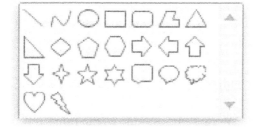

- To draw the shape, drag the pointer.
- To draw a shape with equal sides, press and hold the **Shift** key as you drag the mouse. For example, to draw a square, click the Rectangle , and then press and hold the **Shift** key and drag the mouse.

Change the Appearance of Your Ready-Made Shape

Use Outline Tools

With the shape still selected, you can use tools in the **Shapes** group to change its appearance.

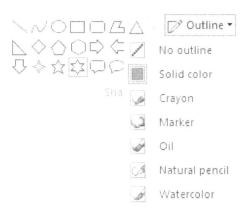

To change the line style, in the **Shapes** group, click **Outline**, and then click a line style.

If you don't want your shape to have an outline, click **Outline**, and then click **No outline**.

To change the outline size, click **Size**, and then click a line size [thickness].

Use Color Tools

With the shape still selected, you can use tools in the **Colors** group to change its appearance.

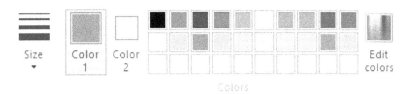

In the **Colors** group, click **Color 1**, and then click a color for the outline.

In the **Colors** group, click **Color 2**, and then click a color to fill the shape.

Use Fill Tools

With the shape still selected, you can use tools in the **Fills** group to change its appearance.

To change the fill style, in the **Shapes** group, click **Fill**, and then click a fill style.

If you don't want your shape to be filled, click **Fill**, and then click **No fill.**

Use Polygon to Make a Custom Shape

Use the Polygon tool ⬜to make a custom shape with any number of sides. This can be useful for creating figures made of two or three types of shapes, or even to build logos.

- On the **Home** tab, in the **Shapes** group, click the **Polygon** tool ⬜.
- To draw a polygon, drag the pointer to draw a straight line. Then, click each point where you want additional sides to appear.
- To create sides with 45- or 90-degree angles, press and hold the **Shift** key as you create each sides.
- Connect the last line to the first line to finish drawing the polygon and to close the shape.

With the shape still selected, you can do one or more of the following if you want to change the appearance of it:

To change the line style, in the **Shapes** group, click **Outline,** and then click a line style.

If you don't want your shape to have an outline, click **Outline**, and then click **No outline**.

To change the outline size, click **Size**, and then click a line size [thickness].

In the Colors group, click **Color 1**, and then click a color for the outline.

In the **Colors** group, click **Color 2**, and then click a color to fill the shape.

To change the fill style, in the **Shapes** group, click **Fill**, and then click a fill style.

If you don't want your shape to be filled, click **Fill**, and then click **No fill**.

Try it!

Draw a four-point polygon, then add a line [as we learned earlier] to any one of the sides. Below is a simple example.

Rotate and Flip Images

In the **Arrange** group on the ribbon, click **Rotate**.

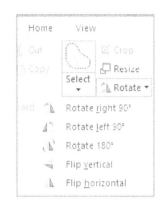

Click one of the following:

- Rotate Right 90°, Rotate Left 90° or Rotate 180°
- Flip vertical or flip horizontal.

Here's the same object, now rotated left 90°.

Saving Your Paint File

If you want to use your new image in other software programs, you will need to save the file. In Paint:

- Click **File.**
- Click **Save.**
- In **Save As**, click **Desktop** in the left navigation pane.
- Make up a name for your file, such as My File.
- Click **Save.** You are new image is saved to the Microsoft Windows desktop.

Summary

Using the tools in Microsoft Paint, you can create images such as a simple figure, diagram, or logo. Have fun experimenting!

Unit Summary

In this unit, you have learned about the following topics:

- Use the keyboard and mouse to control the computer
- Manipulate text and graphics
- Use graphic tools to create or modify images consisting of patterns, figures, or logos.

Practice Questions and Activities

1. Define the meaning of a cursor, and describe or show three types of cursors commonly seen in a Microsoft Windows software application.

2. What is meant by keyboard shortcuts — and how can they help you as you use a computer?

3. Using the polygon tool and Microsoft paint, create a logo for a sports team of your choice, or for the made up company "ABC widgets".

4. Demonstrate your understanding of image tools in Microsoft Paint as follows:

    a. Open Microsoft Paint

    b. Insert an object of your choice

    c. drag the object somewhere else on the screen

    d. Apply color and fill effects of your choice

    e. Rotate the object 90°, then flip it

    f. In the same document, draw a picture such as the Jamaican flag — or another object of your choosing

    g. Save the file and exit Paint.

5. Given a document from your teacher that includes text and one or more images, demonstrate your proficiency with the keyboard and mouse as follows:

    a. Select some text

    b. Make the text bold

    c. Italicize the text

    d. Press F1 [Help], and enter "keyboard shortcuts". Click the first link. Select an option to display keyboard shortcuts. Write one keyboard shortcut of your choice, and explain its function.

    e. Scroll to the top of the document, and then to the bottom of the document

    f. Delete any one sentence in the document

    g. Rotate an image, then flip it

    h. Save the file and exit the application.

Learning Objectives

This unit is designed to provide you with a general knowledge of popular business software and its function. Upon completion, you should be able to:

- Define the term software, and explain its purpose
- Differentiate function and purposes of system software and application software
- Describe the purpose of a word processor, and list three functions it can perform with text
- Describe the key operating systems and differences in their functionality.

What Is Software?

Computer software is a collection of programs that direct the operation of the computer. Programs are a set of instructions that produce a result.

Categories of Software

There are two types of software; **operating system** software and **application** software.

Operating System Software

Operating system software, also called system software allows the parts of a computer to work together by performing tasks such as transferring data between memory and disks or rendering output onto a display device. It also provides a platform to run high-level system software and application software. Examples of popular system software include Microsoft Windows, Mac OS X, and Linux. System software includes:

- **Utility programs** that help to analyze, configure, optimize and maintain the computer.
- **Device drivers** such as computer BIOS and device firmware that provide basic functionality to operate and control the hardware connected to or built into the computer, such as a printer.
- A **user interface** so you can interact with the computer. Since the release in 1985 of Windows 1.0, the graphical user interface [GUI] has become over time the most common user interface technology for personal computing.

Application Software

An application software program is software that causes a computer to perform useful tasks beyond the running of the computer itself. A specific instance of such software is called a software application, application program, application, or app.

The term is used to contrast such software with system software, which manages and integrates a computer's capabilities but does not directly perform tasks that benefit the user. The system software serves the application, which in turn serves the user.

Examples of application software include accounting software, enterprise software, graphics software, media players, and office suites. Many application programs, especially word processing deal mainly with documents. Applications may be bundled with the computer and its system software, or published separately.

What Is a Word Processor?

A word processor is a computer software application that, as directed by the user, performs word processing: the composition, editing, formatting and sometimes printing of any sort of written material. The term originated at IBM's Böblingen, West Germany Laboratory in the 1960s, and the application has evolved over the last 50 years. Typical features of a word processor include:

- Text entry and the option to use automatic text correction
- The functionality to copy text, cut [remove] it, or to paste it elsewhere in the document
- The selection of fonts [typefaces] and point size
- The application of attributes; applying bold, italics, underlining
- The use of bulleted or numbered lists
- Spell and grammar checking
- A built-in thesaurus.

Brands of Word Processing Software

The most widely used commercial software in the world is **Microsoft Word**®. Corel **WordPerfect**® is also used extensively by law firms and at academic institutions. Apache's **OpenOffice** is a completely free software suite that includes a robust word processing application. It can be downloaded and used completely free of charge for any purpose.

The Word Processing User Interface

We'll use Microsoft Word as an example of the user interface. To launch Word from Windows 7:

- Click the **Start** button in the lower left corner of your screen.
- Click All Programs.
- Click the program group **Microsoft Office**, and then from the submenu, choose **Microsoft Office Word [Year]**. The user interface for Microsoft Word's displays.

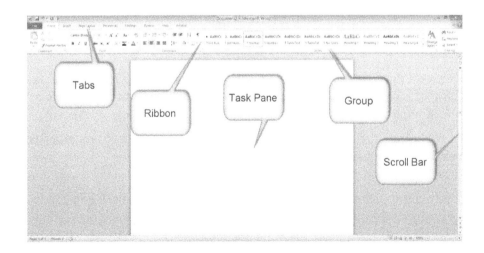

Note: If you use a different version of Windows, you will take similar steps to launch Word.

We'll describe some key functionality of the Microsoft Word window below.

A **ribbon** is a set of toolbars placed on several tabs; in Word, it's been available since 2007. The ribbon contains tabs that display different sets of controls, eliminating the need for many parallel toolbars from earlier versions.

Contextual tabs are tabs that appear only when the user needs them in context with the task to be performed. For instance, in a word processor, an image-related tab may appear when you select an image in a document so you can work with that image. Each tab contains many buttons for using Word's features. To display a different set of commands, click the tab name. For example, to view the Page Layout options, click the Page Layout tab.

Buttons are organized into groups according to their function. To access a feature, click its button. When you hover your mouse cursor over a button on the tab, a **Screen Tip** provides information about the button. Most buttons also contain a dialog box launcher in the bottom right hand corner. This button will open a **dialog** [small window with specific purposes] containing features related to that group.

Creating a New Document

To create a new, blank document, the easiest way is to press **Ctrl + N** [shortcut] on your keyboard. Or you can click the **File** menu and then click **New** as shown here.

A blank task pane opens providing a new, unnamed document.

The mouse cursor appears as a vertical bar that looks like this: |. This means the document is ready for text entry.

Entering Text and Applying an Attribute

An attribute in application software is a characteristic. Simple examples of an attribute are underline, italicize, or bold. Let's apply the bold attribute.

- Type a few short paragraphs of your choice.

- Hover your mouse cursor over one of the paragraphs, then **click** your mouse three times. [In Word lingo, this is called a triple-click.] The text in the entire paragraph is now selected.

- In the font group on the ribbon bar, click the **B** button. Notice that the paragraph now displays in **bold**.

To underline the text instead, keep the text selected, click the B button again to unbold the text, then click the **U** button.

Try it!

Experiment with other attributes in the font group. Remember that when you hover your mouse cursor over a button, a tooltip appears.

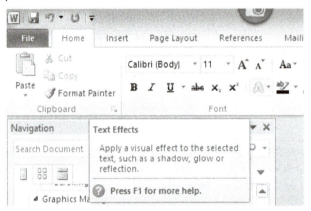

Save Your First Document

- Click the **File** menu option.
- Click **Save**.
- Enter a file name in the text field toward the bottom of the screen.
- Click the **Save** button in the lower right corner of the screen.

More about Operating Systems

As mentioned earlier, a personal computer or laptop operating system [OS] is a collection of software that manages computer hardware resources and provides common services for computer programs. Below are tasks that an operating system performs.

- Manage hardware and software resources of the system, including internal memory
- Provide a user interface, and run applications
- Send messages to applications or the user about the status of operations, or about errors
- Store, retrieve, and manipulate files
- Provide system tools called programs to monitor computer performance, debug, problems, or maintain parts of the system
- Manage information sent to output devices.

Examples of Operating Systems

Below is a description of operating systems in use today for personal computing.

OS	Description
Microsoft Windows	Microsoft Windows 1.0 was released in 1985. It replaced their command-based DOS operating system described below.
	There are drop-down menus, scroll bars, icons, and dialog boxes that make programs easier to learn and use. You're able to switch among several programs without having to quit and restart each one. Windows 1.0 ships with several programs, including MS - DOS file management, Paint, Windows Writer, Notepad, Calculator, and a calendar, card file, and clock to help you manage day-to-day activities.
	Later additions of Microsoft Windows were 2.0, 3.1, Windows for Workgroups 3.11, Windows NT [for an IT audience], Windows 95, 98, XP, Vista, and 7. The latest version, released on October 26, 2012. A free upgrade for a Windows 8 users to version 8.1 was released on October 17, 2013. Windows 8 and 8.1 provide a new user interface that permits the user to interact with the computer through a touchscreen.
MS-DOS	MS-DOS was released by Microsoft in a single user, single processing operating system created by Microsoft for use in personal computers.
	MSDOS uses a command-driven interface. It introduced a whole new language to the general public. Typing "C:" and various cryptic commands gradually became part of daily work. People discovered the use of the backslash [\] key.
	MS - DOS was effective, but also proved difficult to understand for many people. However the commands and MS-DOS remain in force as the foundation on top of which Windows operating system has been built.
UNIX	Ken Thompson, Dennis Ritchie, M. D. McIlroy, and J. F. Ossanna in 1969. Their goals were to develop a good operating system and to foster an environment for communication between its users.
	UNIX runs on many different types of computers. It's a multitasking operating system with both single user and network capabilities. Servers use to power Internet

	sites often run on UNIX. UNIX is not easy for a typical PC user to understand however, and there are few application software programs like The Microsoft office suite that run on UNIX.
Linux	Linux was created in 1991 by Linus Torvalds in Finland as a new free operating system kernel. Initially, Linux was based on the C programming language and is now available for free distribution under the GNU General Public License. Linux is used by many types of industries; government, education, business and nonprofits, scientific institutions, and home users with a technical bent.
OSX	OS X is the newest of Apple Inc.'s Mac OS line of operating systems. It is a Unix operating system built on technology developed at NeXT through the second half of the 1980s. Apple purchased the company in early 1997. Mac OS X v10.0 was released in March 2001. Since then, six more editions of Mac OS X were released, thereafter starting with Mac OS X v10.7 Lion. The most recent version OS X 10.9 Mavericks was first made available on October 22, 2013. OS X runs only on Apple computers. Although it offers operating system functionality similar to Microsoft Windows, the command structure and feature terminology are quite different.

Unit Summary

In this unit, you have learned about the following topics:

- Two main types of software are written for the computer; operating system software runs the computer, and application software allows you to perform tasks of different types.
- A word processor allows you to compose, edit, format and print either any sort of written material.
- Using features in the Microsoft Word ribbon, menus, and buttons, you can apply attributes to text that you have entered.
- Five operating systems exist today for use on personal computers and laptops.

Practice Questions and Activities

1. What is a tooltip?
2. When was Microsoft Windows 8 released?
3. What type of operating system software is used to control the functioning of the printer?
4. On what brand of computer does OS X run?
5. Why is MS-DOS in use today on computers running Microsoft Windows?
6. Discuss the main two types of software for a personal computer, and describe their general functionality.
7. Fill in the blanks in this sentence: Three brand names for word processing software are: _____, _____, and_____.
8. List four types of organizations or professions that use Linux.

9. Describe three attributes that can be applied to text using Microsoft Word.

10. What causes conceptual tabs to appear in Microsoft Word?

11. Use a word processor application to create one or two documents to demonstrate your understanding of using various features and tools such as select, bold, and underline. Explain how word processing makes it easy for you to change these attributes.

12. Find and circle 12 terms below about which you learned in this unit.

Unit 2 Terms

B	W	I	N	D	O	W	S	X	H	N	P
A	U	O	P	E	R	A	T	I	N	G	A
P	O	L	M	I	C	R	O	S	O	F	T
P	P	B	L	P	O	S	X	M	E	C	T
L	E	N	E	E	N	Q	L	E	K	N	R
I	N	S	O	F	T	W	A	R	E	G	I
C	O	I	N	T	E	R	F	A	C	E	B
A	F	L	H	D	X	I	S	G	G	Q	U
T	F	O	R	Z	T	B	E	O	F	N	T
I	I	M	M	B	U	B	C	N	Q	P	E
O	C	S	T	C	A	O	W	K	O	A	U
N	E	B	H	F	L	N	J	K	X	P	R

Windows	Attribute	Ribbon
OS X	Software	Contextual
OpenOffice	Application	Interface
Operating	Microsoft	Bullet

Learning Objectives

This unit is designed to help you develop skills in basic file management using both command-driven and graphical user interface operating systems. Upon completion, you should be able to:

- Enter commands using the MS-DOS command line
- Navigate in Windows Explorer and understand how to work with files and folders the Microsoft Windows Operating system
- Understand the purpose and use of common file extensions.

Use MS-DOS

MS-DOS, short for Microsoft Disk Operating System, is an operating system for x86-based personal computers. It was the most commonly used member of the DOS family of operating systems, and was the main operating system for IBM PC compatible personal computers during the 1980s to the mid-1990s. Then over time it was replaced by operating systems offering a graphical user interface [GUI], in particular by various generations of the Microsoft Windows operating system.

On a Windows computer, you can still use the MS-DOS command line to perform basic tasks files and folders in the operating system.   From the Windows 7 desktop, access the MS-DOS operating system as follows:

- Click **Start**.
- In the Run window, type **cmd** and press **Enter**. The command window appears. Notice that the default location is your own user directory on the C drive.
- Type **cd** and press **Enter.** The system is now pointed to the boot of the C drive.

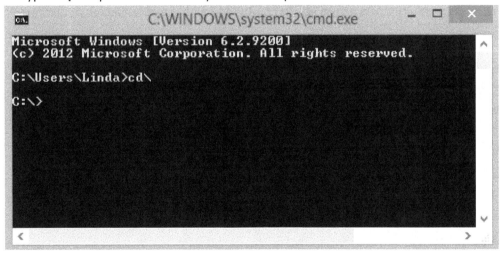

Tip! When you work with MS-DOS, take care to be very precise about how you type commands on the computer.

Formatting a Floppy Diskette

- Insert a floppy diskette into the A drive on the computer.
- Type **FORMAT A:** The computer formats the disk.

- At the prompt for a volume label, enter a name of up to 11 characters.
- Press **Enter**. You are prompted to format another disk.
- Type **Y** for yes, or **N** for no. If no, remove and label your newly formatted floppy diskette. If yes, repeat the format process.
- At the command prompt, type **Exit** to leave the MS-DOS command line. Your screen returns to the Windows desktop.

```
C:\WINDOWS>FORMAT A:
Insert new diskette for drive A:
and press ENTER when ready...

Checking existing disk format.
Verifying 1.44M
Format complete.

Volume label (11 characters, ENTER for none)?

    1,457,664 bytes total disk space
    1,457,664 bytes available on disk

        512 bytes in each allocation unit.
      2,847 allocation units available on disk.

Volume Serial Number is 153F-17D1

Format another (Y/N)?
```

For the remaining MS-DOS commands, you will see a brief explanation and then an example. Below that, there may be relevant notes.

Creating a Text File

This command starts the MS-DOS editor, which creates and allows you to change ASCII files.

> **edit C: soccerteam**

Notes.

> By default, MS-DOS appends the file extension of .txt after the filename.

> Windows 7 and 8 do not support an ASCII editor. The edit command should work with Windows Vista and earlier versions. In Windows 7, you can create a text file readable by DOS by using the Notepad utility.

Creating a Directory

You must first tell MS-DOS where you want to make the directory using the change directory command. Therefore two commands are required.

> **cd \users\owner**

> **md Sportsteam**

This creates a directory in the subdirectory owner called sportsteam. It will look like this:

\users\owner\sportsteam

Moving Within the Directory Structure

CD stands for change directory.

cd \users\owner

Copying a File from the Hard Disk to Other Secondary Storage Devices

Is command copies one or more files to another location.

copy c:\users\owner\soccer.txt e:

Note: Your target device may be represented by a letter different than E. Check this in the navigation pane in Windows Explorer.

Copying a File from a Secondary Storage Device to the Hard Disk

The copy command copies one or more files to another location.

copy e: soccer.txt c:\users\owner

Note: This is the reverse of the DOS command above.

Copying Files from One Directory to Another

The copy command also copies one or more directories to another location.

copy c:\users\owner\soccer.txt c:\users\public

Making a Copy of a Diskette [Disk Copy]

This command allows you to insert a floppy [the source], have MS-DOS copy its contents, and then remove it. When you are prompted to the target diskette, it will copy the stored contents automatically to the second disk [the target].

diskcopy a:

Important! Disk copy works only with floppy diskettes; it does not work with CDs, DVDs hard drives, or USB flash drives.

Copying All Files Within a Directory to Another Directory

With this command, you can copy every file in a source directory to a target directory.

diskcopy a:

Deleting Files, Directories, and Sub Directories

A directory must be empty before it can be deleted. To empty a directory:

cd \users\owner

del *.*

rmdir c:\users\owner

Note: Del *.* deletes every single file contained in the owner subdirectory. Use this command with caution!

Renaming a File or folder

This command allows you to rename a file or files.

ren \users\owner\soccer.txt \users\owner\football.txt

Note: You cannot specify a new drive or path for your destination file. Use MOVE to move files from one directory to another, or to rename a directory.

Backing Up and Restoring Files

The backup command places every file on the floppy diskette.

> **backup c:\users\owner*.* a:**

Note: This places every file from the owner's subdirectory at the root level on the floppy diskette, A: .

Use WINDOWS to Work with Files and Folders

The graphical user interface [GUI] in Microsoft Windows makes working with files and folders more visual and in MS-DOS.

 A **file** is an item that contains information—for example, text or images or music. When opened, a file can look very much like a text document or a picture that you might find on someone's desk or in a filing cabinet. On your computer, files are represented with icons; this makes it easy to recognize a type of file by looking at its icon.

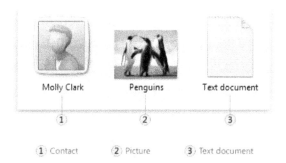

1 Contact   2 Picture   3 Text document

A **folder** is a container in which you can store files. If you had thousands of paper files on your desk, it would be nearly impossible to find any particular file when you needed it. That's why people often store paper files in folders inside a filing cabinet. On your computer, folders work the same way.

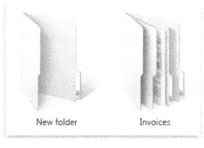

An empty folder (left); a folder containing files (right)

Understanding the parts of a window

Folders can also store other folders. A folder within a folder is called a subfolder. You can create any number of subfolders, and each can hold any number of files and additional subfolders.

Creating a Text File

- Click the **Start** button.
- In the search box, type **WordPad.**
- In the list of results, click **WordPad**.
- In WordPad, type your text. Note: Working with your text, you can change the font and point size, apply paragraph attributes, and insert images.
- Click the **File** menu, and then click **Save**. WordPad gives the document a default name and a file type of RTF [Rich text file, which is compatible with Microsoft Word]. But if you prefer, click the drop-down arrow in the **Save As Type** field, and select a different file type.
- Accept the default folder location, or use the navigation pane on the left to locate and select a different folder.
- Click **Save**.

Creating a Folder

You can create any number of folders, and store folders inside other folders [subfolders].

- Go to the location [such as a folder or the desktop] where you want to create a new folder.
- Right-click a blank area on the desktop or in the folder window, point to **New**, and then click **Folder**.
- Type a name for the new folder, and then press **Enter**. The new folder will appear in the location you specified.

Moving Within the Folder Structure

Windows Explorer provides an easy way to work with folders.

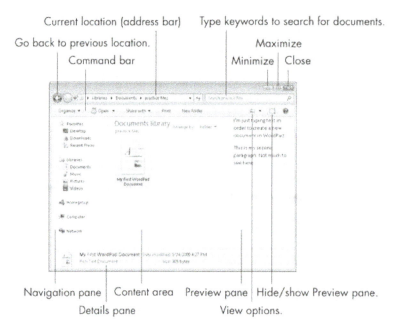

Current location (address bar)   Type keywords to search for documents.

Go back to previous location.   Maximize

Command bar   Minimize │ Close

Navigation pane │ Content area   Preview pane │ Hide/show Preview pane.

Details pane   View options.

By default, your folders are stored in the **Documents** folder in the **Libraries** section in the navigation pane.

- Click the **Documents** folder. All subfolders are displayed in the content area to the right.
- In the **content** area, double-click a folder to files it contains.

Copying a File from the Hard Disk to a Secondary Storage Devices [Universal Serial Bus]

- Plug a USB device such as a flash drive into an open USB port on the computer.
- Notice that Windows Explorer opens; the USB drive name appears with a letter in the Computer area of the navigation pane.
- Use the navigation pane to search for and locate the folder or computer location where the file is stored.
- Double-click the folder. The file opens in the content area.
- Carefully drag the file down to the USB drive as shown in the navigation pane. The device drive name is highlighted. [See illustration below.]
- Release the left mouse button. A copy of your file has been made on the USB drive.

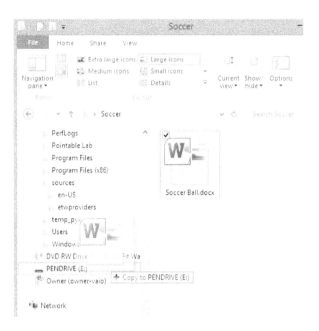

Copying a File from a Secondary Storage Devices to the Hard Drive

We will use Windows commands to demonstrate another way to copy files from device to device.

- Plug the secondary storage device into an open USB port on the computer.
- Notice that Windows Explorer opens; the USB drive name appears with a letter in the Computer area of the navigation pane.
- Double-click the secondary device name. Your file should appear in the content area.
- Point to the file and right-click. In the fly out menu that opens, click **Copy**.
- Navigate to a folder on the hard drive.
- Point to the folder and then right-click. Choose **Paste**.

Copying Files From a Folder to Another Folder

- Use the navigation pane to search for and locate the folder where the files are stored.
- Double-click the folder. The files open in the content area.
- Press and hold **Shift**. Click each file icon or filename you want to copy. [Each selected file should now be highlighted.]
- Right-click and select **Copy**. [Windows makes a copy of the two files.]
- Use the navigation pane again to locate the folder where you want to copy the files.
- Point to the folder, right-click and choose **Paste**. Your selected files have been copied to the destination folder.

Copying All Files Within a Folder to Another Folder

- Use the navigation pane to search for and locate the folder where the files are stored. [This is the source folder.]
- Double-click the folder. The files are displayed in the content area.
- Point to any one of the files, and press **Ctrl + A**. [All of the files should now be highlighted.]
- Right-click and select **Copy**. [Windows makes a copy of the two files.]

- Use the navigation pane again to locate the folder where you want to copy the files. [This is the destination folder.]
- Right-click and choose Paste. Your files have been copied to the destination folder.

Making a Copy of the contents of an External Device Using Disk Copy

Use the Live File System format when you want to burn a data disc that will play in a computer with Windows XP or later.

- Insert a writable disc, such as a CD-R, CD-RW, DVD-R, DVD-RW, or DVD+RW disc, into your computer's CD, DVD, or Blu-ray Disc burner.
- In the **AutoPlay** dialog box that appears, click **Burn files to disc using Windows Explorer**. Note: If the AutoPlay dialog box doesn't appear, click the **Start** button ⬤, click **Computer**, and then double-click your disc burner.
- In the **Burn a Disc** dialog box, type a name for this disc in the **Disc title** box, click **Like a USB flash drive**, and then click **Next**. [This is the option for burning a disc that uses the Live File System disc format. It might take several minutes for the disc to be formatted. When the formatting is complete, an empty disc folder opens.]
- Open the folder that contains the files you want to burn, and then drag the files into the empty disc folder. Note: To select more than one item, press and hold **Ctrl**, and then click the files you want to burn.
- Notice that as you drag files into the disc folder, they are copied automatically to the disc.

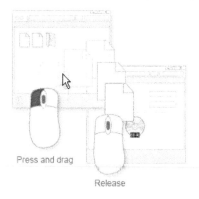

Press and drag

Release

- To close the disk onto which you just copied, in Windows Explorer, click the disc burner drive, and then click **Close Session** on the toolbar.

Tip! Instead of dragging and dropping files as described in the procedure above, you can select the files you want to burn in Windows Explorer, right-click one of the selected files, point to **Send to**, and then click your disc burner drive.

Deleting Files, Folders and Sub Folders

When you no longer need a file or folder, you can remove it from your computer to save space — and to keep your computer from getting cluttered with unwanted files. To delete a file:

- Open the folder or library that contains the file.
- Select the file or folder.
- Press **Delete** on your keyboard.
- In the **Delete File** dialog box, click **Yes**.

Note: Deleted files and folders are placed in the **recycle bin**. You may later restore them as described in the next section.

Restoring Files from the Recycle Bin

Until you take an action to restore them, all of your deleted files and folders remain in the recycle bin. To restore files or folders to their original location:

- Click the **Recycle** bin icon on your Windows desktop.
- Select the files you wish to restore. [The selection method will vary depending on the version of Windows you are using.]
- Click **Restore the Selected Items.** Windows moves the selected items back to their original location, and deletes them from the recycle bin.

Note: The instruction to restore items may differ a bit depending on the Windows version you are using.

Renaming a File or a Folder

You can easily rename files or folders using the Windows Explorer. However to avoid an error message, make sure that any file or folder you want to rename is saved and closed before you attempt this.

To rename a file:

- Open Windows Explorer.
- Right-click the file you want to rename.
- Select **Rename**. A text window opens, with the filename portion highlighted.
- Type a new name for the file.
- Press **Enter** to save the changes.

Important! Make sure that you keep the same file extension so you don't have a problem opening the file later in its native application.

To rename a folder:

- Open Windows Explorer.
- Right-click the folder you want to rename.
- Select **Rename**. A text window opens, with the folder name highlighted.
- Type a new name for the folder.
- Press **Enter** to save the changes.

Tip! Always check to make sure that Windows executed your command properly.

Backing Up and Restoring Files

Use Windows Backup and Restore utility to make a backup of your files and folders, or to restore one or all of them.

Backing Up Files

Open Backup and Restore by clicking the **Start** button ⚪, clicking **Control Panel**, clicking **System and Maintenance**, and then clicking **Backup and Restore**.

Do one of the following:

> If you've never used Windows Backup before, click **Set up backup**, and then follow the steps in the wizard. ⚪ If you're prompted for an administrator password or confirmation, type the password or provide confirmation.

> If you've created a backup before, you can wait for your regularly scheduled backup to occur, or you can manually create a new backup by clicking **Back up now**. ⚪ If you're prompted for an administrator password or confirmation, type the password or provide confirmation.

Notes:

- Back up your files to an external device and not on the computer where the data resides
- Always store media used for backups in a secure place to prevent unauthorized people from having access to your files.

After you create your first backup, Windows Backup will add new or changed information to your subsequent backups. If you're saving your backups on a hard drive or network location, Windows Backup will create a new, full backup for you automatically when needed. If you're saving your backups on CDs or DVDs and can't find an existing backup disc, or if you want to create a new backup of all of the files on your computer, you can create a full backup. Here's how to create a full backup:

Open Backup and Restore by clicking the **Start** button ⚪, clicking **Control Panel**, clicking **System and Maintenance**, and then clicking **Backup and Restore**.

In the left pane, click **Create new, full backup**.

Note: You will only see this option if your backup is being saved on CDs or DVDs.

Restoring Files

You restore files using the Restore Files wizard. You can restore individual files, multiple files, or all files in a backup. You can also restore just your files or files for all people that use the computer.

- Click **Start.**
- Click Control Panel.
- Click System and Maintenance.
- Click Backup and Restore.

- To restore your files, click **Restore my files**.

Manage your backups from this window.

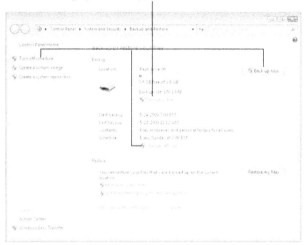

Do one of the following:

- To browse the contents of the backup, click **Browse for files** or **Browse for folders**.
- When you're browsing for folders, you won't be able to see the individual files in a folder. To view individual files, use the **Browse for files** option.
- To search the contents of the backup, click **Search**, type all or part of a file name, and then click **Search**.
- Choose the location to which you want the files restored.

Choose this option, in most cases.

You can either put the files back in their original location or in a new location. Select *In the Following Location* if you want to review the restored file before erasing your new version.

- Choose what to do with any preexisting copy of the file.

Choose what to do with duplicate files.

Select to apply your choice to all duplicates.

If you restore a file to a location that already contains a file of the same name, you'll be asked to choose one of the following:

- **Copy and Replace:** The file currently in the original location will be replaced by the file restored from backup.
- **Don't Copy:** The backed up version isn't restored. Nothing changes.
- **Copy, But Keep Both Files:** The original file will stay as is, and the restored file will include [2] in the filename.
- **Do This for All Conflicts:** Select this check box if you're restoring multiple files and want to apply the same choice to each duplicate filename.
- Click the link to **View Restored Files.** Your files have been restored and the folder containing the restored files opens.
- Click **Finish** to close the dialog box.

Adding a Password When Saving a File

The Windows operating system does not have built-in password protection for folders. However you can password protect Microsoft Office files as you are saving them. Here's an example using Microsoft Word.

Protecting the Document

- Click the **File** menu option.
- Select **Info**.
- Click the **Protect Docu**ment button.

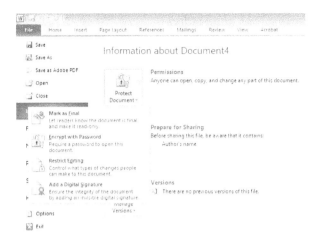

- Click Encrypt with Password.
- Enter a password, then click **OK.**

- Reenter the password as prompted, then click **OK**. Word notes that your document is password-protected.

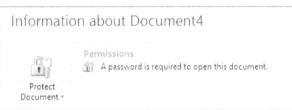

- Save your document as usual.

Using the Password to Open the Document

If you have password protected a file and send it to someone else, be sure to supply him or her with the password so you can be opened.

- Open the file as usual.
- A prompt appears to enter the password.
- Enter the password, and click OK.
- The document displays on the screen.

Note: Other products in Microsoft Office 2010 and above contain similar functionality.

Compressing and Decompressing Files and Folders

Windows has a built-in utility that allows you to compress files or folders in order to conserve file size space. We'll compress a folder as an example.

- In Windows Explorer, right-click the file or folder you want to compress.
- Click Send to.
- Click the compressed folder.
- Click **Yes** to place the compressed folder on the Windows desktop. It adds a file extension of **.zip** to the folder name.

- Double-click the folder to open it. It is decompressed and displayed in Windows Explorer for your use.

Working with File Extensions

All computer files have two-part names; the file name, and the **file extension**.

An extension is a suffix to the name of a computer file applied to indicate the file format of its contents or usage. The file extension identifies the type or category of software that was used to create the file so that the operating system or application software knows how to work with it.

File extensions are usually only three or four letter characters. Here is an example of a file extension, where XXX is the file extension:

myfile.XXX

As an example, for a Microsoft Word document:

- **myfile.doc** indicates a Microsoft Word file version no later than Microsoft Word 2003.
- **myfile.docx** indicates a Microsoft Word file beginning with version 2007.

The table below lists file types commonly in use.

Type:	Used for:
.gif	Graphic interchange format images
.txt	Plain text [created in notepad, WordPad, or saved as text from Microsoft Word]
.pdf	Portable document format file [Most commonly, created using Adobe acrobat]
.doc	Microsoft Word document [Or .docx for Microsoft Word open XML document]
.xls	Microsoft Excel spreadsheet
.zip	Zipped file [File that has been compressed through the use of compression software]
.rar	WinRAR Compressed Archive [Compressed Windows data files]
.com	MS-DOS [A file that issues commands to the MS-DOS system]

.sys	Windows system file [A file used by the operating system as it executes instructions.]
.mdb	Microsoft access database file
.jpg	JPEG image file [Compression for photos created by the Joint Photographic Experts Group]
.exe	Windows executable file [These are always files that execute programs.]
.bmp	Bitmap image [A mapping from some domain such as a range of integers] to bits]
.bat	DOS batch file [A series of commands to be executed by MS-DOS]
.ppt	PowerPoint presentation
.pps	PowerPoint slideshow
.dll	Dynamic link library [A data file in Microsoft Windows that is used by .EXE programs]

Unit Summary

In this unit, you have learned about the following topics:

- Although not used often today as a basic operating system, MS-DOS commands still form a foundation in Microsoft windows software. Commands such as copy allow you to duplicate files or directories.

- Many tasks formerly performed in MS-DOS can be performed more visually using the Microsoft Windows graphical user interface. Examples include navigating within a folder structure, copying files, deleting files, or password protecting individual files or folders.

- All computer files have two-part names; the file name, and the file extension. The file extension consists of period and three or four characters appended just past the filename. The file extension identifies the type software that was used to create the file so that the operating system knows how to execute or handle it.

Practice Questions and Activities

1. Answer these questions about MS-DOS:

   What does MS-DOS stand for?

   When was invented?

   By what company?

2. Working in Microsoft Windows, what action[s] do you take with the mouse to scroll through a document?

a) Click repeatedly in the text area

b) Click Bottom

c) Point to the scrollbar, and then Drag it up or down

d) None of the above.

3. In the Microsoft Windows operating system, what is the term used to identify a folder within a folder?

4. List the steps necessary to restore files from the Microsoft Windows Recycle Bin.

5. Open/Retrieve a document from a specified drive. For example, open a Microsoft Word document on a CD using the appropriate program.

6. Using a document from your class sessions, demonstrate that you can save it to a USB flash drive in the format native to the application. For example, from Microsoft Word, save a picture as either a .bmp or .jpeg file. How do you know that the file was saved successfully on the flash drive?

Learning Objectives

This unit is designed to help you gain develop an appreciation for the contributions made by early developers of computers through the various generations. You will also gain knowledge about various IT careers, and the impact of computers on society. Upon completion, you should be able to:

- State the definition of computer in simple terms
- Discuss the development of early computers
- Classify computers into five generations
- Describe the features of computers associated with each generation, and the differences in technology
- Discuss three purposes for which computers were used in and around the mid-1900s
- List and describe job roles in the information technology [IT] field.

A **computer** is an electronic device that can store, process, retrieve and send out information. Five generations of computing evolution have been classified.

The Five Generations of Computing Evolution

The abacus is noted as the first counting machine. Also called a **counting frame**, it is a calculating tool that was in use centuries before the adoption of the written modern numeral system. It is still used by merchants, traders and clerks in Asia, Africa, and elsewhere.

Then the French philosopher **Blaise Pascal** [1452-1519] invented and built the first adding machine called the PASCULINE. In 1890, **Dr. Herman Hollerith** proposed to the U.S Census Bureau that census data would be fed to the computer on punch cards to avoid tallying it by hand.

First Generation Computers: Vacuum Tubes

1940s-1955. Eventually, in 1946, **John Mauchly** and **J. Presper Eckert** invented the first electronic computer at the University of Pennsylvania. The device used electronic switches and radio vacuum tubes; it was known as the Electronic Numerical Integration and Calculation [ENIAC]. This device signaled the beginning of the first generation of computers. As you can see below, any act more than filled a room!

The CPU consisted of two parts: data processing unit — and the program control unit.

Second Generation Computers: Transistor-Based Computers

1955-1964. This generation was mainly characterized by the shift from vacuum tubes to transistor technology. A **transistor** is a small electronic device containing a semiconductor with at least three electrical contacts, used in a circuit as an amplifier, a detector, or a switch.

Memories were made up of magnetic ferrite cores. Input-Output processors were used to supervise I/O operations, thus allowing the CPU to handle the more important operations. Computer manufacturers began to provide system software such as compilers, subroutine libraries, and batch monitors. The operating system was introduced. Below are two examples of transistors.

Third Generation Computers: Introduction of Integrated Circuits

1964-1971. Transistors were replaced by Integrated Circuits [IC]. This resulted in a substantial reduction in physical size — and cost.

Then semiconductor memories replaced the magnetic ferrite cores in main memory. RAM and ROM became the main memory types. Eventually, there was widespread use of operating systems. Mass production of small lower cost computers called minicomputers began.

Fourth Generation Computers: Large scale Integration/Miniaturization; The chip

1971-2013. Fourth generation computers involve the use of thousands of integrated circuits called Very Large Scale Integration [VSLI]. Very-large-scale integration [VLSI] is the process of creating integrated circuits by combining thousands of transistors into a single chip called a microprocessor. VLSI began in the 1970s when complex semiconductor and communication technologies were being developed, making it possible to fabricate an entire CPU, main memory or similar device with a single integrated circuit that can be mass-produced at a very low cost. This has resulted in new classes of machines such as inexpensive personal desktop computers and laptops, as well as high performance parallel processors that contain thousands of CPUs.

Fifth Generation Computers: Today's Computers

Present-Future. Today we have ultralight notebooks and tablets, as well as smart phones, really just a small computer. However the fifth generation continues. Computing devices, based on artificial intelligence, are still in development, though there are some applications, such as voice recognition, that are being used today. The use of parallel processing and superconductors is helping to make artificial intelligence a reality. Quantum computation and molecular and nanotechnology will radically change the face of computers in years to come. The goal of fifth-generation computing going forward is to develop devices that respond to natural language input — and are capable of learning and self-organization.

In summary, the highlights of each generation are shown below.

Generation	Highlights
First	Vacuum tube; ENIAC at the University of Pennsylvania
Second	Transistor-based computers; input-output processors; software for compiling, subroutine libraries, and batch monitors
Third	Integrated circuits,; semiconductors; RAM and ROM
Fourth	VLSI; single integrated circuits; personal computers; high performance parallel processors
Fifth	Ultralight laptops, tablets; artificial intelligence; voice recognition; nanotechnology; natural language input

Uses of Early Computers

The Census. What was to become the precursor to the electronic computer was developed for the United States Census of 1890. After the 1880 census was done entirely by hand, taking over seven years to complete. Herman Hollerith went about creating a machine that would tabulate the results. The key idea to Hollerith's method was to record all of the data on to cards similar to the original computer punch cards. He got the idea for this method from watching a conductor punch out a description of an individual on a train. " . . . Light hair, dark eyes, large nose, etc." They were making a "punch photograph" of each person. The beauty of Hollerith's method was that once the cards were punched, tabulation was easy. His method cut the census time down from seven years to two and a half years.

Mathematic and Office Calculations. Before the computer entered the office of the modern day business, three key office machines occupied all businesses; the typewriter, a filling system, and an automated adding machine. To produce these mechanical office devices four main suppliers came forward. In 1928, Remington Rand led this business with sales of $60 million, followed by National Cash Register [NCR] with sales of $50 million, and then Burroughs Adding Machine Company with sales of $32 million. In fourth, lagging behind, was IBM which had sales of around $20 million. In the 1930s, with Thomas Watson at the helm, IBM leaped over the other three with sales of $21 billion.

Payroll and Counting. The LEO I [Lyons Electronic Office I] was the first computer used for commercial business applications. Overseen by Oliver Standingford and Raymond Thompson of J. Lyons and Co., LEO I ran its first business application in 1951. In 1954 Lyons formed LEO Computers Ltd to market LEO I and its successors LEO II and LEO III to other companies. LEO Computers eventually became part of English Electric Company [EELM] and then International Computers Limited [ICL] and ultimately Fujitsu.

Lyons used LEO I initially for valuation jobs, but its role was extended to include payroll and accounting, turned inventory. One of its early tasks was the elaboration of daily orders which were phoned in every afternoon by the shops and used to calculate the overnight production requirements, assembly instructions, delivery schedules, invoices, costing, and management reports. LEO series computers were still in use until 1981.

Types of Roles in Information Technology

As the fourth generation of computing has evolved, many work roles in information technology have also evolved. Key positions in IT fields are described below.

Systems Analyst. A systems analyst investigates and analyzes business problems and then designs information systems that provide a solution, typically in response to requests from their business or a customer. He or she gathers requirements and analyzes the costs and the time needed to implement the project.

Key Skills Required: Ability to extract and analyze information; good communication and persuasion skills; sensitivity

Software Engineer or programmer. A programmer or computer software engineer is responsible for the design, development, testing, and deployment of the computer software used in businesses and homes every day. Two primary classifications exist for this role; computer applications engineer, and computer systems software engineers. The computer applications engineer designs programs to run the computer; the computer system software engineer designs software to meet the needs of users of the computer. He or she understands how both software and hardware function and spends time talking with clients and colleagues to understand solutions that are needed.

Key Skills Required: Knowledge of programming, data structure and database system concepts; software testing capabilities; attention to detail; understanding of usability concepts; strong oral and written communications capabilities; analysis; logical thinking; teamwork; attention to detail

Database Administrator. The database administrator [DBA] oversees all aspect of the businesses database structure. This includes architecture, design, implementation, administration, monitoring, tuning, backup, migration, and support. He or she will design databases, architect data warehousing, automate and test database tasks, monitor database utilization and platforms, restore corrupted databases, install and test upgrades and patches, implement security and encryption, and recommend new database technologies.

Key Skills Required: Technical and analytical abilities; an understanding of database architecture; script writing; an understanding of security; good communication skills, especially for work within the IT organization.

Network Administrator. The network administrator oversees the administration, management, and maintenance of computer network systems and data circuits. This may include upgrading installing in troubleshooting networks, network hardware devices, and software. He or she maintains hardware inventory, develops and documents standards for network operations, and recommends and schedules repairs to the network.

Key Skills Required: Technical aptitude; strong analytical skills; solid oral and written communication skills, teamwork, and a sense of confidentiality

Computer Engineer. A computer engineer is responsible for designing, developing, and testing computer hardware, including computer systems, circuit boards, computer chips, keyboards, routers, and printers. He or she supervises the manufacturing, production, installation of the parts.

Key Skills Required: Knowledge of hardware and software component, analysis and evaluation; computerized design skills; testing skills

Computer Technician. The systems engineer is responsible for the oversight of an organization's information systems. He or she coordinates system development tasks including design, integration, and formal testing and oversees all transitions into production. The systems engineer also develops system specifications, and technical and logistical requirements. Is person also creates and maintains documentation about the system and manages and documents system configurations.

Key Skills Required: Technical aptitude; strong coordination, organization, teamwork, and communication abilities; teamwork; ability to work under pressure and deadlines

IT Security Analyst. The person in an IT security analyst role maintains the security and integrity of data throughout an organization. He or she analyzes security measures and determines their effectiveness as well as implementing any training regarding taking proper security measures. This individual works with both IT professionals and organization management to identify, communicate about, and solve systems compromises. Often security analyst also creates documentation to help prevent future security breaches.

Key Skills Required: Strong knowledge of information system security principles and practices; experience with intrusion detection systems; ability to evaluate and develop solutions; an understanding of security for the intranet and extranet; good communication skills to interface with the IT organization

Technical Sales Engineer. Technical sales is possibly one of the least hands-on technical roles, but it still requires an understanding of how IT is used in business. A technical sales person they sell hardware or explain the business benefits of systems and/or services. Work involves identifying customer prospects, meetings, conferences, and drafting proposals. A sales engineer has sales targets and earns commission for completed sales.

Key Skills Required: Product knowledge; persuasion and interpersonal skills; drive, mobility, and business awareness

Software Tester. Bugs can have a massive impact on the productivity and reputation of an IT firm. Testers try to anticipate all the ways an application or system might be used, and how they can fail. They don't necessarily program, but they do need a good understanding of code. Testers prepare test scripts and macros, and then analyze results for the project leader so that corrections can be made. Testers may also be involved at the early stages of projects to anticipate pitfalls before work begins.

Key Skills Required: Technical aptitude; attention to detail; creativity; good organization skills; analytical and investigative thinking; communication skills

Computer Forensics Expert. Forensic specialists uncover digital data such as email, correspondence, or erased files and preserve it for later use as evidence. They also determine how hackers or other unauthorized personnel gain access to information or computer systems, and how they navigated within those systems.

Key Skills Required: Technical skills working with operating a network systems, encryption programs and data retrieval procedures; analytical and investigational skills; communication skills both for use in court, in writing, and with the investigative organization

Web Designer. A web designer designs, creates, and modifies websites. He or she analyzes user requirements and then designs, creates, and modifies websites, often enhancing the content with sound, pictures, graphics, and video clips.

Key Skills Required: Programming; critical thinking; systems analysis; decision-making; strong oral and written communication skills

User Interface Expert. The user interface expert partners with product management and engineering to define, design, and implement solutions for a positive user experience with webpages or a website. This often involves creating wireframes, storyboards, flowcharts, and site maps to communicate interaction and design ideas. He or she also works with end users to evaluate the success and usability of the design. Often this individual will document design guidelines, best practices, and standards.

Key Skills Required: Proficiency using HTML, cascading style sheets, graphics software, and languages such as JavaScript for rapid prototyping; solid visual design skills and presentation skills to share them with others; problem-solving skills, and strong communication skills.

Software Trainer. A software trainer teaches individuals how to use one or more computer programs. He or she must learn to use the software the same manner as the user, and then determine how to present concepts and materials effectively to individuals who may have a wide variety of readiness for learning. Software trainers often partner with instructional designers, training managers, and business partners during the instructional design phase, pilot programs, and evaluation of training effectiveness.

Key Skills Required: Ability to understand concepts, workflows, and nuances of software; teaching skills; flexibility to adapt to different training settings and audiences; strong oral and written communication skills, a high degree of patience, analysis skills training evaluation.

Help Desk or Tech Support Specialist. A help desk or tech support specialist performs troubleshooting for IT hardware, software, and communications problems. These types of specialists work for hardware manufacturers and suppliers solving the problems of business customers or consumers. Many also work for end-user companies supporting, monitoring and maintaining workplace technology and responding to users' requests for help. Some lines of support require professionals with specific experience and knowledge, but tech support can also be a good way into the industry for graduates.

Key skills required: Wide ranging tech knowledge; problem solving; communication/listening; patience; diplomacy.

Technical Writer. A technical writer is a professional writer who analyzes the audience for produces technical documentation for technical, business, or consumer audiences. Documentation includes manuals, user guides, white papers, design specifications, or online help materials.

Key skills required: Technical proficiency with the subject matter; writing skills; analysis skills for task analysis; flexibility, especially if the subject matter is under development; the ability to collaborate with subject matter experts [SMEs] and others who may have responsibility for the successful outcome of the products delivered.

Insights Regarding Today's IT Roles

As computer technology forges ahead, new types of IT roles will evolve. Today's IT professional may work in a very large organization where the job role is highly specialized, or may work in a smaller shop setting where one or more of these roles are combined. And in some IT shops small or large, some of the roles and/or work may be outsourced [contracted out] to fill role gaps.

As business conditions expand and contract, many of these job roles — formerly occupied by in-house employees of companies — have shifted to contractor roles. The work is often similar, but while contractors often make excellent money, they do not enjoy benefits such as health insurance, higher education or training assistance, or necessarily job security.

Unit Summary

In this unit, you have learned about the following topics:

- A computer is an electronic device that stores, processes, sends or receives information.
- The development of the computer as we know it today is based on four generations, beginning with vacuum tubes. The "fifth generation" is in progress.
- Early computers were used for three main purposes; census entry and tabulation, mathematical and office calculations, and payroll and accounting/inventory.
- Many job roles exist in the IT field. For example, one can be a programmer, analyst, engineer, web designer, trainer, or IT support specialist.

Practice Questions and Activities

1. In the matching exercise below, review the listed IT roles. Place the letter of the corresponding job description in the leftmost column.

	IT Role		Description
_____	Computer forensics expert	a)	Analyzes needs; creates websites, often adding sound and visual effects
_____	Software trainer	b)	Secures and maintains integrity of data; analyzes compromises
_____	Web designer	c)	Administers, manages, and maintains computer data systems and data circuits
_____	Systems analyst	d)	Identifies and designs software to meet business needs or solve business problems
_____	IT security analyst	e)	Uncover digital data; preserves it as evidence; writes documentation
_____	Database administrator	f)	Instructs individuals about how to use computer software programs

_____	Software engineer or programmer	g)	Administers architecture, monitoring, tuning, and data integrity of all databases
_____	Network administrator	h)	Designs and develops operating system or application programs
_____	Software tester	i)	Prepares scripts, test software; determines whether it is achieving its purpose

2. List the first four generations of the evolution of the computer including one highlight of each.

3. Research and complete a project that illustrates the generations of computers — and the people who made inventions in each generation. Your project could be a collage, a diorama, or a video.

4. Share the highlights of your project — and one or several of your classmates

5. Construct and use an abacus to perform calculations. Tip: Research types of abacuses and their use in history on internet sites such as Wikipedia – or Google images.

Unit 5: Computer Hardware: Input/Output Devices, Storage, and the Processor

Learning Objectives

This unit is designed to help you understand the role and functions of the processor and input and output devices. Upon completion, you should be able to:

- Describe several types of input devices — and their advantages and disadvantages
- Define and classify output devices according to their function
- Describe the function of the computer's processor and how each component works
- Discuss processing speeds and unit of measurement for a computer
- Explain the relationship between bit, byte, kilobyte, megabyte, gigabyte, and word size
- Describe the arithmetic operations necessary to convert decimal numbers to binary numbers for use in computer processing
- Describe the characteristics of primary and secondary storage devices
- Differentiate between primary and secondary storage devices
- Explain how a computer stores data.

Input Devices

An input device is any piece of computer hardware equipment, known as a peripheral that is used to provide data and control signals to an information processing system such as a computer.

The Keyboard

The evolution of the keyboard began with the invention of the typewriter in 1860s.

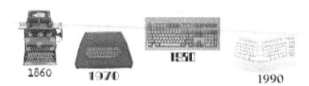

Computer keyboards can be classified by the switch technology that they use. Computer keyboards have 80–110 durable switches, one for each key. For years, the QWERTY keyboard has been the most standard input device for entering information into a computer.

Several different types of keyboards are available on the market today.

Tip! As a computer user, you should always consider the ergonomics of your keyboard. That is, the device should be designed to keep your arms and hands from becoming overtired or from aching, especially if you are keyboarding for long periods.

The traditional keyboard for a desktop computer has been around since the 1970s. In recent years, many keyboards have been made more ergonomic, featuring a softer touch when pressing the keys, more built-in function keys, and even including pointing devices such as a touchpad or trackball.

In a split keyboard, the QWERTY keys are divided in half to provide a more comfortable typing angle for the arms. The spacebar is widened to be easily reachable from either side. Often a wrist rest is built into the keyboard to provide wrist support as you type.

Wired vs. Wireless Keyboards

Traditional keyboards are wired; that is they connect to a computer using a cord that plugs into your computer. A wireless keyboard uses radio frequency [RF], infrared [IR] or Bluetooth technology to communicate with the computer. Often wireless keyboards include or can be paired with a wireless mouse.

Pros and Cons of Wireless Keyboards

Wireless keyboards use batteries for power; the batteries must be recharged periodically. You can mold a wireless keyboard around for increased comfort since it is not attached to the computer.

Wired keyboards do not need to be recharged, but they can only be placed as far as the cord allows from the computer.

Membrane Keyboard

A membrane keyboard is a computer keyboard whose keys are not separate, moving parts. Rather they are pressure pads with only outlines and symbols printed on a flat, flexible surface.

Pros and Cons of a Membrane Keyboard

Membrane keyboards are well suited for places where there is a risk of liquid spilling on the keyboard, such as a lab or manufacturing facility, or where there is dirt, as in a construction project.

Membrane keyboards are not well suited for day-to-day keyboard work at a desk; they do not provide strong touch feedback mechanically to the fingers. Therefore, you may make more typing errors. And they are not very ergonomic.

As an alternative to a keyboard, voice recognition software allows you to talk to the computer, replacing or reducing the need for typing. While there is some learning curve, many people find using their voice quicker than typing text. For people with arm or hand injuries or disabilities, voice recognition may be the only to use a computer at all.

Laptop Keyboards

A typical laptop keyboard layout has typewriter keys, shift keys, function keys, and cursor control keys. There usually isn't room for a number keypad on the right side due to the smaller overall size of a laptop. Laptops include a touchpad, described in the next section, so a mouse is not a requirement.

Input Devices: Pointing Device

There are variety of device types for moving the mouse cursor and selecting buttons or objects.

Mouse or Trackball

A mouse moves the cursor as you slide your arm across a smooth surface. Below the mouse surface is a roller ball with sensors that send information to the computer which then moves the mouse cursor on the screen. An optical mouse works similarly, but uses visible or infrared light instead of a roller-ball to detect the changes in position.

Touchpad

A touchpad is a flat device with sensors inside. As you move your fingers, the sensors transmit signals to your mouse cursor on the computer, allowing it to move. Touchpads are sold separately for use with desktop computers, and they are also included in laptops.

Touchpads can be beneficial to people for whom using a mouse is difficult.

Input devices: Source Data Entry

A **source data entry device** is anything which feeds data into the computer directly from its source. Commonly used source data entry devices are scanners, bar code readers, motion detectors, or light pens. The scanner is the device most commonly used with a computer in an office environment.

Scanner

A scanner is a device that captures images from paper, including pictures, posters, or magazine pages. Most scanners can capture both black-and-white or color images.

You can then use software such as Adobe Photoshop to size or modify the image.

Scanners are also used to create an image of a text page. Once on the computer, the text image can be "read" by optical character recognition [OCR] software and then translated to real text for use in software such as a word processor.

Touchscreen

A **touchscreen** is an electronic visual display that you control through simple or multi-touch gestures by touching the screen with one or more fingers. Using the touchscreen you can react to what is displayed and even control the size of what is displayed.

Many tablet and all-in-one computers running Windows 8 have a touchscreen display.

Touchscreen devices allow you to move the mouse cursor, or open or switch applications. You still need a keyboard for entering text information.

Tablets such as the Apple iPad or the Google Nexus also use touchscreen technology.

Multimedia Input

Multimedia is a mixture of different media — such as text, video, audio, graphics and data — that work together to provide you with all of the computing functions you need. To use multimedia, you rely on a team of input and output devices that are responsible for both transmitting and receiving information between you and the computer.

Input devices include keyboard, mouse, scanner, digital camera or a camera built into the computer.

Terminal Device

A terminal device is a combination of a computer monitor and keyboard to input data and to view it. A terminal does not necessarily include a processor.

Biometric Device

Biometrics involves the identification of a human by his or her characteristics or traits. Biometrics are used in with computers for identification and access control. Most commonly, a biometric reader will examine your fingerprint — or your face.

For your face, a biometric device views an image or video of you and stores it in the computer. It considers many aspects of your facial structure. A fingerprint reader simply takes a picture of your fingerprint and compares it to information about your fingerprint stored in the computer. Just as entering the correct password, if there is a match, you are allowed to proceed to your next task, such as working with the computer.

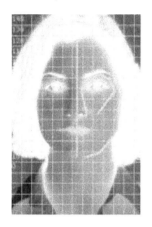 

Cameras and Microphones

Cameras can be built into a computer monitor or laptop. Typically you press a button in a software application to tell the computer to take a picture. The image is taken of whatever's in the front of the screen. A Digital Camera can also serve as an input device to a computer. To move the picture to the computer, you either use a cable to connect the camera to the computer, or remove a storage card from the camera and insert it into or attach it to the computer.

With a **microphone**, you to speak and send sound to your computer. It can be used to add text using a voice recognition software program, or to speak through the computer with another person as part of an online meeting or conference call.

Advantages and Disadvantages of Input Devices

There are pros and cons for each input device. Many have been mentioned earlier in this unit. As you consider the use of device, think about its primary purpose, and your needs. It's quite possible — or even probable that you will need more than one input device; a keyboard, a computer screen, and a pointing device, plus perhaps a microphone and/or a scanner.

Output Devices

An output device is any piece of computer hardware equipment used to send the results of data processing by a computer, converting the electronically generated information into human-readable or viewable form. Below are descriptions of commonly used output devices.

Monitor

A monitor is a television-like device used to display data. Regardless of the type of monitor, the display is made up of illuminated dots called pixels. In 2014, any new monitor purchased will be what is described as a flat panel screen or a flat-panel display. Flat panels are much more lightweight than the old monitors, have much better graphics resolution, and can be moved easily to another workspace if necessary.

A **pixel** is the smallest amount of the screen that can be changed by the computer; a single point in a graphic image.

Resolution refers to the sharpness and clarity of the image. It is a measure of the number of pixels displayed on the screen, such as 1024x768. This means that the screen can display 1024 distinct dots on each of 768 lines, depending upon the size of the monitor. The higher the resolution of the pixels, the greater the detail that can be displayed.

Printer

A printer is a computer peripheral that places text or a computer-generated image on paper. Several terms are important to understand about printers.

Print speed is a description of how many pages can be printed per minute.

Print quality describes how well-formed the characters are when printed; examples are draft, normal, best or custom quality.

Print Resolution is a measure of the number of dots per square inch. For example, a 300-dpi [dots per inch] printer is capable of printing 300 distinct dots in a line one inch long. This means it can print 90,000 dots per square inch.

Print buffer is a storage area, usually in the printer, which receives the information to be printed and stores it until it is printed.

Printers for everyday use come in two types; laser printers and ink jet printers. Although they may look the same on the outside, there are differences in how they produce print.

An **inkjet** printer uses ink which it sprays onto paper in a series of tiny dots as the printer head moves across the paper to recreate the text or image. **Laser printers** use toner, electrically charged powder, which is fused with the paper fibers to produce an image. This fusing process means laser printouts will not smudge or blur because unlike an inkjet printer, the paper does not need to dry.

Toner for laser printers is more expensive than ink for inkjet printers, but laser printers will print more pages for a longer amount of time because of the larger size of a toner cartridge compared with a small inkjet cartridge, as seen below.

Inkjet Printer   **Laser Printer**

Plotter

A plotter is an output device which moves one or more pens across paper to produce an output of graphical data. Printing is achieved by the drawing of continuous lines. Architects, surveyors and engineers use plotters to output their work – maps, charts, or engineering drawings. Some of the images that would had been printed to a plotter in the late 1990s or early 2000s are now instead printed to a large-format inkjet printer.

Multimedia Projector

A **multimedia projector** is an output device that projects an image from a computer onto a screen. Images transmitted from the device are then transmitted into a special digitized light that is reflected on thousands of mirrors in the projector, which shines the image onto a screen. Multimedia projectors, often referred to as LCD projectors, are used most commonly to make presentations in a training session or meeting. The projector is connected to a computer through a special cable equipped to handle in transfer the graphics to the projector.

Ultra-light multimedia projectors often weigh very little and can fit in a laptop that; they are ideal for people who frequently use projectors for presentations away from the office. **Conference room projectors** are heavier and brighter, making them better suited to large rooms.

Document Camera

A document camera is an image capture device for displaying printed information or a multi-dimensional object to an audience. Document cameras are similar to sophisticated web cameras, but they are mounted on arms so they can be placed over object or a page. Typical applications for a document camera include classrooms, meetings, training sessions, videoconferences, courtrooms or medical applications.

Audio Output Devices

The term **audio output device** refers to an audio device that attaches to a computer for the purpose of playing sound, such as music or speech. Examples include speakers, headphones, or earbuds. Regardless of the type, each attaches to the computer, typically either through a "line out" jack – or a USB port.

Speakers	Headphones	Earbuds
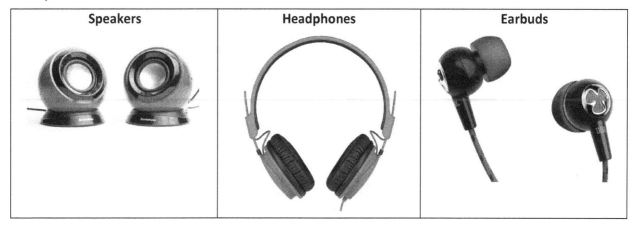		

Virtual Reality Devices

Virtual reality [VR] is a computer-simulated environment that can simulate physical presence in places in the real world — or imagined worlds. Virtual reality is a very sophisticated medium that is not yet in use in everyday computing. One benefit of virtual reality is that it can bring this medium to a business, academic, medical, or military environment without the expensive cost of actually creating or being in the situation. By time you graduate, you should expect to see the use of virtual reality devices to grow.

Advantages and Disadvantages of Output Devices

As with output devices, remember that there are benefits and disadvantages for each. Most frequently, in the work world, you will use a monitor, a printer, and possibly speakers or earphones. But as with input devices, as you explore the use of specific type of output device, consider your purposes.

The Role of the Processor

A **central processing unit** [CPU] is the hardware within a computer that carries out the instructions of a computer program by performing the basic arithmetic, logic, and input/output operations of the system. All computers – desktops and laptops – have a CPU and the other components described below.

Processor Components and Their Functions

The **control unit** in the computer reads, interprets and directs the system to execute a software program.

The **arithmetic & logic unit**, ALU, is a digital circuit that performs integer arithmetic and logical operations. Every CPU contains an ALU. In the illustrations below, the CPU is on the left; it is inserted onto computer's "motherboard", shown on the right.

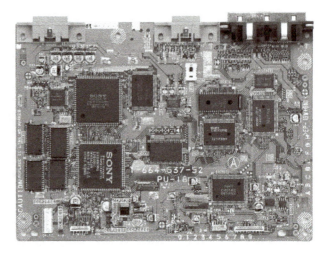

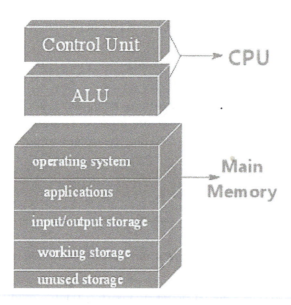

Processing Speeds and Their Unit of Measurement

The term **megahertz [MHz]** represents one million cycles per second. This is a measurement of the transmission speed of the computer. A one-megahertz clock [1 MHz] means that some number of bits [1, 4, 8, 16, 32 or 64] can be manipulated at least one million times per second. A two-gigahertz clock [2 GHz] means at least two billion times. The "at least" is because multiple operations often occur in one clock cycle.

Gigahertz [GHz] represents 1,000,000,000 cycles per second.

Both MHz and GHz have been used to measure CPU speed. Early computer processing speed was measured largely in megahertz. Computers in the second decade of the year 2000 are measured using gigahertz since speeds have increased so significantly since the development of the personal computer in the 1980s. Both MHz and GHz are used to measure CPU speed. For example, a 1.6 GHz computer processes data internally, calculating, comparing, and copying information twice as fast as an 800 MHz machine.

The Computer Machine Cycle

Four basic operations are performed by a computer to work with data; **fetching, decoding, executing and storage**. That is, the computer receives the data from an input source, decodes or understands it, performs a process with it, and stores or saves it in a specified location. This cycle is repeated continuously by the CPU beginning when you boot [turn on] the computer – and until you shut it off.

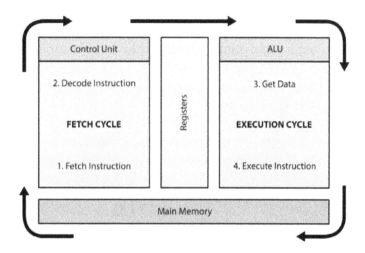

Arithmetic Operation from Decimal to Binary

A computer is constructed of digital electronics, meaning that its electronic circuits can exist in only one of two states: **on** or **off.** Most computer electronics use voltage levels to indicate their present state. For example, a transistor with five volts would be considered "on", while a transistor with no voltage would be considered "off."

The decimal number system that people use every day contains ten digits, 0 through 9. If you begin counting in decimal: 0, 1, 2, 3, 4, 5, 6, 7, 8, 9, you run out of digits after nine. So to continue counting, we add a second column of digits, worth ten times the value of the first column. When we get to 20, must add another column, and so on.

We can also show this by writing decimal numbers in expanded notation. This makes the value of each column clear. For example:

365 is equal to 3×100 + 6×10 + 5×1
1032 is equal to 1×1000 + 0×100 + 3×10 + 2×1

The binary number system works in the exact same way as the decimal system, except that it contains only two digits, 0 and 1. Start counting in binary: 0, 1. But there are no more binary digits. In order to keep counting, we add a second column worth *twice* the value of the column before. We continue counting again: 10, 11...Hmm, time to add another column again. Counting further: 100, 101, 110, 111, 1000, 1001, 1010, 1011, 1100, 1101, 1110, 1111.... If you look at the pattern of 1s and 0s, you see that binary as decimal, but with fewer digits. Binary uses two digits, so each column is worth twice the one before.

This fact, coupled with expanded notation, can be used convert between from binary to decimal. In the binary system, the columns are worth 1, 2, 4, 8, 16, 32, 64, 128, 256, and so forth.

To convert a number from binary to decimal, simply write it in expanded notation. For example, the binary number 101101 can be rewritten in expanded notation as $1 \times 32 + 0 \times 16 + 1 \times 8 + 1 \times 4 + 0 \times 2 + 1 \times 1$. By simplifying this expression, you can see that the binary number 101101 is equal to the decimal number 45.

With numeric data written as binary, the computer can easily manipulate the information using circuits that can add, subtract, multiply, divide, and do many other things with numbers.

Adding and Subtracting Using Binary

Follow these steps to add binary numbers:

- Align the numbers you wish to add as if you were adding decimal numbers.
- Begin with the two numbers in the far right column.
- Add the numbers following the rules of decimal addition. **[1+0 = 1, 0+0 = 0] unless both numbers are a 1. [1+0 = 1, 0+0 = 0] unless both numbers are a 1.Add 1+1 as "10" if present.** [It is not "ten", but "one zero"]. Write "0" below and carry a "1" to the next column. **Add 1+1 as "10" if present.** [It is not "ten" but "one zero"]. Write "0" below and carry a "1" to the next column.
- Add 1+1 as "10" if present. [It is not "ten", but rather "one zero"]. Write "0" below and carry a "1" to the next column.
- Start on the next column to the left.
- Repeat the steps above, but add any carry. Remember that 1+1 = 10 and 1+1+1 = 11. Remember to carry the "1".

Examples of addition with binary:

111 + 100 = 1011

101 + 110 = 1011

1111 + 111 = 10110

Remember…

You can only use the digits 0 and 1.

If you find yourself using 2 or any other digit, you did something wrong.

Don't forget to carry.

Follow these steps to subtract binary numbers:

- Align the two numbers as you would in decimal subtraction.
- Add one or more zeroes [called meeting zeroes] if necessary to represent both numbers with the same number of digits. For example, convert 101-11 to 101-011 so that both have three digits.
- Apply two's complement to the second term: For each digit in the number, change every 1 to 0 and every 0 to 1.
- Add 1 to the number.
- Add the complemented number to the first term. Now the original 101 - 11 has become 101 + 101 = 1010.
- The sum in the previous step should have one more digit than you started with. Remove the most significant digit from the sum to get 101 - 11 = 010. If you don't have an extra digit, you tried to subtract a larger number from a smaller one.

Examples of subtraction with binary:

$111 - 101 = 10$

$110 - 11 = 11$

$1100 - 101 = 111$

Comparison of Data Sizes

When working with files or considering the storage requirements of a computer, it is important to understand the meaning of the relationship between data size measurements.

Data Size	Size/Use
Bit	The smallest unit of data that a computer uses. It can be used to represent two states of information, such as Yes or No.
Byte	A group of bits; usually 7 or 8 A byte contains 8 bits and represents a single character
Kilobyte	Approximately 1,024 Bytes [2^{10} = 1,024] Kilobytes are most frequently used to explain a data file size.
Megabyte	Approximately 1,000 Kilobytes, or 1 million bytes [2^{20} = 1,048,576] Megabytes are frequently used to explain file sizes.
Gigabyte	Approximately 1,000 Megabytes or one thousand million bytes [2^{30} = 1,073,741,824] Gigabytes describe the size of storage devices that hold data.
Terabyte	Approximately one trillion bytes, or 1,000 Gigabytes Terabytes are the number of bits that a CPU can process at one time.
Word Size	Word size describes the natural unit of data used by a particular processor design.

	A word is basically a fixed-sized group of digits [binary or decimal] that are handled as a unit by the instruction set and/or hardware of the processor. Also, word size is number of bits in each word, such as 8, or 16 or 32 or 64.

Here's a simple comparison between the sizes of a byte – and a word.

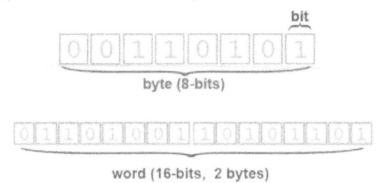

Primary Storage Devices; Advantages and Disadvantages

Primary storage, also known as main storage or memory, is the main area in a computer in which data is stored for quick access by the computer's processor. There are four types of primary storage in the computer. Note: Primary storage devices are embedded in small electronic devices known as chips that are mounted on the motherboard of a desktop computer or laptop.

Examples of primary storage devices are described below, along with their advantages and disadvantages.

Primary Storage Type	Purpose and Notes
RAM	RAM stands for random access memory. It holds programs and data being used by the CPU. Any address in RAM can be accessed equally quickly.
	Using RAM does not slow down the computer very much.
	During the execution of a program, RAM address locations store the intermediate or final results of processing.
	Advantage: RAM is always available to the CPU, assuming it is not full.
	Disadvantage: Any data stored in RAM is lost if power to the computer is turned off for any reason.
ROM	ROM generally holds data programmed when the computer was made; it is not intended to be changed. Some types of ROM can be erased and reprogrammed when not using the computer.
	Programmable ROM and PROM can be custom-programmed by the user one time using special circuitry.
	Erasable-Programmable ROM [EPROM] can also be programmed and erased by the

	user with ultraviolet light and special circuitry outside the computer. Electrically Erasable PROM [EEPROM] can be erased and reprogrammed by special circuitry within the computer by software program. **Advantage:** Data in ROM is preserved even if computer power is turned off. **Disadvantage:** ROM is not user-friendly; changes must be made by experts.
Cache	Cache is a French term meaning to hide. In computer jargon, cache is an amount of memory that stores data so that computer can reuse it. When you issue an instruction to the computer, it checks the cache first. **Advantage:** Cache speeds computer performance by not be running information that may be reused. **Disadvantage:** Cache is erased if the computer power is turned off.
Buffer	A buffer is a region of a physical memory storage used to temporarily store data while it is being moved from one place to another. Typically, the data is stored in a buffer as it is retrieved from an input device such as a microphone or just before it is sent to an output device such as speakers. A buffer may also be used when the computer is moving data between processes. **Advantage:** A buffer frees RAM for more important processing. **Disadvantage:** If power is lost, information in the buffer may be lost depending on when the power was shut off and how the buffer was being used.

Secondary storage is used to store a large amount of data at lower cost per byte than primary memory. In addition, secondary storage does not lose the data when the device is powered down—it is non-volatile. Secondary storage differs from primary storage; it is not directly accessible by the CPU. Instead, it is by input/output channels of the computer, although this is done more slowly than with primary storage. Secondary storage is also referred to as media. Examples of secondary storage devices are described below, along with their advantages and disadvantages.

Secondary Storage Type	Purpose and Notes
Hard Drive	Hard disk drive [HDD] systems [hard disks or hard drives for short] are used for permanent storage and quick access. They typically reside inside the computer and can hold more information than other forms of storage. **Advantage:** Fixed inside the computer, and therefore protected. **Disadvantage:** Replacing a hard drive is a complicated process. Also, hard drives add weight to a laptop.
CD-ROM	A CD-ROM is a thin, flat, round disc used to store data, music, or images. The drive into which you insert a CD-ROM can either be one that records once [CD-R], or one that allows rewriting

	[CD-RW] more than once. CD drives are rated by their data transfer speed. Early drives ran at 150KBps. Soon after, CD drives rated as "2X" drives appeared at 300KBps. this system of ratings continued up until the 8X the 150K bps standard. A CD-ROM can store up to 650 MB of data, so it is best used for computer application file or music storage rather than movies. **Advantage:** CDs are thin so you can store them relatively easily. They are also easy to mail because they are lightweight. **Disadvantage:** Computer files are getting larger every year; often one CD is does not have enough capacity to save a group of data should be kept together.
DVD-ROM 	A DVD-ROM is a thin, flat, round disc used to store data, music, or images. It looks just like a CD-ROM. You cannot record to a DVD-ROM. DVD discs also come as DVD-R and DVD-RW. Movies are pressed to a DVD; you can play them in your computer or using your media entertainment center. Note: You must play a DVD in a DVD drive, not a CD drive. **Advantage**: DVDs also store easily. You can still buy some software applications on DVD. **Disadvantage:** Computer files are getting larger every year; even a DVD may not have enough capacity to save a group of data should be stored together.
USB Drive [USB Thumb Drive] 	USB stands for universal serial bus. The first USB drives appeared in the year 2000, and stored 8 MB of data. Today's USB drives typically range from 2 gigabytes to 1 terabyte. Early transfer speeds for USB 1.0 were slow; today's USB 3.0 drive speed moves data at as much as 200 MB/sec. **Advantage:** Tiny; very portable; inexpensive **Disadvantage:** Because of its small size, a USB drive can be lost or stolen easily.
SD Card	The SD standard, launched in 1999, stands for secure digital. SD is a non-volatile memory card format used in some portable devices such as mobile phones, digital cameras, GPS navigation devices, and tablet computers, desktop and laptop computers, and printers. There are four families of SD: • Standard-Capacity [SDSC]

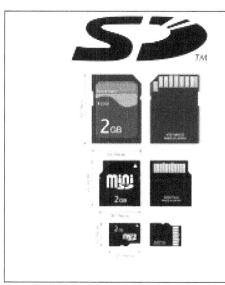	<ul><li>High-Capacity [SDHC]</li><li>eXtended-Capacity [SDXC],</li><li>SDIO, which combines input/output functions with data storage.</li></ul>Three sizes exist; standard SD, about the size of a postage stamp; mini SD, and micro SD. There are four classes of speed. Each varies because of the type of application such as still pictures, video and/or data that the card supports. **Advantage:** Tiniest size, inexpensive, with increasing amounts of storage size developed constantly. **Disadvantage:** Easily lost; you may need multiple sizes for your different devices. But, adapters are available.

Unit Summary

In this unit, you have learned about the following topics and concepts:

- An input device is any computer hardware peripheral that provides data and control signals to a computer.
- An output device is any piece of computer hardware that the results of data processing via electronically generated information to a device with a human-readable or viewable form.
- Four functions are performed in sequence by a computer's processor as it works with data and instructions.
- Megahertz [MHz] represents one million cycles per second of computer transmission speed, while Gigahertz [GHz] represents 1,000,000,000 cycles per second. Modern computers are measured using gigahertz; typically around 3.0 GHz for today CPU.
- Computer data is measured in terms of bit, byte, kilobyte, megabyte, gigabyte, and word size.
- Decimal numbers can be converted to binary format for machine-readable use by a computer processor.
- There are four types of primary storage devices. Each has a different purpose with the function of memory.
- Input and output devices are necessary in order to interact with the computer. Input devices provide data and control signals to the computer; output devices send the results of the data processing from the computer.

Practice Questions and Activities

1. Listed below are computer input and output devices. In the column on the right, write "input" or "output" to classify the type of device.

Printer	

Mouse	
Touchpad	
Microphone	
Biometric device	
Camera	
Keyboard	
Multimedia projector	
Headphones	
Monitor	
Plotter	

7. What are the four functions performed by a computer as it moves through and then repeats its processing cycle?

8. The two terms used to measure computer transmission speed are _____ and _____ .

9. List the four types of primary storage, and the main purpose of each.

10. How many megabytes are contained in a gigabyte?

11. What is the term for the type of number format in which computer must process information?

12. How does a laser printer differ from an inkjet printer? Which type of ink is more expensive?

13. When would you choose to use an ultralight projector for a presentation?

14. Using what you've learned about specifications for a computer system, identify the following: processing speed, input devices, storage capacity [primary and secondary], and output devices.

15. Make a scrapbook showing examples of each of these devices.

16. Collect pictures about the types of output devices to highlight their features.

17. Create a collage that displays all the output devices.

18. Make and solve a crossword puzzle including the types of input and output devices.

19. Design a binary conversion chart and use it to solve problems.

20. Given a list of terms by your teacher, match the terms with their correct definitions.

21. Research and create a report about the relationship between a bit and a byte.

22. Investigate the tables of values for base two and base ten. Explain what you learned.

23. Use the symbols 1 and 0 to write base two numbers.

24. Identify the differences between primary and secondary storage; show these differences on a two column table.

25. Create a collage or diorama showing the generations of computers -- and the people who invented each generation.

26. Discuss a project you've worked on, and one on which a classmate worked. What did you each learn?

27. Construct and use an abacus to perform calculations.

28. Make a scrapbook with pictorial examples of input and output devices.

29. Cross word puzzles on the types of input and output devices

30. Identify from a list of specifications for a computer system, the following:

    Processing speed, input devices, storage capacity [primary and secondary], and output devices.

31. Design a binary conversion chart and use it to solve problems

32. Provide students with a list of terms and definitions and have them make the correct match.

33. Create a report that describes the relationship between a bit — and a byte.

34. Investigate the tables of values for base two and base ten.

35. Use the symbols 1 and 0 to write base two numbers.

36. Find out the differences between primary and secondary storage and show these differences on a two column table.

Unit 6: Perform Research

This unit is designed to help you understand the importance of research, and how to formulate questions to conduct effective and efficient research. Upon completion, you should be able to:

- Define the term research
- Identify purposes for performing research
- List a variety of potential sources of research information
- Formulate questions based on the information needs of the research
- Use keywords to pinpoint and narrow searches for topics.
- Discuss and categorize methods for validating information and websites.
- Apply evaluation criteria of relevancy, suitability, authority, objectivity, and currency to determine the relative value of search results.
- Present information regarding content and references according to established writing format such as APA [American Psychological Association] or MLA [Modern Language Association].

What Is Research?

The term research originates from old French; "Recercher", to search closely. In simple terms, research is the process of conducting an investigation to find answers or a solution to a problem.

Research is used to identify or confirm facts, confirm the results of previous work, solve new or existing problems, support theorems, or develop new theories. As an individual, research allows you to pursue your interests, to learn something new, to hone your problem-solving skills, and to challenge yourself in new ways.

Primary and Secondary Research Sources

A **primary source** is an original object or document. It is first-hand information; source material closest to what is being studied. Primary sources vary by discipline. They may include historical and legal documents, eye witness accounts, results of an experiment, statistical data, pieces of creative writing, and art objects. In the natural and social sciences, the results of an experiment or study are typically found in scholarly articles or papers delivered at conferences; these are considered primary sources.

A **secondary source** is something written about a primary source. Secondary sources include comments on, interpretations of, or discussions about the original material. Sources of secondary information include articles in newspapers or popular magazines, book or movie reviews, or articles found in scholarly journals that evaluate or criticize the original research of another.

Sometimes it's not easy to determine the difference between primary and secondary research. For example, much that you read in the newspaper is secondary research. However if a reporter is writing about an eyewitness account because he or she was embedded as a journalist in place of war, the reporter's article is likely a primary information source. Also, a scholarly journal article could include a review of published work of another researcher. That article is considered as secondary research. It is important, therefore to read the material thoroughly. If in doubt, you can always ask a reference librarian questions about the source.

In addition to knowing whether the material you're looking at is a primary or secondary source, there are a few other considerations that will help you determine the suitability of the content as reference information for your project.

Scope. Ask yourself about the scope of the article, book, website or other material. Is it a general work providing an overview of the topic, or is it focused only on a single aspect of your topic? Does the scope of the content match your own expectations? Does it span the time period in which you are interested?

Audience. Who is the intended audience for this source? A scholarly researcher, or general audience? Is the material too technical or too clinical? Or is it too elementary — or basic?

Purposes for Conducting Research

Different types of research are performed by organizations and individuals for specific purposes.

Academic Research

Academic research comprises investigation and writing based upon the idea of scientific inquiry or the scientific method. Based on the assumption that everything in the universe is linked by cause and reaction, the scientific method assumes that they are is a logical explanation for all observed behavior.

A researcher using the scientific method of inquiry begins by creating a **hypothesis**, and assumption or group of assumptions about what he or she expects to find after conducting research on a topic. Researchers typically talk about a **null hypothesis**, meaning that there is no meaningful relationship between two observed phenomena. The researcher then develops a methodology that will prove or disprove the null hypothesis.

Research may be qualitative or quantitative. In quantitative research, mathematical tools are used to analyze data collected during the research. If this method is not used, then the research is considered to be qualitative. In either case, the research is completed, and the results are analyzed.

Business Research

Business research involves the conducting of specific activities designed to gather data to solve a problem. Unlike pure academic methods for fields such as chemistry, business research methods may include questionnaires, interviews, focus groups, surveys, reading journals, and/or observation. For example, businesses may perform research to answer these types of questions:

- What are our customers' current solutions?
- Do they make or buy these solutions? If they buy them, from whom?
- How can we help our customers solve their problems?
- Can customers afford our solutions?
- What external factors can affect our success? Examples include standards, competition, market conditions, and regulation.

Large technology companies such as IBM, Apple, Microsoft, and AT&T perform massive amounts of research. Many of these companies have their own research divisions and/or foundations dedicated solely to researching new products, or to determine how their products can better the world in some way. One example is the Bill and Melinda Gates Foundation; one of the foundation's goals is to expand educational opportunities – and access to information technology. http://www.gatesfoundation.org/ Note: Mr. Bill Gates is a co-founder and former CEO of Microsoft Corporation.

Recreational Research

Recreational research, sometimes termed original or individual research is research that is not exclusively based on a summary, review or synthesis of earlier publications on the subject of research. This material is typically of a primary source character. The purpose of the original research is to produce new knowledge, rather than to present the existing knowledge in a new form.

Recreational research for an individual might include a genealogy project, researching travel plans, or looking for plans to build a gazebo. And the internet is often used by consumers to research potential tech purchases such as gadgets, computer software, tablets, or mobile phones.

Potential Sources of Research Information

There are many sources of research information. Sometimes it's evident whether content in a specific type of material is primary or secondary, however sometimes it takes a bit of sleuthing to determine this.

Material Type	
Books	Books can serve as both a primary and a secondary source of research information.
Magazine Articles	As with books, magazines may represent primary or secondary sources as well. With magazines, it's important to examine the date of publication. If the date of publication is close to a time when the topic situation occurred, it may represent learning that took place near the publication date. However in a recent magazine article that looks back at a situation that occurred in the past, the information could be considered to be secondary.
Scholarly Journal Articles	Scholarly journal articles almost always contain primary research sources, however as mentioned above, there may be articles included in a journal that review the work of another person, making the information a secondary source.
Newspaper Articles and Opinion Pieces	Newspapers often contain both factual content and opinion content. "News reporting" from well-established news outlets is generally considered to be reliable for statements of fact, though even the most reputable reporting sometimes contains errors. News reporting from less-established outlets is generally considered less reliable for statements of fact. Opinion pieces, whether written by the editors of the publication — editorials – or by outside authors [called "op-eds"] are reliable primary sources for statements attributed to that editor or author, but are rarely reliable for statements of fact.
Websites	Of all of the types of research sources, websites require the most scrutiny as to whether they represent primary or secondary research sources, or are not valid at all. See the next several sections for strategies you can use when

	working with information found on the Internet.
Other Materials	Material such as statistical articles from industry, academic, research and trade organizations are often primary reference information sources.

Formulating Questions Based on Your Information Needs

Below are eight questions to ask as you begin a research project.

- What is my research hypothesis or topic?
- What are the essential issues, problems, or challenges regarding this hypothesis?
- How will I state my research questions? What terminology and/or keywords will I use?
- What primary data sources are available for me to perform my research?
- What research methods will I use to test my hypothesis?
- What data have I gathered?
- What have I learned from an analysis of the data?
- What are the results, and what do the results mean in terms of my hypothesis?

Strategies for Successfully Locating Internet Information

Use Keywords

Keywords are the words and phrases used on internet search engines that produce results based on your query. The keywords you use will vary depending upon the kind of information with which you are dealing. For example, if you want to research cricket teams in the Caribbean, you could reasonably expect results specific to those keywords as our sample shows below.

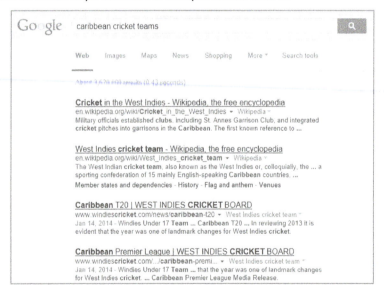

Many publishers of website information publish keywords to optimize the possibility that the search engines will pick up keywords when a user creates a search in a search engine such as Google, Yahoo, or Bing. In the example above, notice that Google indicated that there were 3,620,000 possible results from a search using the keywords "Caribbean cricket teams". The results that occur on the first page have been keyword-optimized so that when those keywords are typed, those particular sites will appear within the top results of the search.

If our cricket keyword search above produced 3,620,000 possible results, it's possible that your research topic might produce even more. Therefore, you should develop keywords that are as specific as possible so that search engines narrow the search focus to the most appropriate results. Below are some tips for creating keyword search statements, also called search strings.

- Use nouns and objects whenever possible
- Place the most important terms first.
- When feasible, use at least three keywords in your query.
- Combine keywords into phrases when possible.
- Avoid common words such as *the, or, an* unless they are part of your search phrase.
- Think about words you'd expect to find in the body of the page, and use them as keywords.
- Write down your search statement and revise it before you type it into a search engine.

Note: Enter keywords as lowercase text.

Use Boolean Logic

Boolean logic takes its name from British mathematician George Boole [1815-1864], who wrote about a system of logic designed to produce more accurate search results through the formation of precisely stated queries. Three words [operators] of this logic are **AND, OR, and NOT**, which are used to link words and phrases for more precise queries.

Operator	Search Result Impact
And	Narrows your search by retrieving only sources that contain every one of the keywords you enter. Take care; the more terms you enter, the narrower your search results. *Sample search statement:* **horse and burro**
Or	Expands your search by returning sources in which either or both keywords appear. Since the OR operator is usually used for keywords that are similar or synonymous, the more keywords you enter, the more results you will retrieve. *Sample search statement:* **horse or burro**
Not /and Not	Limits your search by returning only your first keyword, but not the second, even if the first word appears in that result, too. *Sample search statement:* **horse not burro**

Three additional search parameter types can help you narrow or broaden your search results.

Operator	Search Result Impact
+ and -	Use in front of words to force their inclusion [+] and/or exclusion [-] in searches. Note: Do not use a space between the sign and the keyword. *Sample search statement:* **+lake –fish**
" "	Use around phrases to ensure they are searched exactly as is, with the words side by side in the same order.

	Sample search statement: **"Red Cross donations "** red cross donations Web News Images Shopping Maps More ⁻ Search tools About 46,300,000 results (0.40 seconds) Ads related to **red cross donations** ⓘ Red Cross® Official Site - Support the Red Cross - RedCross.org www.redcross.org/Donation ▾ 1 (855) 989 2232

*
 	
[wildcard]
symbol]
	Use a wildcard expression, *, to look for variations in spelling and word form.
	
	Sample search statements:
	
	    librar* returns results for library, libraries, librarian
	
	    colo*r returns results for colour

Note: You can combine phrases with keywords using the double quotes and the plus [+] and minus [-] signs. For example, + cricket + players-" Cayman"

Validating Information from a Website

Much of the information on the Internet is not reviewed by a credible authority. Unlike more traditional media such as books, scholarly journals, or magazines which undergo editing, website page content need not be approved by an individual or organization before it is posted for public use. Therefore, any individual can conceivably post anything. With research, you must avoid the assumption that if you see it on the Internet, it must be true. Use the tools that you are learning in this course to evaluate each and every Internet source you read, summarize, or quote in order to properly support your research.

Types of Internet Domains

Like the three or four letter file extensions at the end of a computer file, every Internet domain must have an extension that identifies its type of site.

Domain Extension Type	Type of Publishing or Publisher
.edu	Education
.org	Nonprofit organization
.com .biz	Commercial Sites
.net	Network Infrastructure
.jm .jp .gov	Country domain; Jamaica, Japan, and US federal or state government

Personal Web Pages

Often it's challenging to determine if a website you are viewing is actually the personal page of an individual. Here's an example: http://www.jhu.edu/~jsmith/sports.html

In the URL, **.edu** indicates the domain is an institution of higher education; Johns Hopkins University. While it would be easy to assume that the entire URL stems from the University, the **tilde [~]** after the type of domain usually indicates that the page or pages you see on the screen represent a personal web page, rather than part of the organization's official web site.

In this example, the site is a file about sports in the folder of someone named jsmith. J. Smith could be an instructor or coach affiliated with University who has valuable information to share. However J. Smith may also be a student attending the University with privileges to create a personal page and someone who wants to share an opinion about sports. Therefore, you must always apply extra scrutiny to website addresses in general, but especially when you see a tilde in the URL.

Applying Evaluative Criteria to Determine Relative Value of Information

Much information on the Internet is not reviewed, or "filtered", whereas traditional media such as books, magazines, and videos are read or reviewed by an editor. As a student who will be accountable for information you use based on research, it is your responsibility to make sure that information and citations you use are credible. Below are five criteria that, if followed, will help you evaluate what you see – and determine whether you should consider using it in your work. They are relevancy, suitability, authority, objectivity, and currency.

Relevancy

Though many search engines rank material according to their idea of what is "relevant", that doesn't mean the material is relevant to your needs — or that it is reliable. Further, web coverage frequently differs from coverage in print.

Questions to Ask

- Is the information applicable to your topic?
- Do you believe that it is useful to you?
- Does this site have information that you cannot find elsewhere?
- How in depth does the material seem to be?

How Can I Tell?

- Thoroughly read the content at the website; follow any included hyperlinks to compare the content with what you see on the main page of the site.
- Try to determine if the information you have found can be verified; ask a reference librarian for help if necessary

Suitability

Any source you use and cite in your research must be suitable to the topic.

Questions to Ask

- Whose perspective on the topic or issues are included?
- Is an important perspective on the topic or issues excluded?
- Is there evidence of bias? [Note that opinion pieces are intended to express a particular bias; check whether opinions are backed up by solid evidence.]
- Is there evidence of undue exaggeration, prejudice, over-generalization, or opinion misrepresented as fact?

How Can I Tell?

- Read through/scan all webpages.
- Ask a Reference Librarian if the information you have found can be verified elsewhere.
- Does the source include all the information you need? What time period is included? Does the source only include information since a certain date?
- When was the information last updated?
- Who is the audience?

Authority

Authority refers to whether or not an individual, organization, or an agency is recognized as an expert in a field — and if that body is knowledgeable, qualified, and reliable. An example of a reliable authority would be a university or a government agency. Authority is an extremely important criterion when evaluating internet resources.

Questions to Ask

- Does the information have a complete list of works cited and which reference credible, authoritative sources?
- If the information is not backed up with sources, what is the author's relationship to the subject to be able to give an "expert" opinion?
- Is the work scholarly or popular? Is the methodology used for the research described? Are sources of information cited in text or bibliographies?
- Does it omit important and relevant information, or have an emotional writing style? These are possible clues about the author's bias
- Is the author/information provider clearly identified? Is data included about the author/information provider?

How Can I Tell?

- Is the author/information provider affiliated with a recognized institution/organization?
- Is the author a person you recognise as an expert in his or her field?
- Can you find references to the author or authors elsewhere?
- Are there other websites or pages by the same author or authors?
- Is an individual named as a contact person, with a method for contact?

Objectivity

Often, websites are influenced by advertisers. Also, bias can be introduced into website content. Make sure that you have made every effort to screen for advertising influence and bias.

Questions to Ask

- Does the information show a minimum of bias, promoting one more strongly than others?
- Is the page a presentation of facts — and not designed to steer opinion?
- Is the page free of advertisements or sponsored links?

How Can I Tell?

- Is the material presented selectively or in an unbalanced manner? Is only one side of an issue presented? Has some information been left out?
- Are other points of view explored, keeping the content unbiased?
- Does the word "I" appear? This may indicate a lack of objectivity.
- Has been content been written in a way to try to get me to change my mind?
- Is the text well-written, free of spelling errors, and grammatically correct?
- Are research methodologies adequately explained?

Currency

Like printed sources, some work is not time-sensitive, such as history, or a novel. Other work, such as in science, has limited useful life because of new discoveries, or in technology because of the rapid evolution of hardware, software, and services. Also, a site may be updated or revised only partially, meaning that not all of the information has been revised. Be careful to note when the information was first created, and if applicable, last updated so that you can determine its value in your research.

Questions to Ask Yourself

- Do I have a publication and revision date[s] for the information?
- Are there links to other sites that produce results rather than dead ends?

How Can I Tell?

- Read through and scan the text to see if the author attributes information/facts to a particular year.
- Scan through the bibliography or list of references; see how current is each item? [Be concerned if there isn't one!]
- Is there a footer where the author has included a date?
- Are the links up to date and working?

Using an Established Writing Format

There are two predominate organizations that have developed writing formats used for written works:

- APA [American psychological Association]
- MLA [Modern language Association].

Each association has distinct types of writing audiences, however there is some overlap. Over the years, both associations have published style guides which are updated periodically.

Some of the areas of a written manuscript for which styles are provided in both organizations are:

APA Style

The American Psychological Association was established in 1929. The APA style is an academic format specified in The Publication Manual of the American Psychological Association, a guide that offers academic authors guidance on various subjects for the submission of papers to the publications of APA. The APA states that the guidelines were developed to assist reading comprehension in the social and behavioral sciences, for clarity of communication, and for "word choice that best reduces bias in language". APA Style establishes standards of written communication concerning:

- The organization of content
- Writing style
- Reference citations
- How to prepare a manuscript for publication in certain disciplines.
- In addition to APA publications, APA style is widely used for writing including scientific, medical, and public health journals, textbooks, and academia, for papers written in classes. Examples of professionals who use APA include researchers, educators, social workers, nurses, business people, and individuals. Here are the basic formatting principles for an APA reference citation.
-

- Indent all lines after the first line of each entry one-half inch from the left margin. This is called hanging indentation.
- Authors' names are inverted [last name first]; give the last name and initials for all authors of a particular work for up to and including seven authors. If the work has more than seven authors, list the first six authors; use ellipses after the sixth author's name. After the ellipses, list the last author's name of the work.
- Alphabetize list entries by the last name of the first author of each work.
- For multiple articles by the same author, or authors listed in the same order, list the entries in chronological order, from earliest to most recent.
- Present the journal title in full.
- Maintain the punctuation and capitalization that is used by the journal in its title.
- For example: ReCALL not RECALL or Knowledge Management Research & Practice not Knowledge Management Research and Practice.
- Capitalize all major words in journal titles.
- When referring to books, chapters, articles, or Web pages, capitalize only the first letter of the first word of a title and subtitle, the first word after a colon or a dash in the title, and proper nouns. Do not capitalize the first letter of the second word in a hyphenated compound word.
- Italicize titles of longer works such as books and journals.
- Do not italicize, underline, or put quotes around the titles of shorter works such as journal articles or essays in edited collections.
-

You can learn more about the APA style guide, Publication Manual of the American Psychological Association, [6th ed., 2nd printing] and access some free tutorials at www.apastyle.org .

Below is a sample entry from a bibliography formatted in APA style. Note the use of commas, periods, and spacing after the periods.

Gay, L., & Airasian, P. (2000). Educational Research Competencies for Analysis and Application (Sixth.). Prentice-Hall.

MLA Style

The Modern Language Association of America [Modern Language Association or MLA] was founded in 1883. It is the principal professional association in the United States for scholars of language and literature. The organization includes 30,000 members in 100 countries, primarily academic scholars, professors, and graduate students who study or teach language and literature, including English, other modern languages, and comparative literature. Today, the MLA style is most commonly used to write papers and cite sources within the liberal arts and humanities disciplines. Here are the basic formatting principles for an MLA reference citation.

Basics

- Begin your list of works cited at the end of the paper on a new page with the centered title, Works Cited.
- Alphabetize the entries in your list by the author's last name, using the letter-by-letter system [ignore spaces and other punctuation.] If the author's name is unknown, alphabetize by the title, ignoring any A, An, or The.

- For dates, spell out the names of months in the text of your paper, but abbreviate them in the list of works cited, except for May, June, and July. Use either the day-month-year style 22 July 1999) or the month-day-year style [July 22, 1999]. Be consistent. With the month-day-year style, be sure to add a comma after the year unless another punctuation mark belongs there.

Use of Underlining or *Italics*

- When reports were written using typewriters, the names of publications were underlined because most typewriters had no way to print italics.
- For a bibliography written by hand, you should still underline the names of publications.
- Working on a computer, use italics for publication names.

Hanging Indentation

- All MLA citations should use hanging indents; the first line of an entry should be flush left, and the second and subsequent lines should be indented 1/2".

Capitalization, Abbreviation, and Punctuation

- The MLA guidelines specify using title case capitalization; capitalize the first words, the last words, and all principal words, including those that follow hyphens in compound terms.
- Use lowercase abbreviations to identify the parts of a work [e.g., *vol.* for *volume*, *ed.* for *editor*] except when these designations follow a period.
- Whenever possible, use the appropriate abbreviated forms for the publisher's name [*Random* instead of *Random House*].
- Separate author, title, and publication information with a period followed by one space.
- Use a colon and a space to separate a title from a subtitle.
- Include other kinds of punctuation only if they are part of the title.
- Use quotation marks to indicate the titles of short works appearing within larger works [e.g., "Memories of Childhood." *American Short Stories*]. Also use quotation marks for titles of unpublished works and songs.

You can learn more about the MLA style guide, MLA Handbook for Writers of Research Papers [7th edition] at www.mla.org .

Below is the same sample entry from a bibliography as above, formatted in MLA style. Note the use of commas, periods, spacing after the periods, parentheses or their lack — and the word "and" versus "&".

Gay, L., & Airasian, P. (2000). Educational Research Competencies for Analysis and Application (Sixth.). Prentice- Hall.

Using and Comparing MLA and APA

The best way to learn to build your bibliography references in either style is to use the basic rules for the style as a checklist as you write your first reference.

Below is one reference written first in APA, and then in MLA style.

Gay, L.R., and Peter Airasian. Educational Research Competencies for Analysis and Application. Sixth. Prentice-Hall, 2000.

Gay, L., & Airasian, P. (2000). Educational Research Competencies for Analysis and Application (Sixth.). Prentice- Hall.

For an excellent side-by-side comparison of content in both MLA and APA styles developed by a university, open this document: **MLA_APA_Side_by_Side.pdf** .

You can find comprehensive information about both styles at a site maintained by Purdue University: **https://owl.english.purdue.edu/owl/ /**

Unit Summary

In this unit, you have learned about the following topics and concepts:

- The meaning of the term "research"
- Reasons for performing research
- The variety of potential sources of information; books, periodicals, and the Internet
- Steps to follow to develop successful strategies for locating information on the Internet. This includes the use of key words to focus on and narrow the results returned.
- Types of website domains domain types such as .edu, .com, and .gov that provide credible sources of research information
- Evaluation criteria to determine the relative value of the research information found for relevancy, suitability, authority, objectivity, and currency
- Use of the established APA and MLA style formats to cite bibliographical references for a research paper

Practice Questions and Activities

1. Use a reference source to find the answer to a question proposed by your teacher, such as "What is the importance of ICT [information and communications technology] in schools"?

2. Describe the main difference between a primary and secondary research source.

3. The five evaluative criteria that you can use to determine the relative value of research information are:

a.
b.
c.
d.
e.
f.

4. For each information source listed below, write several benefits of the source and also one or two concerns about its use as a research source.

Information source	Benefits	Concerns
Books		
Magazine Articles		
Scholarly Journal Articles		
Newspaper Articles and Opinion Pieces		
Websites		
Other Materials		

5. Practice using keywords to narrow information results.

    a. Think of a fun research topic. List one keyword for your search.
    b. Perform an Internet search using only the one keyword. How many results does your web browser find? [Hint: Google shows the number of results at the top of the webpage.]
    c. Add a second keyword and repeat the search. How many results appear now?
    d. Now add an operator. For example, Caribbean AND food. What happens to the number of results? For your topic, how do the results on the first page of the search compare with your expectations regarding results for your topic?

6. Visit the websites listed below. List two things you can expect to find on this site based on the home page.

Domain	Two Expected Information Topics
www.ucci.edu.ky	
http://www.nlm.nih.gov/medlineplus/	
www.caymanislands.ky	
www.microsoft.com	

7. List at least four differences between the APA and MLA bibliography formats.

8. Given several Internet sites selected by your teacher, analyse each and note the evaluative criteria you would apply to determine their credibility as reference material.

9. Class Exercise. Here's a fun class activity that simply and visually shows the impact of using the Boolean search operators *And, Or, and Not*. Began the exercise with all students sitting at their desks. Then announce the instructions for each search operator. Watch as students stand up and sit down! :-)

AND

- All students wearing glasses stand up
- All students wearing glasses AND who are girls stand up
- All students wearing glasses AND who are girls AND with a name that starts with "A" stand up

OR / And OR

- All students wearing glasses OR shoes stand up
- All students wearing glasses AND shoes OR watches stand up

NOT

- All students wearing glasses but NOT watches, stand up
- All students who are boys and NOT wearing watches, stand up

10. Team Exercise. Which team can below most quickly identify the most formatting differences in the APA and MLA reference citation below?

MLA

"Italy." *The New Encyclopaedia Britannica: Macropaedia*. 15th ed. 2000. Print.

APA

Italy. (2000). In *The new encyclopaedia Britannica: Macropaedia* (Vol. xx, pp. xxx-xxx). Chicago, IL: Encyclopaedia Britannica.

Learning Objectives

This unit is designed to help you appreciate the importance of data communication to the wider community — and its impact on society's development. Upon completion, you should be able to:

- Define the meaning of the term data communication
- Identify different communication devices and their uses
- Describe the appearance of various transmission media and identify appropriate for each
- Understand the application of communication technology in everyday life
- Discuss the different types of networks.

What Is Data Communication?

Simply put, data communication is a process in which two or more computers or devices transfer data, instructions, and information.

Components Necessary for Successful Data Communications

Several components are necessary in order to be able to communicate successfully. They are:

- The **sending device** that initiates an instruction to transmit data, instructions or information, also known as the **sender.**
- The **sending communications device** that connects the outbound data to the communications channel. The sending device encodes the information for more effective transmission. The sending device is also called an **encoder.**
- The **communications channel**, or transmission media on which the data, instructions or information travel. One example is an email message.
- The **receiving communications device** that connects the inbound data to a receiving device. The receiving device is also called a **decoder.**
- The **receiving device** that accepts the transmission of data, instructions, or information, also known as the **receiver.**

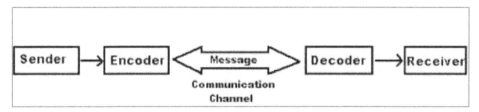

Simple model of data communication process, found on Google

Types of Communication Devices and Their Uses

Modem

Modulation is the process of conveying a message signal, for example a digital bit stream or an analogue audio signal, inside another signal that can be physically transmitted. A modulator is a device that performs modulation.

Demodulation is the opposite of modulation; the process of demodulation restores the information as it existed before modulation, placing it within the receiving device.

The word **modem** is a contraction of the words modulator and demodulator. A modem can perform both operations. A modem is typically used to send digital data over a phone line.

Modems grew out of the need to connect teleprinters over ordinary phone lines, instead of the more expensive leased lines which had previously been used. In 1942, IBM adapted this technology to their unit record equipment and were able to transmit punched cards at 25 bits/second.

The US Air Force began using mass-produced modems in 1958 as part of an air defense system, connecting terminals at various airbases, radar sites, and command-and-control centers.

AT&T introduced a Bell 103A modem that transmitted it 300 bps [bits per second] over ordinary phone line. After that, acoustic couplers were developed to allow the connection of the telephone handset with these early modems.

The *Novation CAT* acoustically coupled modem

In 1981, the Hayes smart modem was introduced, eliminating the need for the acoustic coupler, and allowing a computer to connect directly to telephone lines through what was called a **dial-up connection**. Over the years, the 300–baud speed increased; modems have remained in use in the ensuing 40-odd years. Although their use has been overshadowed dramatically in developed countries by broadband technology, many people still access the Internet using a modem capable of downloading data at 56k bits [56,000 bits per second], capable of downloading data to the computer at the effective rate of 53.3k bits, regulated to that speed in the U.S.

The original model 300-baud Smartmodem

Telephone [Mobile telephones, Smart phones, Computers PDAs]

Invention of the Telephone

Alexander Graham Bell is credited with the first US patent in 1876 for his invention of the telephone. At that time, this meant transmitting the human voice over existing telegraph wires. The Bell Telephone Company was created in 1877, and by 1886, more than 150,000 people in the U.S. owned telephones.

Bell at the opening of the long-distance line from New York to Chicago in 1892.

Over the years, the telephone became a household institution in developed countries, and competitors emerged.

Mobile or Cellular Phones

It wasn't until the 1990s that wireless telephones became useful as consumer technology. The phones were described as cellular phones because of the transmission cells which wirelessly connected the caller through the telephone company's central office, and back out to the recipient.

In 1992, the first text message was sent from a cell phone by employees of Logica CMG. And by 1995, there were more than 33 million cellular telephone subscribers in the United States. As adoption of cell phones has grown, governments of developed countries have worked with telecommunications providers to make increased amounts of transmission bandwidth available.

Smartphone

Smartphone is a term for distinguishing mobile phones with advanced features from mobile phones with basic features. Early smartphones typically combined the features of a mobile phone with those of another popular consumer device, such as a personal digital assistant [PDA], a media player, a digital camera, and/or a GPS navigation unit. Modern smartphones include all of those features – plus some features of a laptop, including web browsing, Wi-Fi, and 3rd-party apps [applications] and accessories. The most popular smartphones today are powered by Google's Android and Apple's iOS mobile operating systems, with the Windows CE OS coming in at a distant third. Below is a brief history of the rapid evolution of the smart phone, beginning in 1993.

Year[s]	Development
1993	IBM Simon, a very early smart phone
1996-2000	Nokia Communicator 9000 series
1997	Erickson "Smartphone" GS88; first device labeled as smart phone
2000	Erickson R380; first touchscreen phone
2001-2003	Palm's new Palm OS [operating system]; models PalmOne, Kyocera, and Treo
2002	RIM Blackberry 5810; first smartphone optimized for wireless email use
2002	Microsoft Windows CE, Compact Edition
2007	Apple's iPhone introduced
2008	iPhone 3G; Android operating system; HTC Dream smartphone; Open source OSs
2009	Motorola Droid, licensed to Verizon wireless
2010	Continued evolution of operating systems; iPhone 4
2011	Smart phones power mobile operating systems from companies such as Apple, Samsung, Motorola, Erickson, HP
2012	iPhone five
2013	Apple's iPhone 5C and 5S. And the Apple iPhone is the top-selling phone of all time in the United States, Japan, and other countries

Computer

Computers today are equipped with two ways to communicate. Most desktop and laptop computers have a report to support ethernet, a cable that uses broadband transmission to connect to a digital modem — or to a network. Any new or recently-built computer also has support for wireless technology, the ability for the machine to connect wirelessly with the local area network. These technologies are explained in the next several sections.

Tablet

A tablet is a general-purpose computer contained in a single panel. The built-in touchscreen touch screen serves as the input device. Modern tablets are operated by fingers and optionally, the use of a stylus, a pointed instrument used as an input device on a touchscreen. All tablets have the capability to connect to the Internet wirelessly through built-in wireless technology.

Types of Transmission Media

Signals

There are two types of transmission signals, analogue and digital.

- An **analogue signal** is a continuous electrical wave
- A **digital signal** consists of discrete electrical pulses that represent bits.

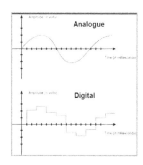

Physical and Wireless Transmission Media

Media is required to transmit a signal. Transmission media can be physical or wireless.

Physical Media

Physical Media Type	Description
Twisted Pair Cable	Twisted pair cable has four pairs of wires inside of a jacket. Each pair is twisted with a different number of twists per inch to help eliminate interference from other pairs and electrical devices. The tighter the twisting, the higher the supported transmission rate – and the greater the cost per foot. Twisted pair can be shielded and unshielded. The disadvantage of UTP [unshielded twisted pair] is that it may be susceptible to interference from radio and electrical frequencies. Twisted pair, with a data rate of 1-100mbps, is a commonly used medium in a telephone network. It is much less expensive than other physical media types, but it is more limited in terms of distance and transmission rate.
Coaxial Cable [coax] RG-59 flexible coaxial cable composed of A. Outer plastic sheath B. Woven copper shield C. Inner dielectric insulator D. Copper core	Coaxial cable, or coax, is a type of cable patented by English engineer and mathematician Oliver Heaviside in 1880. It has an inner conductor surrounded by a tubular insulating layer, surrounded by a tubular conducting shield. Many coaxial cables also have an insulating outer sheath or jacket. The term coaxial comes from the inner conductor and the outer shield sharing a geometric axis. Coax connects devices in home video equipment, ham radio setups, and measurement electronics. It was common for implementing computer networks, in particular Ethernet, but twisted pair cables have replaced them in most applications except in the consumer cable modem market for broadband Internet access.
Fibre Optic Cable	Fiber optic cable contains one or more optical fibers. The optical fibre elements are usually individually coated with plastic layers and housed in a protective tube adapted for the environment

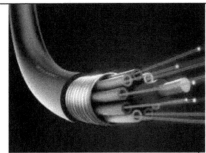	where the cable will be installed. Fibre optic cable can contain up to a thousand fibers in a single cable, with bandwidth potential in terabytes per second. Not all fibers in the cable are required for an individual transmission; companies may leave some cables "dark" for later use. Fibre supports telecommunications, making wiretapping more difficult and reducing electrical interference. Fibre is increasingly used in military and transportation applications as it offers increased performance, greater bandwidth and better security for signals — at a lower cost.
Ethernet 	Ethernet is an IT industry standard developed in the 1970s and supported by manufacturers of network equipment in order to easily connect devices. End connectors are called RJ45. Three standards of cables exist: **Cat 5.** Older standard; supports speeds up to 100mbps **Cat 5e.** Supports speeds up to 1 Gbps **Cat 6.** Supports up to 16bps; capable of supporting higher speeds as they evolve. Ethernet cables connect computers routers and switches on a local area network.

Wireless Media

Wireless Media Type	Description
Microwave 	Microwave transmission is the technology of sending information or energy by using radio waves. The wavelengths are measured in small numbers of centimetres called microwaves. Frequencies range from 1.0 GHz to 30 GHz. Microwave transmission is widely used for point-to-point communications such as are used by the military because the small wavelength allows antennas point the signal in narrow beams and with less interference. Microwave has a bandwidth 30 times of the radio spectrum below it. A disadvantage is that microwaves are limited to line of sight transmission; they cannot pass around hills or mountains as can lower frequency radio waves.
Satellite Communication	A communications satellite or comsat is an artificial satellite sent to orbit in space to support telecommunications. For fixed, point-to-point services, communications satellites relay microwaves complementary to that of communication cables. Satellites also support mobile transmission such as military communication, communications to ships, vehicles, planes and hand-held terminals, TV and radio broadcasting, and for Internet

| | connections to remote areas. |

| **Cellular Radio**  | A cellular network or mobile network is a wireless network distributed over land areas called cells, each served by at least one fixed-location transceiver, known as a cell site or base station. Each cell uses different frequencies so that there is no interference, and to provide guaranteed bandwidth in each cell.

Cells that are joined together provide radio coverage over a wide geographic area, allowing a large number of portable transceivers such as mobile phones or pagers to communicate with each other. Using base stations, these devices also communicate with fixed transceivers and telephones anywhere in the network, even while transceivers are moving through more than one cell while transmitting.

Cellular networks provide greater capacity compared with a single large transmitter. And because cell towers are closer together, less power is used. The towers cover a larger area than a single transmitter; cells can be added, and transmission isn't limited by the horizon.

Voice and data cellular networks are found worldwide so that mobile phones and portable devices can connect to the public switched telephone network – and public Internet. Private cellular networks are used for research, and for fleet dispatch. |
| **Bluetooth**  | Bluetooth is a wireless technology standard invented by Ericsson, a telecommunications company, in 1994. The standard governs the exchange of data over short distances using short-wavelength microwave transmissions from fixed and mobile devices. Bluetooth is managed by the Bluetooth Special Interest Group [SIG] which includes over 19,000 telecommunications, computing, networking, and consumer electronics companies. The SIG oversees the development of the specification, manages the qualification program, protects the trademarks, and issues licenses for qualifying devices.

Bluetooth serves well in simple applications where you wish to connect two using minimal configuration. Connection is accomplished through "pairing" whereby two Bluetooth-capable devices within range discover each other. Bluetooth applications include wireless headsets for cell phones, connecting mobile phones with car stereo systems, wireless control of and communication with tablets and speakers, and connecting wireless |

	keyboards, mice, and microphones with computers.
Infrared 	Infrared was discovered in 1800 by astronomer William Herschel. Infrared is a short range signal that is sent wirelessly; it is the same technology that is used in a TV remote control. You can connect a computer and other devices equipped with infrared ports by holding the infrared ports on the two devices so they can "see" each other, then using an infrared connection utility. In addition to remote control applications, infrared [IR] light is used in industrial, scientific, and medical applications. Night-vision devices using active near-infrared illumination allow people or animals to be observed without the observer being detected. Infrared thermal-imaging cameras are used to detect heat loss in insulated systems, to observe changing blood flow in the skin, and to detect overheating of and electrical apparatus.

The Application of Communication Technology in Everyday Life

A day in the life of the student through the wonders of communications technology…

It's early Friday morning. The alarm rings. No, it's not your old alarm clock. Remember, when it broke, you started setting the alarm on your smartphone to wake you. Before breakfast, you remember that you're expecting an email from one of your classmates about a project on which you're both working, so you log into your email account. Working from your tablet or computer through the wireless Internet connection your family recently installed makes this a snap.

When you get to school, you log on to the Internet in the library before class starts to do a final bit of research for your current project. Because you expect to work on it this evening, you send a copy of some new results to your printer at home because it's been set up to communicate wirelessly with your home network.

During study hall, you check several newsgroups you subscribe to online to see if there any new developments to support your project. And your class may have a videoconference with a peer class in another classroom, city, or country.

In science class, you're assigned a task with your learning team; to use groupware, also known as collaborative software to pose questions to ask when a fellow team presents the results of their project research.

During the weekend, you want to conference with your cousin who just entered university. You fire up your computer or tablet, launch your Skype Internet conferencing application, and find out how he likes his new classes. Using a technology called voice over Internet protocol [VoIP] that is built into Skype, you can talk with him for free or at low cost — without making a telephone call. Or, you might instead decide to use the FaceTime app on your iPad, because like you, your cousin also has an iOS [Apple] device. And then the club to which you belong is planning get together, and you're in charge of special events, so you open up your instant messenger and exchange a few ideas. You remember to save them off in the file, so you can work on them further.

Later, you and a friend decide to walk to the local McDonald's; you send your mother an SMS text message [short message service] from your smartphone letting her know what time you'll be home.

On Sunday evening, your family decides to try a new restaurant, so you turn on the GPS [global positioning system] in the car or on your mobile phone to check the directions. From your phone, you leave a voicemail with the restaurant to see if you can get an earlier table. After dinner, you take a picture of the family and send it to your cousin through your smart phones multimedia messaging service [MMS]. Next time, you promise yourself, you'll send him a video instead.

Then it's time to set your smartphone alarm to be ready for Monday morning – and a new week.

Whew! It's almost dizzying, isn't it? But can you imagine living without all these amazing connectivity devices and tools that make life more connected, more efficient — and often more fun?

Networking Concepts

A computer network or data network is a telecommunications network that allows computers to exchange data. In computer networks, networked computing devices pass data to each other through data connections. The connections [network links] between nodes are established using either various types of cables — or wireless media. Networks exist for the sole purpose of sharing information between people or machines. To share information, however, rules must be followed to so that the all the different types of devices, transporting mechanisms, hardware, and software can communicate efficiently and smoothly.

Why Use a Network?

Without access to networks of various types, users of a computer, smartphone, or tablet would have to work in isolation from outside information — and other people. Through networks, people and organizations can share information, access centralized file storage, or communicate by email or messaging with others. Networks enable people to perform everyday tasks and activities; perform research, conduct business electronically make purchases, check and airline arrival status, send and receive email, or play games.

Types of Networks

Local Area Network [LAN]

A **LAN** is a system that connects network devices over a relatively short distance. A networked office building, school, or home may contain a single LAN, though sometimes one building will have a few small LANs, and occasionally a LAN will connect a group of computers located in nearby buildings. Devices can be connected to the LAN either through the use of wires – or wirelessly.

A LAN has two basic elements; the **topology,** the method of hardware connection, and the **protocol**, a standard set of rules describing how data is communicated between the devices.

A LAN is made up of the following components:

- **Server.** A file server is a computer attached to a network, dedicated to providing a location for shared storage of computer files that can be accessed by the computers [often called **clients**] attached to the same network. A file server does not typically performed computational tasks, and may not run programs on behalf of its clients. The file server also provides data security for data throughout the network, often through a combination of antivirus, anti-phishing, and malware software protection as well as hardware devices dedicated to security.
- **Communications links**. A network must have a method to connect the clients in the network with the server, and also with each other. Communications links include fibre optic cables, telephone wires, coaxial cable, satellite, infra-red, and wireless connections.
- **Software.** Software consists of computer programs that establish the connection through the communications links between the server and the clients, or other peripherals such as printers. This type of software program is called a network operating system [NOS].

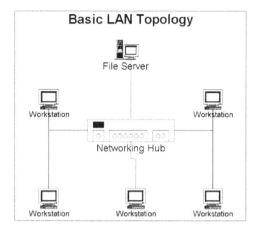

Basic LAN Topology

Notes:

- In larger networks, a networking hub may be used to connect many desktops and laptops — as well as printers — to the file server.
- Larger networks may have multiple file servers.

Benefits of the LAN to Individual Users

- **Data Sharing.** The ability to share data, if the network administrator has allowed this. [Often, certain folders and files are made available to specific departments or workgroups across an organization.]
- **Resource Sharing.** Users typically have access to common peripherals such as printers, scanners, and fax services.
- **Communications.** Often users on computers and laptops are permitted to with each other.
- **Working remotely.** Often networks are configured to allow some or all users to access their files from outside of the physical walls of the organization, when traveling, working at another location, or logging in from home.

Benefits of the LAN to the Organization

- **Centralized Access.** Simultaneously access centrally located processors, data, or programs [instruction sets];
- **Cost.** Since less equipment is needed, organizations often realize lower overall cost to provide an IT platform to its members.
- **Productivity.** Users all access the network the same way, and their files are backed up nightly on the file server, reducing the possibility of lost data.
- **Security.** Many layers of security can be implemented using the network operating system. This includes logins, passwords, file access by user, and also the ability to control who can access the Internet – and to what extent.
- **Network Administration.** One or more individuals are charged with the responsibility for architecting and maintaining the network. They are also the individuals who will troubleshoot network connectivity issues, and provide consulting to the organization regarding network systems.

LAN Topologies

When local area networks first emerged, there were three predominant topologies.

Topology Type	Architecture	Advantages and Disadvantages
Star	All of the computers are connected to a central server. 	*Advantages:* • Easy to add devices • If one computer fails or a cable becomes damaged, the rest of the network devices are usually not effected Disadvantages: • Requires more cabling • If the server fails, the entire network is affected
Ring	Ring topologies are similar to bus topologies, except they transmit in one direction only from station to station. Typically, a ring architecture uses separate physical ports and wires for transmit and receive; more than one ring is usually used to enable bi-directional communication. 	*Advantages:* • Communication is usually faster than with a line network • Easy to configure Disadvantages: • If the main cable is damaged the entire network goes down • Difficult to maintain
Bus	A single cable forms the backbone, with nodes at different points. Data is sent along the line in packets. 	*Advantages:* • Less hardware to set up • Easy to configure Disadvantages: • If the cable fails, the entire network goes down • Collisions of data packets result in data loss Note: Bus technology is not widely used anymore because of its

		disadvantages.

WAN Technology

A WAN, wide area network, is a network in which computers are separated by large distances and therefore must be serviced via modems rather than network cards. Companies with multiple locations and larger city governments are two examples of organizations that use a WAN.

The largest WAN is the internet, a collection of networks and gateways linking millions — possibly billions — of computer, smartphone, and tablet users worldwide.

Wide area networks are connected by several different types of communication systems. These communication paths are referred to as links. Individuals connect to a wide area network in different ways.

- Individuals in homes use a broadband connection provided by their local phone, cable TV, or satellite TV company.
- Some home users still connect to a WAN network such as the Internet using a dial-up modem. However with the stream sizes of digital images and movie streaming, it is difficult or impossible to download these massive amounts of data through a dial-up modem.
- Users in schools, companies, and government typically use high-speed connection lines. A digital modem makes the connection, so no analog conversion is needed, resulting in faster display of data and images. WAN connection technologies include leased lines, packet switches, and cell relays.

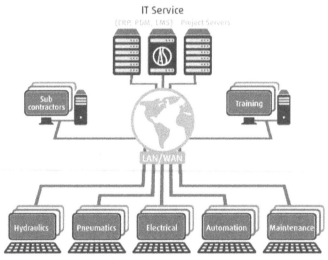

Corporate Departments

Unit Summary

In this unit, you have learned about the following topics and concepts:

- The meaning of the term data communication
- Identification of different communication devices and their uses
- The appearance and function of transmission media
- Types of networks and the advantages of each
- How communication technology benefits individuals in everyday life

Practice Questions and Activities.

1. What is the difference between analog and digital signals?

2. List the five components necessary to use data communications:

3. _____

4. _____

5. _____

6. _____

7. _____

8. What two processes are combined within a modem?

9. What is the transmission media that is replacing physical methods?

10. What are three benefits gained by an individual when using a network?

11. Have ten students play telephone, whispering a message representing a component of a successful communication to the next student.

12. Show a variety of communication devices; and have the students identify the type of device and the types of communication that can occur over the medium.

13. Have students create a model of a telecommunication network using four materials; plastic, string, paper and an empty soda can.

14. Ask students to keep a log for one week tracking the different communication devices they use — and for how long they use each device. After sharing their results, conduct a discussion about the time periods, and the impact on students' day-to-day lives.

15. Have students form small teams to complete the crossword puzzle on the next page.

16. s

Across:

2. Information sent through radio wave

3. Cells which wirelessly connect voice calls

6. A network topology

Down:

1. Method for connecting computer to Internet

4. Method of transmission media witho cable

5. Single panel general-purpose comp

7. Mobile phone with advanced feature

8. Cable for connecting multimedia de

Learning Objectives

This unit is designed to help you appreciate the ethics relating to ICT and its impact on society. Upon completion, you should be able to:

- Define ethics terms; including copyright, intellectual property, hacking, piracy, privacy invasion
- Describe the implications of computer ethics on society
- Identify consequences resulting from copyright infringement on intellectual property, invasion of privacy, and hacking
- Demonstrate an understanding of paraphrasing and citing sources
- Identify types of computer crimes; as target, instrument, or crimes associated with the prevalence of computers
- Identify security threats and the safeguarding of computers
- Describe the social responsibilities of using electronic devices, including lab ethics

A Definition of Computer Ethics

Computer ethics are a set of moral principles that govern the use of computers. Some common issues surrounding computer ethics include copyright, intellectual property, hacking, piracy, and the invasion of privacy.

What is Copyright?

Copyright provides its holder with the right to restrict unauthorized copying and reproduction of an original expression such as a literary work, a movie, music, a painting, or computer software. The violation of copyright law can be addressed in the United States through civil or criminal courts. Punishment varies among countries.

What is Intellectual Property?

Intellectual property represents creations of the mind such as musical, literary, and artistic works; inventions; symbols, names, images, and designs used in commerce, including copyrights, trademarks, patents, and related rights. Under intellectual property law, the holder of one of these abstract properties has certain exclusive rights to the creative work, commercial symbol, or invention by which it is covered. Unauthorized use, called infringement, may be a breach of civil or criminal law, depending on the type of intellectual property and the violation committed.

What is Hacking?

Hacking is defined as the access of someone else's computer system without permission in order to obtain or change information. In the U.S., three federal agencies may be involved in an investigation of hacking: the FBI local office where the hacking occurred, the U.S. Secret Service, and the Internet Crime Complaint Center, a partnership between the FBI and the national White collar crime Center.

What Does Piracy Mean?

Piracy is the unauthorized copying of software property. Specific types of piracy are described below.

Type of Piracy	Example
Counterfeiting	Duplicating and selling unauthorized copies of software
Soft Lifting	The purchasing of a single licensed copy of software and loading it on several machines
Hard Disk Loading	Selling computers pre-loaded with illegal software. In most cases, the PC manufacturer will not supply the installation media, license agreement, manual, or other documentation.
Bulletin Board Piracy	Putting software on a bulletin-board service for anyone to copy, or copying software from a bulletin-board service which is not shareware or freeware.
Software Rental	The rental of software for temporary use. In the US, the Software Rental Amendments Act of 1990 prohibits the rental, leasing, or lending of original copies of any software without the express permission of the copyright owner. Similar laws exist in other countries.

Most developed countries in the world have laws to protect software publishers from violations of software piracy.

What is Software Privacy?

Privacy is the protection given to information to conceal it from unauthorized persons having access to it. With the proliferation of laptops followed by tablet computing and smartphone use, there are many opportunities for the compromise of personal and commercial privacy of electronic information. Here are just three examples of situations when information privacy can be compromised:

- Working in public places or environments such as coffee shops, buses, trains, or airplanes where prying eyes might capture enough information to compromise your information integrity
- When using unsecured Wi-Fi networks to connect to the Internet, and logging into sites such as online banking
- Accessing business information from an unsecured device such as a public computer.

Software that records your keyboard and mouse activity [key logging or keylogger programs] can be downloaded in secret to your computer in order to make a physical copy of all keystrokes you press when logging into Internet sites. This can results in the compromising of private information.

Examples of Privacy Compromise

In late 2013, Target Brands, Inc. based in Minneapolis, MN announced a security breach with an invasion of information privacy affecting upwards of 40 million customers. Whomever compromised the security of the Target site and/or its customer information databases now holds massive amounts of private consumer information. This data can be sold to other criminals for purposes such as identity theft and credit card fraud. The potential damage implication of this recent privacy exposure can cost Target Brands, Inc. – as well as consumers – billions of dollars, and may have far-reaching negative effects for years. Adobe Systems also sustained a breach of customer credit card data in mid-2013. In addition to the public losing trust for a retailer to appropriately protect information, affected companies also must go to great lengths to try to secure data even more stringently. On a smaller scale, but no less detrimental, individual privacy is also an exposure.

What is Computer Crime?

Computer crime, or cybercrime, is a purposeful action to steal, damage, or destroy computer data without authorization, and the access of a computer system and/or user account without authorization.

Types of Computer Crime

Computer crime involves any criminal act that affects a computer and/or a network. Many forms of computer crime exist. And as beneficial as computers and the Internet are to billions of people, some people regrettably choose to use their knowledge and skills in ways that are unethical in order to try to make money or cause problems for others. People like this do not seem to care whether the target is an individual, an organization -- or an entire nation. Several overarching types of criminal activity exist; we will discuss each below.

- Crimes that target an individual computer
- Crimes that use an individual computer as an instrument to facilitate criminal activity
- Crimes facilitated by computer networks or devices.

Crimes Targeting an Individual Computer

Malicious software aimed at an individual computer user can be written. The malicious software downloads when the user logs into a compromised website, clicks a link without investigating its purpose, or uses an Internet connection that is not secure.

Viruses execute instructions that the user did not authorize. Damage to the computer may include deleting, copying, blocking or modifying data, or altering the way in which the computer performs. To protect yourself, install antivirus software, and keep it up-to-date. If the software detects any malicious code, it should quarantine, or isolate the information so that any malicious programs cannot be executed.

Also, be cautious at any website if pop-ups appear offering to provide free software to "maintain" your computer. There may be a virus payload hidden in the download. Once a computer is infected, it is extremely difficult, time-consuming, and often expensive to remove the malicious software and restore the system to normal. And if a recent data backup is not available, one also risks partial or complete loss of data.

Crimes Using a Computer as an Instrument to Enable Criminal Activity

There are many ways in which individuals utilize a computer to commit one or more crimes. Below are several examples, all of which occur in today's computer-prolific environment.

Phishing. Phishing is the act of trying to obtain information such as usernames, passwords, and credit card data by pretending to be a trustworthy entity. Most phishing attempts arrive in the form of an email message from a familiar source such as your bank or credit card company. The criminal provides a story suggesting that you must take action immediately or something will occur, such as closing down your account. He or she provides a link to the supposed site where the victim is to log in. The site, however, is phony, and the criminal has gained and individual's private information with which to commit identity theft or to compromise a bank account.

Wire Fraud. Wire fraud is any fraudulent scheme to purposefully deprive an individual of property or honest services through the use of mail or wire communication. Wire fraud has been a federal crime in the United States since 1872, currently with a penalty of imprisonment of up to 20 years. Today, computers often provide the electronic communication medium for wire transfers.

Digital Counterfeiting. Criminals have learned how to use computers and laser printers to create fake paper currency, and counterfeit checks. Violators of counterfeiting law can be prosecuted for charges such as attempted theft by fraud, and forgery. If you suspect you have been given counterfeit currency or a counterfeit check, take it to your local police station.

Child Pornography. An unfortunate result of the proliferation of the Internet and chat rooms has been an increase in the conduct of child pornography through electronic means. Images are stored on personal computers, and then sent by email to other people or posted on Internet sites such as peer-to-peer networks, where members make all or some of their information available to other members. Most developed countries have federal law which makes child pornography activity a crime punishable by jail terms and fines.

Crimes Associated with the Prevalence of Computers

Zombie Networks. A **bot**, short for robot, is a unique type of computer virus that infects and compromises the security of several computers. The bot takes control of them and creates a network of "bots" to be managed remotely as a "zombie" network. The criminal then uses the zombie network in several ways; to create a denial of service attack against a site such as an online retailer.

Distributed Denial of Service Attacks [DDoS]. In a denial of service attack, the file servers of an Internet site are bombarded with repeated login requests from bots throughout a zombie network. These requests overwhelm the traffic capacity of the servers, making it difficult or impossible for legitimate individuals to login. Shutting down the access requests and restoring a server to a functionality represent wasted time, and loss of business potential.

Bulk Spam. Criminals use spambots, or software search engines designed to find and collect email addresses. They then create a fake email name and email address and create a subject line that is designed to bypass spam-checking software. Millions of spam are sent out each day across the globe, causing email providers, corporate IT team members, and computer users much time and energy trying to block spam, or simply to dispose of it.

Consequences of Breaking the Laws

Many countries, provinces, states, and jurisdictions have created laws to punish convicted computer criminals who violate copyright, invade individual or business privacy, or gain unauthorized access into a computer or system by hacking. After all, these criminals have taken something that doesn't belong to them, and used it for their own betterment, or to willfully provide damages to others. This is theft.

Cybercrime laws are updated often as the criminals become more sophisticated about ways in which to break laws. People who are caught conducting computer crime face prosecution. Depending on the severity of the crime, penalties include fines, jail time, and/or probation. As an example, in the United States in 2010, a person convicted of the felony of accessing a computer to "defraud and obtain value" one face a minimum prison sentence of five years, and a maximum of 10 years.

If at school you become aware of any unauthorized computer activity – or activity that you suspect is illegal – please report it to your teacher.

Malware Security Threats

Malware, short for malicious software, is software that is used to disrupt computer operations, gather sensitive information, or gain access to private computer systems. Malware can appear as programming code, scripts for execution by a computer, active content, or other software variants. The most prevalent types of malware are described below.

Type of Malware	Examples
Virus	A computer virus is a type of malware that, when executed, replicates by inserting copies of itself into other computer programs, data files, or the boot sector of a computer's hard drive, infecting the normal operation of the computer in one or more ways.
Worm	A computer worm is a standalone malware computer program that replicates itself in order to spread to other computers. Often, it uses a computer network to spread itself, relying on security failures on the target computer to access it. Unlike a computer virus, a warm does not need to attach itself to an existing program. Worms almost always cause some type of harm to the network such as consuming bandwidth as opposed to viruses that almost always corrupt or modify files on a targeted computer.
Trojan Horse	A Trojan horse is any program that entices the user to run it, concealing harmful or malicious programming code. The code may take effect immediately, and can lead to many undesirable effects, such as deleting a user's files — or installing additional harmful software.
Rootkit	A rootkit is concealed software that modifies a computer's operating system so that the malware is hidden from the user. Rootkits can prevent a malicious process from being visible in the system's list of processes, or keep its files from being read. Party boy Florida
Spyware	Spyware is software that is installed on the computer in secret, gathering information about a person or organization. It may send such information to another entity without the user's consent, or that asserts control over a computer without the user's knowledge.
Adware	Adware, or advertising-supported software, is any software package which automatically renders advertisements in order to generate revenue for its author. The advertisements may be in the user interface of the software — or on a screen presented to the user during the installation process. Functionality may be designed to analyze which Internet sites the user visits and to present advertising pertinent to the types of goods or services featured there.

Security Safeguards

As the Internet grows and computer criminals find new ways to hack into systems, it's critical to take measures to apply protections to personal and commercial data. Below are several important actions you must always take to maximize the security of electronic information.

- Install and maintain current antivirus software on every computer or laptop. Make sure that the computer on which you work is protected by a firewall, a software and/or hardware barrier that protects a home or business network from penetration by an unauthorized user or software program.

- Consider installing software such as Ad-Aware, which protects against adware and spyware.

- Use unique passwords that are not easily figured out, but something that you can remember. Work to create strong passwords that include a combination of letters and numbers, but together in random order. Do not use the same password for every single account login.

- If you work on a network, remember to sign off the computer when you are finished working.

- Always question the origin of any email you receive. If you do not know the sender or are unfamiliar with the nature of the subject line, delete the message.

- Never click a link contained in the body of an email message. Instead, write down the URL information and login through the provider's login screens.

- Open only email attachments sent to you by someone you know – or from a trusted source. If you cannot verify the source, immediately delete the email attachment.

Paraphrasing

Paraphrasing is a restatement of a text or passage in another form or other words. Using paraphrasing, you are:

- Presenting your own version of important information and ideas written by another person, written in a new way

- Using one legitimate method to borrow from a source, as long as you add accurate citation documentation

- Distinguishing the material from a summary, a passage that focuses briefly on one main idea, rather a comprehensive restatement.

Below are steps to follow when working with information that you intend to paraphrase.

17. Review the original content; be sure you comprehend it fully.

18. Write your paraphrase without looking at the original.

19. Make a few notes near the paraphrase as a reminder about how you think you want incorporate the material. Add a key word or phrase to remind you about the subject of your paraphrase.

20. Compare your paraphrase content with the original to ensure that you have accurately expressed all the key information in a manner that is new.

21. If you borrow any term or phrase directly from the source, be sure to insert quotation marks.

22. Write down the source and the page with your notes in case you decide later to include it and appropriately credit source.

Aside from the legalities, paraphrasing provides you with several advantages:

- It is preferable to quoting information from a mediocre portion of text.
- It helps you avoid the temptation to perform too much quoting.
- By reviewing the material, and then writing the paraphrasing separately, you gain a more full comprehension of the original source.

Citing Sources Properly

Paraphrased electronic content must always be properly cited, According to the Purdue Owl Online Writing Lab. The citation below conforms to the MLA format. The "Owl" explains that the URL is no longer required, however you may still include it at the end of the citation, surrounded with angle brackets.

> Russell, Tony, Allen Brizee, Elizabeth Angeli, Russell Keck, Joshua M. Paiz, and Purdue OWL Staff. *"MLA Works Cited: Electronic Sources". The Purdue OWL.* Purdue U Writing Lab, 14 Dec. 2012. Web. 29 Jan. 2014. <https://owl.english.purdue.edu/owl/resource/747/08/>

Remember! It is important to take notes when you encounter and are working with a source. It's always better than returning later – and having to retrace your steps.

Using Electronic Devices in a Socially Responsible Way

Schools and universities go to great length and expense to create and maintain computer labs for use by students. Labs are provided at no cost to you to foster learning. Computer equipment in labs should be used only for academic purposes. As a student, it is your responsibility to make sure that you understand the rules – and follow them.

In the school computer lab, prohibited activities include:

- The making, viewing, and or distribution of inappropriate videos and pictures such as depiction of violence, pornography, or other socially offensive materials.
- The distribution of inappropriate text, including jokes, chain email messages, or distributing any text that does not support academic or research purposes.

Check the lab in your school for policies applicable to your lab environment.

Unit Summary

In this unit, you have learned about the following topics and concepts:

- The meaning of ethics terms; copyright, intellectual property, hacking, piracy, and privacy invasion
- The implications to society when computer ethics are compromised
- The consequences resulting from copyright infringement on intellectual property, invasion of privacy, and hacking
- An understanding of paraphrasing and citing sources
- the identification of types of computer crimes; as the target, the instrument, or crimes associated with the prevalence of computers
- identification of security threats – and the safeguarding of computers
- The social responsibilities of using electronic devices, including lab ethics

Practice Questions and Activities

1. List three types of malware that can affect a computer. Add a brief description of each type.

A.
B.
C.

2. Participate in a class discussion about how ethical considerations discussed in this unit impacts your school, your daily life outside school, or your country.

3. Form small groups. Debate any or all of the consequences resulting from:

    a. Copyright infringement on intellectual property,
    b. Invasion of privacy
    c. Hacking
    d. Electronic eavesdropping.

4. Given an example of a portion of copyrighted text, work alone or in small groups to practice your paraphrasing skills and how to cite the source of the work.

5. Based on the content of this unit, prepare questions and then conduct interviews with IT and other business or government executives to learn about efforts and the impact of computer ethics on their company/organization.

6. Divide into teams. List and prioritize at least three consequences to an organization when its systems are infected by malware. In a large group discussion after the exercise, compare notes with fellow teams.

7. Individually or in groups, create a list of lab rules and ethical behaviours when an individual does not behave according to them. What should the consequences be?

8. Write a one to two page paper that explores the concept of the invasion of privacy. Consider how criminals do this, and the damage that is caused. Conclude by listing efforts an individual can take to protect information privacy.

Learning Objectives

This unit is designed to help you understand the process of basic problem-solving. Upon completion, you should be able to:

- Define the term "problem"
- Identify the steps in order to solve a simple everyday problem
- Demonstrate your ability to solve a simple everyday real-world problem.

What is a Problem?

Problem-solving is the process of investigating to find answers or a solution to a problem. As you continue with your education, you will be presented with problems that need to be solved. It's important to have an approach to help you find a solution in an orderly way.

Steps to Solving a Problem

Problem-solving requires a methodical, rational approach. Here are four basic steps:

1. Understand and explore the problem
2. Gather related information
3. Use the related information to solve the problem
4. Look back and reflect on the applicability of the solution

When you follow specific steps toward solving the problem, and generate a solution that works, you have the confidence and satisfaction of knowing that the process worked. And if your chosen solution turns out to be not the best one, you can always re-evaluate your potential solutions and arrive at a better solution.

Solving Simple Real World Problems

Ordinary people are confronted with problems every day, all over the world. For you, as a student, the nature of problems can vary widely, from something basic such as "what clothes should I wear today?" to something more complex like "how I do complete my science homework?"

Let's try this together. Since we're thinking about clothes, how about using it as our problem?

And, oh, let's assume it's the weekend, Saturday, just in case you wear a uniform to school. [Wearing a uniform possibly rules out a lot of questions you might want to ask about your clothes for school.] :-)

Problem Statement: "It's Saturday. What clothes should I wear today?" Let's apply this problem to our model. We'll tackle this as a class working together. Think of your teacher as your problem-solving expert. After all, he or she has had many more years than you to work on problem solving. :-)

Try Brainstorming

Brainstorming is the act of generating ideas by holding a spontaneous group discussion, recording all ideas, categorizing them, and then analyzing them. Steps involved in a brainstorming session are:

1. Set up the area so that everyone can see each other, and so everyone can see what is being recorded on a marker board, flip chart, or using a projector.

2. Assign one person as the recorder. He or she will document all contributions.

3. Go over the rules. One person speaks at a time, all participants should contribute, all responses will be recorded, no answers are "wrong", and no one should insult or criticize another for a particular response.

4. Introduce the topic about which the group will brainstorm.

5. Determine a goal that everyone would like to have accomplished by the end of the session such as, a minimum number of ideas, everyone have at least two suggestions, or something similar.

6. As people are sharing their ideas, the recorder should try to group them in categories or sub-categories so the information is somewhat organized.

7. Once the brainstorming session is over, the group should analyze the list and evaluate each idea. When examining the responses, the group should combine repeated or similar ideas – and eliminate answers that do not fit. [Combining is called lassoing, just like a lasso; the rope thrown to catch a calf at a rodeo.]

Solve a Problem Together

With the results of brainstorming completed, ideas about related information have now been gathered and can be plugged back into problem-solving step number three.

Let's get started! Below are the four steps in the problem-solving process, along with some suggestions to get everyone started.

1. Understand and explore the problem

What exactly is the problem?

Why do decisions have to be made about this on Saturday morning?

??

??

2. Gather related information

What will the weather be today?

??

??

3. How can we use the information we've gathered to arrive at a solution, thus solving the problem?

What do we know now?

How to we apply it?

??

??

[See the Practice Questions section for a recording sheet for potential solutions.]

4. How did we do?

Once solved, it's a best practice to look back at the solution and reflect on its appropriateness for solving the problem.

Class discussion... with teacher as facilitator.

Unit Summary

In this unit, you have learned about the following topics and concepts:

- The meaning of the term "problem"
- Steps to take to solve the problem
- The ability to think through the steps in order to solve a simple everyday problem.

Practice Questions and Activities

1. Use sources such as your textbooks and/or Internet to research a definition for the term 'problem' and the steps to solve a problem

2. Summarize the steps to solve a simple everyday problems.

3. Work the steps below to solve this problem: **How to make a glass of lemonade.**

Step 1. Understand and explore the problem
Step 2. Gather related information
Step 3. Use the related information to solve the problem
Step 4. Looking back

Possible solution:

Step 2: Get required ingredients [glass, lemon, water, sugar, ice, spoon, knife]; Use utensils to combine ingredients

 Step 3:

Fill the glass ¾ way with water; Put three spoonfuls of sugar in glass; Use knife to cut lemon in halves; Squeeze half lemon to extract juice into glass; Use spoon to stir/mix until sugar is dissolved; Add three cubes of ice into glass

Step 4: Looking Back: Is the lemonade to my taste? Do I need to add more sugar, water, ice or lemon?

The Problem:

_____

Possible Solution	Pros	Cons
1		
2		
3		
4		
5		

My/Our Solution:

_____

Did the solution work?

- If yes, terrific!
- If no, I/we need to choose another solution.

Notes…

Unit 9B: Intermediate Problem Solving

Learning Objectives

This unit is designed to help you develop the knowledge and skills to solve more complex problems. Upon completion, you should be able to:

- Define the problem
- Identify the steps to take to solve a problem
- Solve a simple real world problem
- Define the term algorithm
- Write an algorithm to solve a simple real world problem
- Demonstrate the use of the algorithm as you solve a problem.

What is a Problem?

Problem-solving is the process of investigating to find answers or a solution to a problem.

Problem-Solving Steps

In unit 9A, we followed four basic steps to solve a simple problem. Let's review them.

1. Understand and explore the problem
2. Gather related information
3. Use the related information to solve the problem
4. Look back and reflect on the applicability of the solution.

We used picking out our clothes for a Saturday as the problem we wanted to solve. We stated the problem, gathered ideas from the group to analyze alternatives, and then generated solutions, selecting one. Finally, we took a look back to consider how applicable the chosen solution was for solving the problem.

Solve a Simple Real World Problem

Today, let's apply these steps to brushing your teeth, something we all do every morning.

Try It!

- As a class or in small groups, follow the process and arrive at a solution for this problem: I need to brush my teeth when I wake up. How do I accomplish that?
- Afterward, look back. How did the process go? Was the solution achieved? Was it the appropriate solution?

What is an Algorithm?

An algorithm is a procedure or a set of rules for solving a problem.

Use Algorithms to Solve Simple Real World Problems

We can use an algorithm to apply structure to the steps we follow to solve a problem. We will use a similar process as before, but we'll add the structure of the algorithm:

1. Understand and explore the problem

2. Gather related information

4. Use the related information to solve the problem, placing it in the algorithm.

5. Look back and reflect on the solution.

Here's an example.

Step	Process
1. Understand and explore the problem	Make a phone call using a cell phone with a prepaid plan. Related information: • Know the name of the person you're calling • Know the person's phone number
2. Gather related information to solve the problem	How do I dial a number and make a call? Where do I hear the voice of the person I'm calling? How will I know that the call was connected? What will the speaker sound like? How do I end the call?
3. Build an **algorithm** that lists the instructions to solve the problem, using the information you gathered **Important!** Start every statement in the algorithm with a verb, indicating an action will happen.	Pick up the cell phone Use the keypad to dial the number Press the send/go button Place the phone next to your ear Wait while the call is connected Wait for the person to pick up the phone Speak with the person Press the stop/end button to terminate the call
4. Look back and reflect on the solution to the problem	Questions can include: Did I know how to dial the keypad?

	What if the keypad was locked?
	Are the Send or Go button easy to find?
	Was the recipient of the call easy to Hear?
	End! [Problem solved]

Try It!

- Using the model above, follow the steps process to explain how to fry an egg, including an algorithm to follow.

- When complete, compare your algorithm with those written by your classmates.

- How did the algorithm make the process of solving the problem more concrete?

- Discuss results with your classmates.

Unit Summary

In this unit, you have learned about the following topics and concepts:

- A definition of the term problem
- The steps to follow to solve a problem
- Solving simple real world problem
- Defining the term algorithm
- writing an algorithm to solve a simple real world problem
- Demonstrating your understanding of the use of the algorithm as you solve a problem.

Practice Questions and Activities

1. Define the term algorithm.

2. Do some research about algorithms. In what ways other than what we explored are they used?

3. Demonstrate your understanding of the use of an algorithm to solve a problem by defining a problem, and then following the process we followed in this section. What did you learn? Share your results with your classmates.

Learning Objectives

This unit is designed to assist students in developing the requisite knowledge and skills to solve problem. Upon completion, you should be able to:

- Define problem
- Identify the steps in solving a problem
- Solve simple real world problem
- Define the term algorithm
- Write algorithms to solve simple real world problems
- Discuss the concept and purpose of a flow chart
- Identify, draw and explain flow chart symbols
- Use flow charts to solve a problem.

What is a Problem?

Problem-solving is the process of investigating to find answers or a solution to a problem.

Problem Solving Steps

The following steps allow you to follow the process of investigation to find answers or solution to a problem.

5. Understand and explore the problem

6. Gather related information

7. Use the related information to solve the problem

8. Look back and reflect on the solution

Try It!

- Decide upon a problem you want to solve.

- Follow the problem-solving process, including writing an algorithm as you did in unit 9B.

What is an Algorithm?

An algorithm is a procedure or a set of rules for solving a problem. Different types of steps that can be part of an algorithm include:

Sequential. Steps to follow in order; when one is completed, the next is started.

Conditional. Whether a step is completed depends on a specified condition that must be met. If the condition is met, the process continues as planned. But if the condition is not met, something else will happen.

Repetitive. Anything that happens over and over again. A synonym for repetitive is "loop".

Euclid, an Ancient Greek in 300 BC, also known as Euclid of Alexandria, was a Greek mathematician, often referred to as the "Father of Geometry". His theories regarding geometry were actively followed until the late 19th or early 20th century. Below is a simple program written to express the steps to follow to find the greatest common divisor for a specified number, one of Euclid's major theories, or algorithms. What's important here is the fact that the program follows an algorithm; a procedure or a set of rules for solving a problem.

- Notice that beginning with line number 6, there is a step-by-step listing of rules to follow to get to the end, line 90.

- Also notice that certain instructions are represented by an active verb; in this program, **print**.

```
5 REM Euclid's algorithm for greatest common divisor
6 PRINT "Type two integers greater than 0"
10 INPUT A,B
20 IF B=0 THEN GOTO 80
30 IF A > B THEN GOTO 60
40 LET B=B-A
50 GOTO 20
60 LET A=A-B
70 GOTO 20
80 PRINT A
90 END
```

What is a Flow Chart?

Simply put, a flow chart is a graphical representation of a set of activities performed to solve a problem. Defined another way, a flowchart is a type of diagram that represents an algorithm or process, showing the steps as boxes of various kinds, and their order by connecting them with arrows. Flowcharts are used in various fields to analyze, design, document, or manage a process or program. Here is an example of a flowchart for a solution to a problem of wanting lunch.

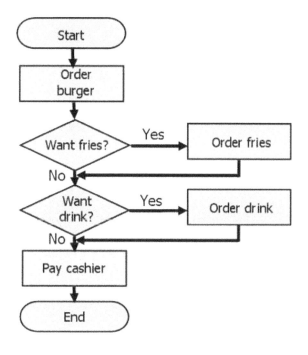

Flow Chart Symbols

The symbols below are basic symbols that you will find in just about every flowchart that involves computerized system. These symbols can also be used to document statements in an algorithm that is used to solve a problem or to complete a process.

Symbol	Purpose
	Start or End
	Input/Output
	Process
	Storage
	Decision

	Data Flow

Use a Flow Chart to Solve a Problem

In Unit 9B, we wrote a simple algorithm to list the instructions to follow to place a cell phone call. We can use that information to build a flow chart.

Action	Flow Chart Diagram Result	
Pick up the cell phone	Start	
Use the keypad to dial the number. [We assume you know the number.]	Input/Output	
Press the send/go button	Process	
Place the phone next to your ear	Process	
Has the person answered the phone? If yes, move on. If no, wait.	Decision	
Have the conversation.	Process	
End the call.	End	

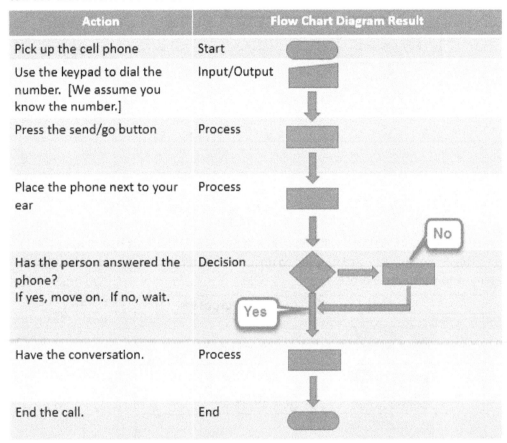

Try It!

- Discuss the flow chart above. Does it follow the process? What, if anything might you want to add based on your understanding of the problem — and the process?

Unit Summary

In this unit, you have learned about the following topics and concepts:

- Defining a problem
- Identifying the steps necessary to solve a problem
- Solving simple real world problem
- Defining the term algorithm
- Writing algorithms to solve simple real world problems
- Discussing the concept and purpose of a flow chart
- Identifying, drawing and explaining flow chart symbols
- Using flow charts to solve problem.

Practice Questions and Activities

1. Use sources such as textbook or Internet to research a definition for the term problem, the steps to solve a problem and algorithm.

2. Select any everyday problem you might encounter. Write steps that allow you to solve this simple real world problems.

3. Create a flow chart that represents the solution to a problem such as putting on socks and sneakers, or finding the sum of two numbers and calculator. First, write the steps of the problem, then build your flowchart diagram. Finally, check your diagram to be sure it represents the correct activities and flow.

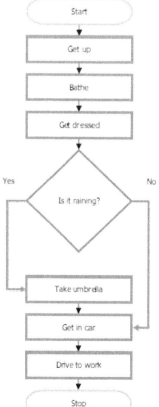

Here's an example of how your finished work should look:

Problem

Does Janice need her umbrella?

Background

It is Tuesday morning. Janice gets up, bags, dresses for work, and must make a choice whether to take her umbrella before she heads out for work. She will take her umbrella if it is raining. Write an algorithm that represents the activities that Janice performed on Tuesday morning. Then design a flowchart for these activities.

Solution, in Steps

Start

    Get up

    Bathe

    Dress

    If it is raining, then take umbrella

Get into car

Drive to work

Stop

Solution as Flow Chart

Unit 10A: Introduction to Word Processing

Learning Objectives

This unit is designed to teach you how to use a word processor to enhance text and document settings. Upon completion, you should be able to:

- State the purposes of word processing software
- Identify software products available for word processing
- Identify the different components and features of the word processor window
- Use word processing features to enter and manage text
- Use tab settings to create columnar data
- Apply font attributes to text.

Note: The procedures and illustrations in Units 10, 10B and 10C are based on Microsoft Word 2013. If you are working with an earlier version, you should find that most features work similarly. You can always press **F1** to get help specific to your product version.

Purpose and Examples of Word Processing

A word processor is a computer software application that allows you to take actions with words, sentences, and paragraphs.

Word processing was one of the earliest tools developed for a personal computer. Corel **WordPerfect**, older than Microsoft Word, was originally developed in 1979 at Brigham Young University in Utah to be used on Data General computers. With the release 5.1 in 1989, WordPerfect had become a standard in the DOS market, bypassing any other offerings.

Microsoft began development of **Word** in the early 1980s, but didn't gain much traction with the PC computing market until 1990, when they released the first edition of Word for Windows. WordPerfect followed shortly, however Word sales have outpaced WordPerfect sales from then on.

For those who want a free option, **Writer** is a word processor in Apache's OpenOffice software suite.

In addition to the ability to enter, move, and edit text, today's word processing software includes many other functionalities:

Feature	Brief Description
Page Layout	The page layout functions let you decide how each page will be set out.
Text Presentation	The appearance of text can be easily altered. Different fonts and styles can be

	used and the size of text can be varied.
Text Editing	Text editing functions are used to revise and change text you have entered.
Text Block Handling	The style and position of selected blocks of text can be changed.
Text Analysis	The word processor can look at your document and highlight errors such as spelling or grammatical mistakes.
Templates	Template files let you save favourite document layouts that you have created so that you can use them again later.
Mail Merge	A word processor allows you to combine information such as names and addresses with content such as a letter for mass mailings.
Reference Management	Features include a table of contents generation, creating footnotes and endnotes, formatting style for citations and bibliographies, adding figures and captions, indexing, and building tables of authorities.

Now let's launch **Microsoft Word** and take a tour.

- Launch Word from your Windows desktop or by clicking the **Start** button.
- Click **Blank document**.

A new document screen opens.

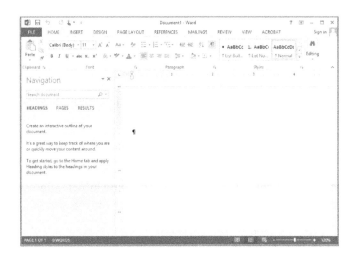

Parts of the Word Processor Window

The ribbon appears at the top of Microsoft Word 2007 and later versions. It is designed to help you quickly find the commands you need to complete a task. Commands are organized in groups located under tabs. Each tab relates to a type of activity, such as writing — or laying out a page.

To reduce clutter, some tabs are displayed only when needed. For example, the **Picture Tools** tab is shown only when a picture is selected.

Buttons are organized into groups according to the functions they perform. To access a feature, click its button. As you hover your mouse pointer over a button, a Screen Tip appears to provide information about the button.

Most groups on the ribbon also contain a small arrow in the lower right hand corner.   For additional features related to that group, click the arrow.

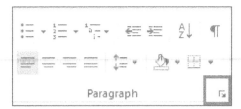

Below are the main features and functionality that appear when you launch **Word**.

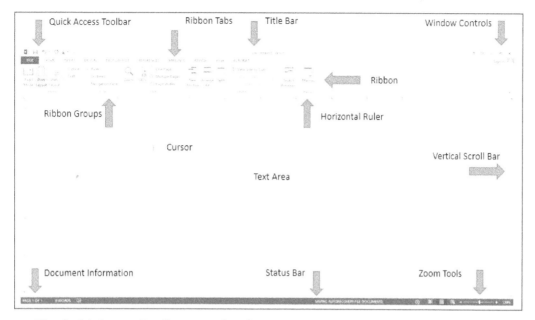

- The **Quick Access Toolbar** provides shortcuts to commonly used features.
- The **Ribbon contains Tabs** that organize tasks according to the future you are using, such as Font.
- **Ribbon Groups** provide commands applicable to the commands in the tab in which are working.
- The **Title Bar** at the top of the screen displays the name of the document in which you are working.
- The **Horizontal Ruler** serves as a guide when working with paragraphs, images, and tables.
- A **Vertical scrollbar** appears on the right side of your screen display more of your document if necessary. Drag the scrollbar up or down.
- A **horizontal scrollbar** appears if the document is wider than the screen can display. Drag the scrollbar left or right.
- **Document information** is displayed in the lower left corner of your screen
- The **Status Bar** displays information when necessary, such as when you are saving a document.
- The **Zoom Slider** in the lower right of the screen allows you to drag the slider bar to zoom in — or out.

Task Panes

Task panes provide a common area for commands that may require more information or options than the ribbon or its groups can provide. Task panes will open dynamically as you perform a task that requires them. Below, we see an example of the task with options or matting text effects. You won't be using this function again for a while, you can click the X close the pain.

145

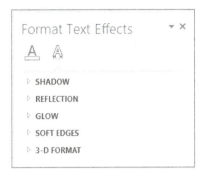

Format Text Effects

SHADOW
REFLECTION
GLOW
SOFT EDGES
3-D FORMAT

Use a Word Processor to Work with Text

Entering Text in a New Document

Follow the steps below to enter text into a new, blank document.

- Click your left mouse button near the cursor, the blinking vertical line.
- Begin typing.

Cursor

Saving a New Document

- Click the **File** tab.
- Click **Save As**.
- Browse to the location where you'd like to save your document.
- Choose a folder under **Computer** – or click **Browse** and locate a folder.
- Click **Save**.
  Word automatically saves files in the .docx file format. To save your document in a format other than .docx, click the **Save as type** list, and then select the file format that you want.

Tip! To save your document as you continue to work on it, click **Save** in the Quick Access Toolbar.

Entering Text in an Existing Document

- Click in the location in the existing text where you wish to add text.
- Begin typing.

Keys to Use When Working with Text

KEY	PURPOSE
Tab	Indent text [By default, in half inches to the right].
Shift	Press to create capital letters, or for symbols, with the appropriate number key representing the symbol
Caps Lock	Press once to turn Shift on; press again to turn Shift off.
Enter	Begin a new paragraph. [Note: Do not do this after each sentence. Word will automatically wrap the text to the next line.]
Backspace	Delete the character to the left of your cursor.
Delete	Delete the character to the right of your cursor.
Arrow Keys	Navigate through your document. [You can also use the scroll bars to do this.]

Cut, Paste, and Copy Text

Cut, copy, and paste are frequently-used functions for working with text.

>**Cutting text** means deleting it from one place.

>**Copying text** means making a duplicate of the text in the Windows clipboard.

>**Pasting text** means you can place text just copied into another location.

Cutting Text

When you cut text, is removed from the document and placed Windows clipboard so you can reuse it. Important! The text will be overwritten the next time you cut or copy text.

1. Select the text you wish to affect by dragging your mouse over it.
2. Choose one of the three methods below to cut the text.

Option	Steps	
Buttons on the Clipboard Ribbon Group	Click the **Cut** button in the **Clipboard** group on the ribbon.	Paste ✂ Cut 📋 Copy ❦ Format Painter Clipboard
Keyboard Shortcuts	Press and hold **Ctrl** while also pressing **X. [Ctrl + X]**	

Mouse Right-Click	Cut Copy Paste Options: Accept Format Change Reject Change Track Changes Hyperlink... New Comment

Right-click your mouse. In the fly-out menu that appears, choose **Cut**.

Copy Text

- Select the text you wish to affect by dragging your mouse over it.
- Choose one of the three methods below. [The text is copied, and placed in the Windows clipboard so that you can reuse it.]

Option	Steps	
Buttons on the Clipboard Ribbon Group	Click the **Copy** button in the **Clipboard** group on the ribbon.	Paste Cut Copy Format Painter Clipboard
Keyboard Shortcuts	Press and hold **Ctrl** while also pressing **C**. [**Ctrl + X**]	
Mouse Right-Click	Right-click your mouse. In the fly-out menu that appears, choose **Copy**.	Cut Copy Paste Options: Font... Paragraph... Define Synonyms Translate Search with Bing Hyperlink... New Comment

Paste Text

- With text already in the clipboard from a previous cut or copy operation, choose one of the three methods below.

Option	Steps	
Buttons on the Clipboard Ribbon Group	Click the **Paste** button in the **Clipboard** group on the ribbon. Choose a paste option	Paste Calibri (Body) B I U Paste Options: Paste Special... Set Default Paste...
Keyboard Shortcuts	Press and hold **Ctrl** while also pressing **V. [Ctrl + V]**	
Mouse Right-Click	Right-click your mouse. In the fly-out menu, choose **Paste Options**. Click **Paste**. [Note: There may be more than one paste option depending on what type of task you are performing.]	Cut Copy Paste Options: A Font... Paragraph... Define Synonyms Translate Search with Bing Hyperlink... New Comment

Formatting Text

You can apply many attributes to enhance the appearance of your text using the buttons in the **Font** group on the **Home** tab in the **Ribbon**.

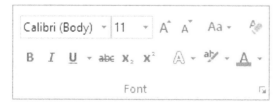

Notes:

- The buttons are toggle functions. That is, click to toggle the attribute on – and click again to toggle off.

- To apply a formatting attribute to existing text, first select it.

- For text you are going to type, you can invoke the attribute first. Any text you enter will be affected until you turn the attribute off by clicking the button again.

Below are the options found in the font group.

Text Attribute	Button to Click
Bold	Applies bold
Italics	Applies italics
Underscore	Applies underscore
Text Effects and Typography	Applies various text effects; outline, shadow, reflection, glow, number styles, ligatures, number styles.
Text Highlight Color	Highlights your text in a color you choose from the palette
Font Color	Changes the color of your font to your choice from the palette

As with text, you can format paragraphs using tools in the paragraph group.

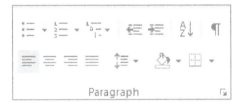

Paragraph Attribute	Button to Click
Bullets	Creates a bulleted list
Numbering	Creates a numbered list
Outlining	Generates an outline
Justification	Aligns the text Left, Center, Right Justify, or Fullly Justified
Indenting	Shifts your paragraph farther in from the left margin
Line and Paragraph Spacing	Determine how much spacing you you have between lines

Use Tab Settings to Create Lists of Data

To quickly set tabs in your document, click the ruler wherever you want to add a tab.

- Display the ruler at the top of your document by clicking **View** > **Ruler**.
- Click the tab selector at the left end of the ruler until it displays the type of tab stop you want.
- Click the bottom edge of the ruler wherever you want the tab.

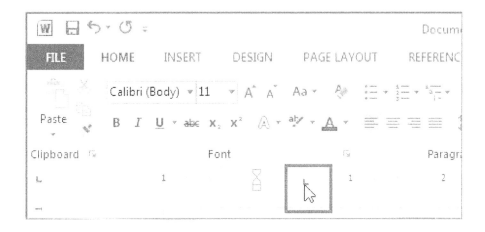

- To adjust the position of the tab, drag it left or right along the ruler, stopping where you want it.
- To remove a tab stop, drag it off the ruler.

Precisely Set Tab Stops Using the Tabs Dialog Box

If you want more precision than you can get with the ruler, or if you want to insert a specific character [leader] before the tab, use the **Tabs** dialog box.

- Click **Page Layout**, and then click the **Paragraph** Dialog Box Launcher.

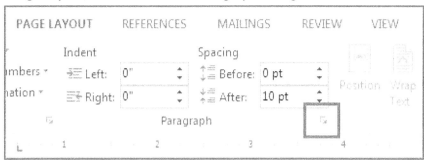

- Click **Tabs.**
- Under **Tab stop position**, type the location where you want to set the tab stop.

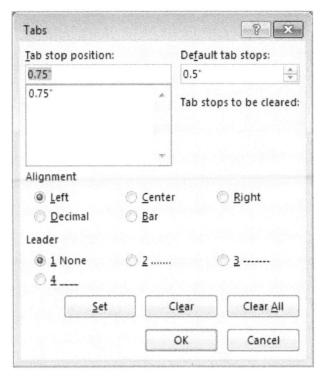

- Under **Alignment**, click the type of tab stop you want.
- To add dot leaders with your tab stop, or to add another type of leader, click the option that you want under **Leader**.
- Click **Set**.
- Repeat steps 3-6 to add another tab stop, or click **OK**.

With your tabs now set, let's see how tabs work with a list of names. We'll create a listing of first and last names.

Type a first name, press **TAB**, then type a last name. Note: you have tab options set in Display Options, a tab symbol, a right arrow will appear on your screen.

John   Doe

Sally   Smith

Change Font Attributes

Change Line Spacing

The fastest way to change the amount of space between lines of text – or between paragraphs for an entire document — is to use the **Paragraph Spacing** button on the **Design** tab. Using these set of tools, you can make both types of changes at the same time.

Change Line Spacing for Selected Text

- Select the text for which you want to make a change to the line spacing.
- Click the **Design** tab.
- Click Paragraph Spacing.

- Move your cursor over each of the spacing options under Built-In, and notice how the line spacing changes.
- Click the option you want. If you want to single space your document, choose No Paragraph Space.

Note: This overrides the settings of the style set you're currently using. If you decide later that you'd like to return to the original settings, click **Design > Paragraph Spacing** again and choose the option under **Style Set**. The option may be **Default**, as shown above, or it will show the name of style set you're currently using.

Change the Line Spacing in a Portion of the Document

- Select the paragraphs you want to change.
- On the Home tab, click the Line and Paragraph Spacing button.

- Choose the number of line spaces you want. Or, click Line Spacing Options at the bottom of the menu, and then select the options you want in the Paragraph dialog box under Spacing.

Adjust Indents and Spacing

When you want to make precise changes to your indents and spacing or you want to make several changes all at once, open the Paragraph dialog box and click the Indents and Spacing tab.

- Select the text you want to adjust.

- Click the Paragraph dialog box launcher on the Home tab or on the Page Layout tab.

- If necessary, click the Indents and Spacing tab.

- Choose your settings and click **OK**.

Modify the Font Size

- Select the text that you want to change.
- On the ribbon, click the **Home** tab.
- In the **Font** group, click the arrow next to **Font Size**, and then click to select a size. The point size of the text changes.

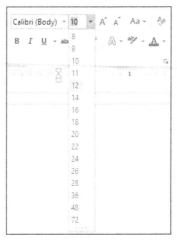

Apply Superscript or Subscript

Superscript and **subscript** represent a number, figure, symbol, or indicator that is smaller than the normal line of type. Superscript is set slightly above the normal line; subscript, slightly below it.

- Select the text that you want to make superscript or subscript.
- On the ribbon, click the **Home** tab.

- In the Font group, click X_2 for subscript, or click X^2 for superscript. Notice that your selected text is now subscripted of or superscripted.

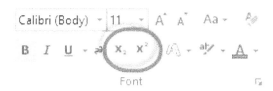

Change the Text Colour

- Select the text that you want to change.
- On the ribbon, click the **Home** tab.
- In the **Font** group, click the arrow next to Font Color, and then click to select a color. The text colour changes.

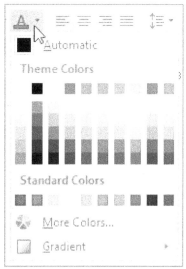

Note: You can also use the formatting options on the Mini toolbar to quickly format text. The Mini toolbar appears automatically when you select text.

Unit Summary

In this unit, you have learned about the following topics and concepts:

- The purposes of word processing software
- Products available for word processing software
- The different components and features of the word processor window
- Using word processing features to enter and manage text
- Creating columnar data using tab settings
- Applying font attributes to text

Practice Questions and Activities

1. List three attributes you can change from the Font group in the Home tab.

2. What keyboard shortcuts are used for cutting and for copying text? In what other one way can you accomplish each of these tasks?

3. Use a prepared text document to change font attributes. For a short paragraph:

   - Apply bold

   - Apply italics

   - Add a shadow or a glow to the text.

4. Using tabs, create a list of your classmates' names, along with a fun fact about each individual.

5. Using the table feature, create a table that compares the sales of three companies during the four monthly quarters of the business year. Set up your table like this:

Company	Jan-Mar	Apr-Jun	Jul-Sep	Oct-Dec
Soccer Sports				
Fun Fishing				
Sally's Salon				

Learning Objectives

This unit is designed to help you use more advanced Word Processing settings in the preparation of documents. Upon completion, you should be able to:

- Create a simple table
- Insert graphics into a word document
- Create a document with two or more columns

Create a Simple Table

Tables provide a much more manageable way to work with and format list information.

- Click **Insert** > **Table** and move the cursor over the grid until you highlight the number of columns and rows you want.
- Click your left mouse button. A new empty table appears in the document.

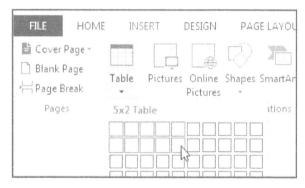

Making Changes in an Existing Table

Table Design

When you select a table, the **Table Design** tab opens and displays the **Table Tools** group.

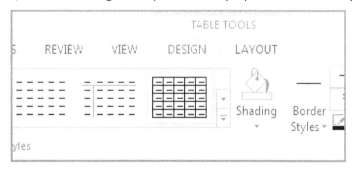

You can style your table by clicking any of the many styles. If you don't like the style, simply click a different one to see the result.

Table Layout

Use the **Layout** tab in **Table Tools** to choose different colours, table styles, and to add or remove a border.

Below are some examples of how to apply colors and borders.

Table Layout Task	Instructions
Choose different colours	Click any color in the **Shading** palette. 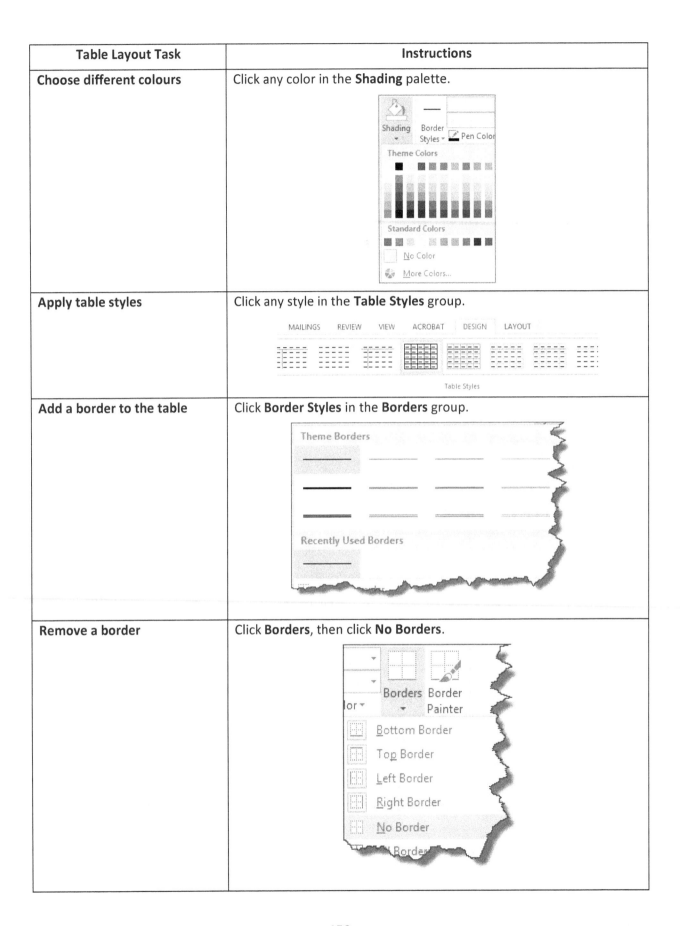
Apply table styles	Click any style in the **Table Styles** group.
Add a border to the table	Click **Border Styles** in the **Borders** group.
Remove a border	Click **Borders**, then click **No Borders**.

Insert or Remove Columns or Rows from a Table

- Select a row or column in the table.
- Right-click your mouse.
- Choose **Insert**.
- Select an insertion type from the flyout menu, such as **Insert Rows Above**.

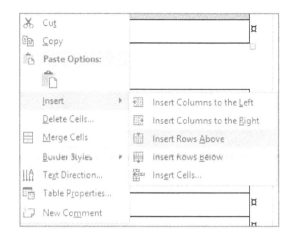

Convert Existing Text to a Table

If you already have text in your document that would look better as a table, Word can convert the text to a table. Below is an example of text in one row, with two columns. Note that a tab has been added as an indicator that there will be two columns.

My text   For a two-column table

To convert this text to a table:

- Select the text.
- Click **Insert > Table**.
- Click **Convert Text to Table**.

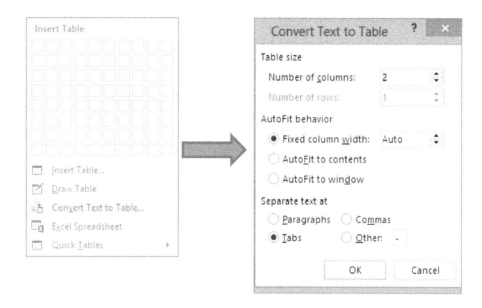

- In the **Convert Text to Table** dialogue, either accept the default column and row settings, or change them.
- Select the **AutoFit** behaviour, and, if you used a tab in your content, accept the default setting of Tabs as the method for separating text.
- Click **OK.**

Word places a table around your text. You can now format the table as you wish.

Below is how our sample table appears using the default settings.

My text	For a two-column table

Try It! Create a Simple Table

Below we've provided some text that needs to be converted to a table. Your result should be 3 columns wide by 4 rows long. If your teacher allows, pair up with a classmate or two!

Red Team	Monday	5pm
Green Team	Tuesday	5pm
Blue Team	Wednesday	5pm
Orange Team	Thursday	5pm

How does your table look? :-)

Insert Images into Documents

In Unit 1, you learned how to create graphic images, working in Microsoft Paint. Now, we will learn how to do this in Word, and how to modify the images you've inserted.

The **Illustrations** group on the **Insert** tab on the ribbon provides many options for inserting graphic images into your Word document.

Insert a Picture

- Click **Insert**. The Insert tab displays.

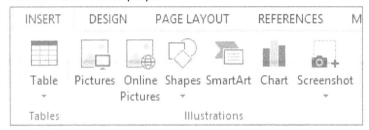

- Click **Pictures** from the **Illustrations** group.

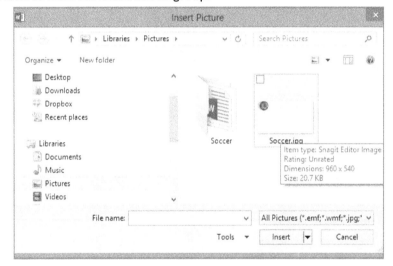

- In the **Insert Picture** dialogue, locate the picture that you want to insert. For example, you might have a picture file in My Documents or in Libraries.
- Double-click the picture that you want to insert.
- Click **Insert**. The picture is placed in the document at the cursor location.

Insert a Shape

- Click **Insert**. The Insert tab displays.
- Click **Shapes** from the **Illustrations** group. The Shapes palette displays.
- Click any shape, such as a flow chart symbol.
- Click in the text area, then drag your mouse. Your chosen shape appears.
- Release the mouse button when the shape reaches a size you like.

Edit Images

Once you have added an image, you can move and modify it.

Move or Size an Image

- To **move** an image, click to select it, then drag it to its new location.
- To **size** an image, drag the small square in any corner. Release the mouse left button when it reaches the size you want.

Change the Colour of a Shape

You can make a shape appear quite different from its default color.

- Select the shape size you want to modify. The **Format** tab appears on the ribbon.
- Click the **Format** tab. The Shape Styles group displays.

- Click the **Shape Fill** button in the **Shapes Styles** group.
- Click a colour from the **Theme Colors** task pane. Notice that the colour of the shape changes.

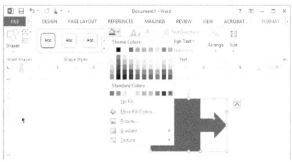

Add Special Effects to a Shape

The **Shape Effects** task panel in the **Shape Styles** provides special effects options you can apply to shapes.

- Click the shape to which you want to add an effect. [To add the same effect to multiple shapes, click the first shape, and then press and hold Ctrl as you click the other shapes.]
- On the **Format** tab, in the **Shape Styles** group, click **Shape Effects**, and select an option.

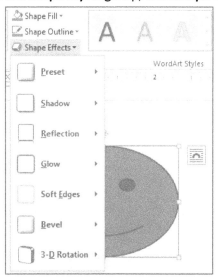

Below is a description of the function of each shape effect.

Effect Type	Function
Preset	Provides a variety already-applied shape attributes
Shadow	Used to apply Inner, outer, or perspective shadow options
Reflection	Creates a reflection of varying degrees
Glow	Applies a glow effect with color choices
Soft Edges	Softens the image edges in increments
Bevel	Adds sloping edges in increments
3-D Rotation	Gives rotation choices with dimensional characteristics

Change Shape Styles

Thematic shapes styles in Word let you quickly change the visual appearance of your shape.

- Click the shape.
- On the format tab in the **Shape Styles** group, click the arrow in the lower right corner.

- From the **Format Shape** task pane, choose to apply **Fill** and/or **Line** attributes.

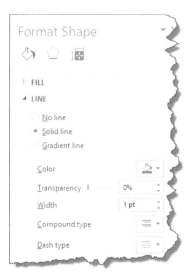

Here's an example of the kinds of results you might see.

Default Shape

Restyled Shape Using Shape Styles

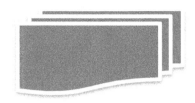

Create a Document with Two or More Columns

Similar to the column layout you see in a newspaper, magazine, or newsletter, you can set up columns and enter text and images in Word. Then, as you input content, Word will flow the contents from one column to the next.

Format a Document with Columns

- Create a blank new document.
- On the **Page Layout** tab, click **Columns**.

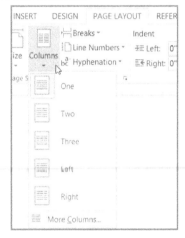

- Click the number of columns that you want. Word automatically sets the column widths to fit your page.
- Enter or paste the text that you want to appear in the columns.

If the presets don't work for your layout, or if you need more than three columns, choose **More Columns** at the bottom of the list – and adjust the settings in the **Columns** dialog box.

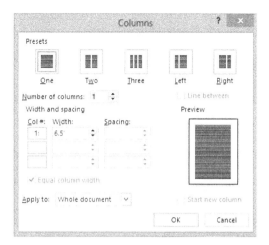

Notes:

- If your document has more than one section, the new layout will be applied only to the current section. [This won't be an issue if you begin with a new document.]
- You can control how text flows between columns by inserting a column break.

    For example, insert a column break to end a paragraph in one column and start a new paragraph at the top of the next column.

- To insert a line between columns, click **Columns** again, and then click **More Columns**. In the **Columns** dialog box, select the **Line between** check box.
- You can also use the **Columns** dialog box to adjust the column width and the spacing between columns.

Sample Two Column Layout with Text

Below, this new document was created by selecting a 2-column layout in the **Page Setup** group of the **Page Layout** tab, then adding text.

Lorem ipsum dolor sit amet, consectetuer adipiscing elit. Maecenas porttitor congue massa. Fusce posuere, magna sed pulvinar ultricies, purus lectus malesuada libero, sit amet commodo magna eros quis urna. ¶

Nunc viverra imperdiet enim. Fusce est. Vivamus a tellus. ¶

Pellentesque habitant morbi tristique senectus et netus et malesuada fames ac turpis egestas. Proin pharetra nonummy pede. Mauris et orci. ¶

Aenean nec lorem. In porttitor. Donec laoreet nonummy augue. ¶

Suspendisse dui purus, scelerisque at, vulputate vitae, pretium mattis, nunc. Mauris eget neque at sem venenatis eleifend. Ut nonummy. ¶

Lorem ipsum dolor sit amet, consectetuer adipiscing elit. Maecenas porttitor congue massa. Fusce posuere, magna sed pulvinar ultricies, purus lectus malesuada libero, sit amet commodo magna eros quis urna. ¶

Nunc viverra imperdiet enim. Fusce est. Vivamus a tellus. ¶

Pellentesque habitant morbi tristique senectus et netus et malesuada fames ac turpis egestas. Proin pharetra nonummy pede. Mauris et orci. ¶

Aenean nec lorem. In porttitor. Donec laoreet nonummy augue. ¶

Suspendisse dui purus, scelerisque at, vulputate vitae, pretium mattis, nunc. Mauris eget neque at sem venenatis eleifend. Ut nonummy. ¶

Lorem ipsum dolor sit amet, consectetuer adipiscing elit. Maecenas porttitor congue massa. Fusce posuere, magna sed pulvinar ultricies, purus lectus malesuada libero, sit amet commodo magna eros quis urna. ¶

Nunc viverra imperdiet enim. Fusce est. Vivamus a tellus. ¶

Pellentesque habitant morbi tristique senectus et netus et malesuada fames ac turpis egestas. Proin pharetra nonummy pede. Mauris et orci. ¶

Aenean nec lorem. In porttitor. Donec laoreet nonummy augue. ¶

Suspendisse dui purus, scelerisque at, vulputate vitae, pretium mattis, nunc. Mauris eget neque at sem venenatis eleifend. Ut nonummy. ¶

Lorem ipsum dolor sit amet, consectetuer adipiscing elit. Maecenas porttitor congue massa. Fusce posuere, magna sed pulvinar ultricies, purus lectus malesuada libero, sit amet commodo magna eros quis urna. ¶

Nunc viverra imperdiet enim. Fusce est. Vivamus a tellus. ¶

Pellentesque habitant morbi tristique senectus et netus et malesuada fames ac turpis egestas. Proin pharetra nonummy pede. Mauris et orci. ¶

Aenean nec lorem. In porttitor. Donec laoreet nonummy augue. ¶

Suspendisse dui purus, scelerisque at, vulputate vitae, pretium mattis, nunc. Mauris eget neque at sem venenatis eleifend. Ut nonummy. ¶

¶

You can insert an image here ¶

Tip! Another way to use columns in a document such as a newsletter or brochure is to begin with a template that already has the layout you want. Then replace the template's placeholder text with your own.   Many free templates for newsletters and brochures are available at the **Microsoft Office.com Templates** web site.

Unit Summary

In this unit, you have learned about the following topics and concepts:

- Creating a simple table and applying formatting
- Inserting images into a word document and manipulating and formatting them
- Creating a publication such as a newsletter or with two or more columns

Practice Questions and Activities

1. What are the two tabs on the ribbon that allow you to manipulate images?
2. Describe the steps you would follow to insert a picture into a document.
3. What is the first thing you must do to move or size an image?
4. What are two purposes for using columns in a Microsoft Word document?
5. Create a table that displays your class schedule at your school by day, time, and subject.
6. Create a new document with two columns.

- Use a prepared text of your choosing in place of the template placeholder text.
- Add an image.
- Add a break between two paragraphs in one of the columns.

7. What happens if the text in the second column exceeds the space on the page?

Spreadsheet Terminology

Spreadsheet applications have own terminology. Key terms are defined below.

Term	Functionality in a Spreadsheet
Argument	A value that provides information to Excel for an action, an event, a method, a property, a function, or a procedure
Cell	A cell is a box that holds data. In the spreadsheet, a cell is referenced by its row and column designations. Cells can contain numbers, text, or formulas.
Cell Range	A cell range is a group of cells that have been selected.
Cell Address	Cell address is the specific row and column designation. For example, the cell address **C1** means that the data is located in **row C, column 1**.
Cell Location	Cell location is another term commonly used for cell address.
Functions	A function is a preset formula in Excel. The function name tells Excel what calculation to execute. Functions begin with the equal sign [=] followed by the function's name and its arguments, instructions enclosed within round brackets. For example, the function AVERAGE[<column>] will calculate an average of data in a specified column.
Formula, Formulae	The formula is any equation entered into a cell in Microsoft Excel. The formula begins with an =, indicating to Excel that a calculation will be executed. For example, according to Microsoft.com: The SUM function adds all the numbers that you specify as arguments. Each argument can be a range, a cell reference, an array, a constant, a formula, or the result from another function. For example, SUM(A1:A5) adds all the numbers that are contained in cells A1 through A5. For another example, SUM(A1, A3, A5) adds the numbers that are contained in cells A1, A3, and A5.
Labels	In Excel, the term label has several meanings. It can refer to a text entry such as a heading used to identify a column of data. Labels are also used to identify the horizontal and vertical axis names in charts.
Range	A range is a group of cells that is referred to collectively. Arrange can include adjacent cells, or non-adjacent cells. With a range, you can make changes to many cells at one time.
Sheet or Worksheet	An array of cells
Syntax	The set of rules that defines the combinations of symbols that are considered to be a correctly structured phrase in that language
Values	Values in a spreadsheet are generally numbers; values can also be plain text, dates or months.

Worksheet	A worksheet is the place where you enter data and make calculations.

Navigating Within a Spreadsheet

Excel, like Word, features a ribbon with tabs and groups with specific commands. As you work, different tabs will appear when necessary, such as when you're creating charts or graphs.

Below is an illustration of the Excel screen — and its key features and functions.

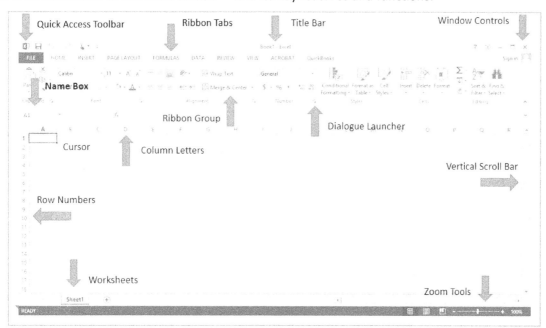

- The **Quick Access Toolbar** provides shortcuts to commonly used features.
- The **Ribbon** contains **Tabs** that organize tasks according to the future you are using, such as Font.
- **Ribbon Groups** provide commands applicable to the commands in the tab in which are working.
- The **Dialogue Launcher** is a small arrow in the lower right corner of many of the groups. It provides access to more features and tools.
- The **Title Bar** at the top of the screen displays the name of the document in which you are working.
- A **Vertical scrollbar** appears on the right side of your screen to display more of your document if necessary. Drag the scrollbar up or down.

- The **Zoom Slider** in the lower right of the screen allows you to drag the slider bar to zoom in — or out.
- The **Cursor** is located in cell A1 when you first open a new workbook.
- The **Name Box** is located above cell A1.
- **Row letters** and **column numbers** allow precise location of cells – or groups of cells. For example, if you type C12 in the name box, the cursor will be placed in cell C12.
- **Worksheets** in which you can work are shown in the lower left of the screen. Default names such as **Sheet1** are given by Excel. You can add new worksheets, delete worksheets — or rename each one.

Movement Commands and Function Keys

You can use both the keyboard and the mouse [or a combination] to issue commands to Excel. Below is a summary of movement commands in Excel.

Movement Command	Options
Move to a different cell	<ul><li>When entering a value, press **Enter** to move down one cell.</li><li>Press **Left Arrow** or **Right Arrow** to move horizontally</li><li>Press **Up Arrow** or **Down Arrow** to move vertically</li><li>Type a cell location in the **Name Box**, located above cell A1.</li></ul>
Move to a different place on the screen	<ul><li>Press Page Up or Page Down</li><li>Drag the **vertical scroll bar** up or down</li><li>Drag the **horizontal scroll bar** left or right</li></ul>
Go Home or Go to End	<ul><li>Press **Ctrl + End** to navigate to the last cell that contains data</li><li>Press **Ctrl + Home** to return to cell A1</li></ul>
Navigate among worksheets	<ul><li>At the bottom of the screen, click the sheet label you want to view</li></ul>
Navigate to A1	<ul><li>Press Ctrl + Home</li></ul>
Select an Entire Row	<ul><li>Click the row number 2 Purple</li></ul>
Select an Entire Column	<ul><li>Click the column letter C Q2</li></ul>

Tools for Creating a Simple Spreadsheet

Create a Blank New Workbook

6. Open Excel. Click the **Blank Workbook** option. A new spreadsheet opens; the cursor appears in cell A1.

Blank workbook

Enter Labels and Values

Enter Values

- In the worksheet, click a cell.
- Type the numbers or text that you want to enter, and then press **Enter** or **Tab**.

Enter Labels

Excel uses the term labels for multiple purposes. In its simplest form, a label is typically text that can be used in the same way as a heading, similarly to a table in Microsoft Word.   In the spreadsheet below, row 1 displays labels for four columns. We'll work with formatting in the next several sections.

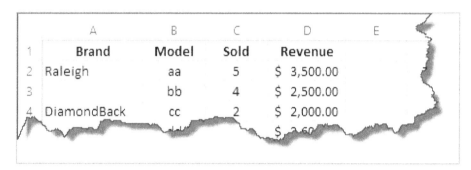

	A	B	C	D	E
1	Brand	Model	Sold	Revenue	
2	Raleigh	aa	5	$ 3,500.00	
3		bb	4	$ 2,500.00	
4	DiamondBack	cc	2	$ 2,000.00	

Enter Dates or Time

- On the worksheet, click a cell.
- Type a date or time as follows:

  To enter a date, use a slash mark or a hyphen to separate the parts of a date; for example, type 9/5/2002 or 5-Sep-2002.

  To enter a time that is based on the 12-hour clock, enter the time followed by a space, and then type a or p after the time; for example, 9:00 p. Otherwise, Excel enters the time as AM.

Tip! To enter the current date and time, press **Ctrl + Shift + ;** [semicolon].

Format Cells

Specifying Decimals, Currency, or Percent

You can quickly apply formatting to numeric values as follows:

- Select the cells you want to format.
- Click an option in the **Number** group on the **Home** tab.

For the number **675** below, notice that we used buttons in the Number group to apply formatting.

For this Result:	Choose this Format Option	By Clicking this Button:
675.00	**Increase Decimal** *twice*	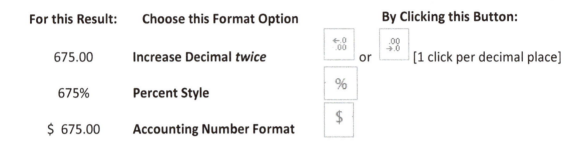 or [1 click per decimal place]
675%	**Percent Style**	
$ 675.00	**Accounting Number Format**	

Set Alignment

In the **Alignment Group**, to align information within the cell vertically, click one of three **vertical** alignment buttons to place data the top, center, or bottom of the cell.

Or, click one of three **horizontal** alignment buttons in the lower row of the group for left, center or right justification of the cell contents.

Wrap Text

To wrap text in a cell, select the cells that you want to format; on the **Home** tab, in the **Alignment** group, click **Wrap Text**.

Original Text	Results after clicking Wrap Text
Sample text I want to wrap	Sample text I want to wrap

Format Text for Cells and Labels

Similarly to Microsoft Word, you can format the font you use, its size, and appearance attributes.

- Select one or more cells, entire rows and/or columns, or even the entire spreadsheet.
- Click any of the attributes in the **Font** group; font, font size, bold, italic, borders, fill, text color, or increase or decrease text size [Large A, Smaller A].

7. For more formatting options, click the arrow in the lower right corner of the Font group.

Create Your First Spreadsheet

Using the tasks discussed in the previous six sections, create a simple spreadsheet.

a. Open Excel and create a blank workbook.

b. Enter the following information beginning in cell A1.
Remember to press the Tab and/or Enter keys to move across and down as you work.
Note! "Diamondback" in cell **4A** is too wide for the column. We'll fix that later.

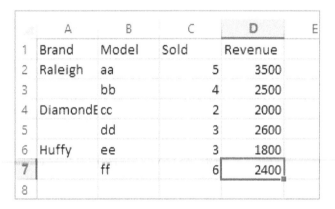

c. Apply **bold** to the labels in cells A1, B1, C1, and D1. Then **center** each one.

d. **Center** the data in cells B1 through B7, C1 through C7, and D1 through D7.

e. Select **column D** and apply **Accounting Number Format to** the values. [Since "Revenue" isn't a number, it will be ignored.] What attributes have changed about these numbers?

f. **Change the width of column A** so that "Diamondback" fits properly. To do this, place your mouse cursor on the boundary between columns A and B. Drag to the right until the entire word fits within the cell, then release the mouse button.

g. Save the spreadsheet as bikesales. Depending on the version of Excel you are using, notice that Excel places an extension such as **.XLSX or .XLS** at the end of "bikesales".

h. Compare your results with the illustration below. How did you do?

	A	B	C	D
1	Brand	Model	Sold	Revenue
2	Raleigh	aa	5	$3,500.00
3		bb	4	$2,500.00
4	DiamondBack	cc	2	$2,000.00
5		dd	3	$2,600.00
6	Huffy	ee	3	$1,800.00
7		ff	6	$2,400.00
8				

If something isn't just right, experiment to see if you can make your spreadsheet look the same.

And don't worry; you will have more opportunities to work with spreadsheets in unit 11 B.   :-)

Basic Spreadsheet System Functions

A function is a preset formula in Excel. The function name tells Excel what calculation to execute. Functions begin with the equal sign [=], followed by the function's name and its arguments, instructions enclosed within round brackets.

Sum

The **Sum** function adds all the numbers that you specify as arguments. Each argument can be a range, a cell reference, a formula, or the result from another function.

The syntax for the sum function is **SUM(number1,[number2],...)**

Below is an example of a simple sum function:

> **=SUM(A1:A5)**   Adds all the numbers that are contained in cells A1 through A5.

And here is a sum that's a bit more complicated:

> **=SUM(A1, A3, A5)** Adds the numbers that are contained in cells A1, A3, and A5. [Notice the commas required after each cell reference.]

Notes:

- When typing function names, uppercase letters are not required.
- If any arguments are error values, or if any arguments are text that cannot be translated into numbers, Excel will display an error.

Below are some examples of the Sum function. [This example was taken from the Excel help files when pressing F1.]

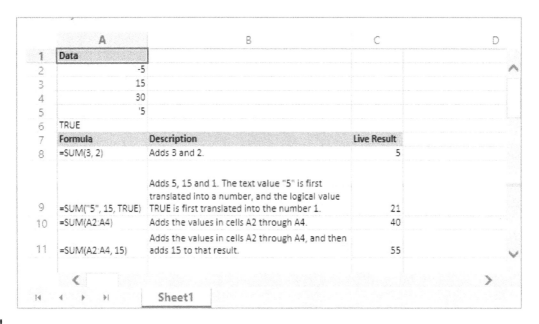

	A	B	C	D
1	Data			
2	-5			
3	15			
4	30			
5	'5			
6	TRUE			
7	Formula	Description	Live Result	
8	=SUM(3, 2)	Adds 3 and 2.	5	
9	=SUM("5", 15, TRUE)	Adds 5, 15 and 1. The text value "5" is first translated into a number, and the logical value TRUE is first translated into the number 1.	21	
10	=SUM(A2:A4)	Adds the values in cells A2 through A4.	40	
11	=SUM(A2:A4, 15)	Adds the values in cells A2 through A4, and then adds 15 to that result.	55	

Sheet1

Try It!

Use the **bikesales** spreadsheet to apply the sum function to the revenue column, as follows.

- Place your cursor in cell **8D**.
- Type **=sum(** Excel begins building the function.
- Drag your mouse down through all of the cells in column D showing revenue.
- Type **)** [right parenthesis] to complete the function syntax.
- Press **Enter**. Excel completes the sum function expression and produces the total.

Excel builds function; you select cells; they are added based on the dragging of your mouse. Then you type **)** and press Enter.	Result after you press Enter
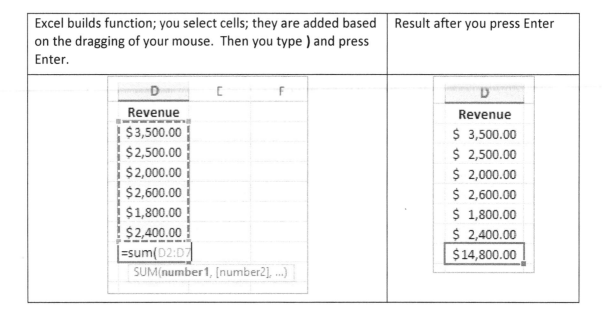	

178

Autosum

Use **AutoSum** to automatically add a quick calculation to your spreadsheet, such as sum or average.

When you click Autosum, Excel automatically enters the **Sum** formula to add the selected cell values.

Here's an example, also from Excel's help files. To add the January numbers in this Entertainment budget, select cell B7, the cell immediately below the column of numbers. Then click **AutoSum**. A formula appears in cell B7, and Excel highlights the cells you're totaling.

SUM		✕ ✓ fx	=SUM(B3:B6)	
	A	B	C	D
1		Jan	Feb	
2	Entertainment			
3	Cable TV	52.98	52.98	
4	Video rentals	7.98	11.97	
5	Movies	16.00	32.00	
6	CDs	18.98	29.99	
7	Totals	=SUM(B3:B6)		

Press **Enter** to display the result (95.94) in cell B7. You can also see the formula in the formula bar at the top of the Excel window.

Notes:

- To sum a column of numbers, select the cell immediately below the last number in the column. To sum a row of numbers, select the cell immediately to the right.

- **AutoSum** is located in two tabs: **Home** > **AutoSum**, and **Formulas** > **AutoSum**.
- Once you create a formula, you can copy it to other cells instead of typing it over and over. For example, if you copy the formula in cell B7 to cell C7, the formula in C7 automatically adjusts to the new location, and calculates the numbers in C3:C6. Cool, yes? :-)
- You can also use AutoSum on more **than** one cell at a time. For example, you could highlight both cell B7 and C7, click **AutoSum**, and total both columns at the same time.

Try It!

Use the **bikesales** spreadsheet to apply the AUTOSUM function to the revenue column, as follows.

- Remove the SUM value from cell 8D by selecting the cell and pressing **Delete**. [The cursor remains in cell D8.]
- Click the AUTOSUM button in the **Insert** group on the **Formulas** tab; then choose **SUM**. Excel adds the function syntax for you.
- Drag your mouse down through all of the cells in column D showing revenue.
- Press **Enter**. Excel completes the sum function expression — and produces the total.

Have you saved several steps by using AUTOSUM as compared with SUM?

Min

The **Min** function returns the smallest number in a set of values. To use Min, select your cells and then:

- In the editing group, click **Home**.
- Click the arrow next to **AutoSum**, then click **Min**.

The syntax for the MIN function is MIN(number1, [number2], ...)

Number1, number2, ... Number1 is optional, subsequent numbers are optional. 1 to 255 numbers for which you want to find the minimum value.

Notes:

Arguments can either be numbers or names, arrays, or references that contain numbers.

Logical values and text representations of numbers that you type directly into the list of arguments are counted.

If an argument is an array or reference, only numbers in that array or reference are used. Empty cells, logical values, or text in the array or reference are ignored.

If the arguments contain no numbers, MIN returns **0**.

Arguments that are error values or text that cannot be translated into numbers cause errors.

The workbook below — also from Excel's help files — displays examples of the results of this function.

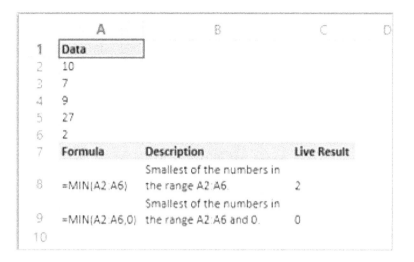

Try It!

Use the **bikesales** spreadsheet.

- Remove any previous function and/or results values from cell 8D.
- In the editing group, click **Home**.
- Click the arrow next to **AutoSum**, then click **Min**.
- Drag your mouse down through all of the cells in column D showing revenue.
- Press **Enter**. Excel completes the Min function expression — and displays the smallest value in the range.

Excel builds function; you select cells; they are added based on the dragging of your mouse. Then you press Enter.	Result after you press Enter
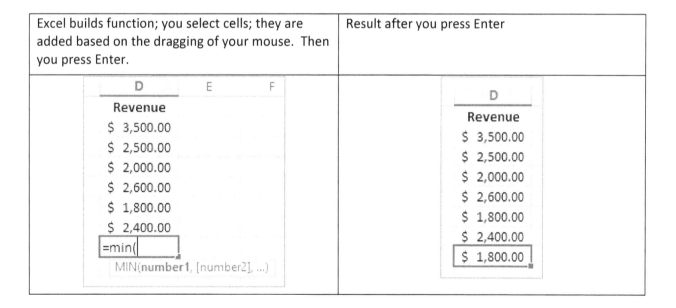	

Max

As opposed to Min, the **Max** function returns the largest value in a set of values. To use Max, select your cells and then:

- In the editing group, click **Home**.
- Click the arrow next to **AutoSum**, then click **Max**.

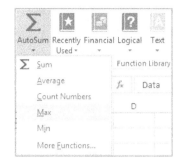

The syntax is **MAX(number1**,number2,...)

Number1, number2, ...   are 1 to 255 numbers for which you want to find the maximum value.

Notes:

- Arguments can be either numbers or names, arrays, or references that contain numbers.
- The function counts logical values and text representations of numbers that you type directly into the list of arguments.
- If an argument is an array or reference, only numbers in that array or reference are used. Empty cells, logical values, or text in the array or reference are ignored.
- If the arguments contain no numbers, Max returns 0 [zero].
- Arguments that are error values or text that cannot be translated into numbers cause errors.

Below is an example from the Excel help files:

	A
1	**Data**
2	10
3	7
4	9
5	27
6	2

Expression	Provides this Result
=MAX(A2:A6)	Largest of the numbers above [27]
=MAX(A2:A6, 30)	Largest of the numbers above and 30 [30]

Try It!

Use the **bikesales** spreadsheet.

- Replace any previous function in cell 8D with a **Max** function.
- Press **Enter**.
- Did the results show you the largest value?

Average

The AVERAGE function calculates the average of numbers that aren't in a contiguous row or column.

The function returns the *arithmetic mean* by adding a group of numbers, and then dividing by the count of those numbers. Note: The AVERAGE function ignores any blank cells.

To use **Average** to average cells A2, A3, A4, and A7, use a formula like this**: =AVERAGE(A2:A4,A7)**
A2:A4 tells Excel where the numbers are. It's the first argument, or piece of data the AVERAGE function needs to run. Notice the comma before the second argument, A7. The result is 7.5 .

Try It!

Use the **bikesales** spreadsheet.

- Replace any previous function in cell 8D with an **Average** function. Include cells D2 through D7.
- Press **Enter**.
- Did the results show you the average value for the selected range?

Count

The **Count** function counts the number of cells that contain numbers, and counts numbers within the list of arguments. Use the Count function to get the number of entries in a number field that is in a range or array of numbers.

For example, you can enter the following formula to count the numbers in the range A1:A20:

=COUNT(A1:A20)

In this example, if five of the cells in the range contain numbers, the result is **5**.

The syntax is COUNT(value1, [value2], ...)

The COUNT function syntax has the following elements:

> **value1**   Required. The first item, cell reference, or range within which you want to count numbers.

> **value2, ...**   Optional. Up to 255 additional items, cell references, or ranges within which you want to count numbers.

The arguments can contain or refer to a variety of different types of data, but only numbers are counted. Notes:

- Arguments that are numbers, dates, or a text representation of numbers [for example, a number enclosed in quotation marks, such as "1"] are counted.
- Logical values and text representations of numbers that you type directly into the list of arguments are counted.
- Arguments that are error values or text that cannot be translated into numbers are not counted.
- If an argument is an array or reference, only numbers in that array or reference are counted. Empty cells, logical values, text, or error values in the array or reference are not counted.

Below are examples of results from the Excel help files, reached by pressing **F1**.

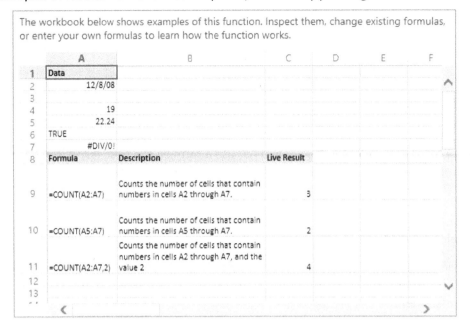

The workbook below shows examples of this function. Inspect them, change existing formulas, or enter your own formulas to learn how the function works.

	A	B	C	D	E	F
1	Data					
2	12/8/08					
3						
4	19					
5	22.24					
6	TRUE					
7	#DIV/0!					
8	**Formula**	**Description**		**Live Result**		
9	=COUNT(A2:A7)	Counts the number of cells that contain numbers in cells A2 through A7.		3		
10	=COUNT(A5:A7)	Counts the number of cells that contain numbers in cells A5 through A7.		2		
11	=COUNT(A2:A7,2)	Counts the number of cells that contain numbers in cells A2 through A7, and the value 2		4		
12						
13						

Try It!

Use the **bikesales** spreadsheet.

- Replace any previous function in cell 8D with a **Count** function. Include cells D2 through D7.
- Press **Enter**.
- Is the result what you expected?

Unit Summary

In this unit, you have learned about the following topics and concepts:

- The definition of term spreadsheet
- Examples of spreadsheet software products on the market
- Purposes for which spreadsheet software is used
- Terms associated with spreadsheets
- Navigating within a spreadsheet
- Creating a simple spreadsheet
- Using basic Excel functions.

Practice Questions and Activities

1. List four keyboard keys that enable navigation around a spreadsheet. Describe what task each key performs.

2. In the matching exercise below, review the terms associated with spreadsheets by placing the letter of the corresponding definition in the leftmost column.

	Term		Description
_____	**Argument x**	j)	An array of cells
_____	**Cell x**	k)	A preset formula in Excel
_____	**Cell Range x**	l)	Data in a spreadsheet is generally numeric, but can also be plain text, dates, or months.
_____	**Cell Address x**	m)	A file where you enter data and make calculations.
_____	**Cell Location x**	n)	The set of rules that defines the combinations of symbols that are considered to be a correctly structured formula or function
_____	**Function x**	o)	A box that holds data in a spreadsheet
_____	**Formula, Formulae x**	p)	A text entry to identify columns or rows, or the name of a horizontal or vertical axis in a chart.
_____	**Labels x**	q)	A term commonly used for the cell address.
_____	**Range x**	r)	The specific row and column designation. For example, the cell address **C1** means that the data is located in **row C, column 1**.
_____	**Sheet or Worksheet ****	s)	Any equation entered into a cell. The formula begins with an "=" sign, indicating that a calculation will be executed.
_____	**Syntax x**	t)	A group of cells that is referred to collectively. A range can include adjacent cells, or non-adjacent cells. With a range,

_____	**Values x**	u)	you can make changes to many cells at one time.
			A value that provides information to Excel for an action, an event, a method, a property, a function, or a procedure
_____	**Worksheet x**	v)	The set of rules that defines the combinations of symbols that are considered to be a correctly structured phrase in that language

- Explain the difference between the **Sum** function and the **AutoSum** function.

- What other functions can you perform using **Autosum**?

- Your teacher will provide you with a spreadsheet for this exercise. Using it, demonstrate your examples of the following in Excel.

  a. Cells

  b. Cell addresses

  c. Ranges

  d. Values

  e. Labels

  f. Rows and columns

  g. Navigation around the spreadsheet, using the mouse/arrow and/or other distance keys

- Create a spreadsheet listing names, subjects and marks. Then create a table with labels for the names, subjects, and marks.

- Demonstrate your understanding of 4 of the 6 following functions by creating a simple spreadsheet and performing each of the following functions. MIN, MAX, AVERAGE, COUNT, SUM, AUTO

Learning Objectives

This unit is designed to develop skills to use more advanced spreadsheet applications. Upon completion, you should be able to do everything you learned in Unit 11A, and also:

- Create a simple spreadsheet on your own
- Format cells by applying attributes
- Sort data through a simple sort, and then a criteria sort
- Create, modify and format a graph such as a pie chart and line and bar graphs.

Spreadsheet Examples

Since the early days of spreadsheets, their uses have grown as software companies add more features. Below are five typical uses.

- Making repetitive and/or complex calculations
- Managing reference or tracking information
- Preparing and monitoring budgets
- Documenting monthly and yearly income and expenses [income statements, balance sheets]
- Performing interest calculations.

Select and Use Predefined System Functions

In addition to the basics, functions often allow you to simplify and shorten formulas on a worksheet. In Unit 11 A, we learned about and practiced using five simple system functions; Sum, Min, Max, Average and Count, all located within the AutoSum category.

There are other functions in the **Function Library** located in the **Formulas** tab, organized by categories.

Below is a short summary of the purposes of function categories arranged in groups in the 2013 library.

Excel Function Option	Brief Description
Recently Used	Displays a list of recently used functions. Note: May also show others not recently used by you.
Financial	Provides options dealing with interest calculations, depreciation, payment coupon amounts and dates, and investment values.

Logical	Allows you to use logic terminology such as And, If, Or, and Not to build programmatic syntax.
Text	Excel's text functions are helpful for working with names, addresses, customer lists, or other text-based data. Examples include Len [Length] and Upper [convert text to uppercase].
Date & Time	Provides many options for manipulating the date and/or the time, and placing results formatted accordingly in one or more cells.
Lookup & Reference	Works with address references and manipulation of values in relationship to cells and ranges of cells, in addition to a hyperlink function.
Math & Trig [Trigonometry]	Provides sophisticated now calculation math manipulation options such as cosine, Roman to Arabic values. Also contains several rounding functions.
More Functions	The remaining categories in the library are grouped as More Functions. Statistical ▶ Engineering ▶ Cube ▶ Information ▶ Compatibility ▶ Web ▶

Many of the function groups contain sophisticated formulae, and many are specific to disciplines such as engineering, mathematics, and finance. However, we will explore a function that performs a true/false test when comparing values.

If Function

The **IF** function returns one value if a condition you specify evaluates to TRUE, and another value if that condition evaluates to FALSE.

For example, the formula **=IF(A1>10,"Over 10","10 or less")** returns "Over 10" if A1 is greater than 10, and "10 or less" if A1 is less than or equal to 10.

The Syntax for the If function is **IF(logical_test, [value_if_true], [value_if_false])**

Of the three logical arguments, only logical_test is required. For the logical test, any value or expression that can be evaluated will return TRUE or FALSE.

For example, **A10=100** is a logical expression; if the value in cell A10 is equal to 100, the expression evaluates to TRUE. Otherwise, the expression evaluates to FALSE.

Below are some illustrations of how the **If** function can be used in a spreadsheet.

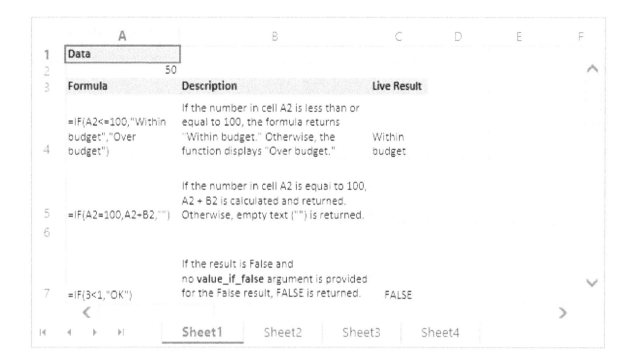

Discuss It!

Try to think of other everyday examples when the IF function could be useful.

Create a Simple Formula to Perform Arithmetic

You can create a simple formula to perform arithmetic functions in Excel; add, subtract, multiply, divide.

- An equal sign [=] instructs Excel to expect a formula; always begin with = .
- You can enter a formula in any unused cell; the cell need not be adjacent to the cells of the function you are performing.

Function	Symbol	Sample equation	Task Function Performs
Add	+	=E1+E2+E3	Adds numbers in cells B1, B2, and B3
Subtract	-	=E4-E5	Subtracts the value of B5 from B4
Multiply	*	=E2*E3	Multiplies the value of B2 times the value of B3
Divide	/	=E2/E3	Divides the value in B2 by the value in B3

Try It!

- Use the **bikesales** spreadsheet you created earlier in this unit.
- Create an arithmetic formula of your choice to perform one of the four arithmetic functions with the sold or revenue columns C or D.

- Do the math on paper, then compare with the result from the function. Do they agree? If so, congratulations! If not, revisit the function's expression to check for syntax accuracy.

Format Cells

You can apply many formatting attributes to enhance the appearance of your text and values using the buttons in the **Font** group on the **Home** tab in the **Ribbon**.

Notes:

- The buttons are toggle functions. That is, click the button to toggle the attribute on – and click again to toggle it off selected information in cells, or before adding your information.

- To apply a formatting attribute to existing cell data, first select the cell, or range of cells.

Below are the formatting options in the **Font** group.

Text Attribute	Button to Click
Font	Choose from the many Windows fonts
Font Size	Select a point size between 8 and 72 points
Bold	Apply bold
Italics	Apply italics
Underscore	Apply underscore
Borders	Choose from 18 border presets plus options in Format Cells
Fill Color	Color the cell background to highlight it
Font Color	Select a font color from the palette

Sort Data

Sorting information helps you more easily see the data the way you want, and to find values quickly. You can sort a range or a table of data based on one or more columns; for example, you can sort employees first by department — and then by last name.

Sort Quickly

Below are the steps to perform for a simple alphabetic sort.

- Select the range of cells you wish to sort, such as C1:C5 [a single column] or A1:D5 [multiple rows and columns].
- On the ribbon, click the **Data** tab.
- Click either the **Ascending** command ![A to Z] to Sort A to Z, or the **Descending** command ![Z to A] to Sort Z to A.

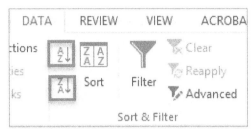

Notice the original and sorted results below. In the sorted version, the Blue team now appears as the first sales team. All of the values in rows two through five were also included in the sort. And the heading was excluded from the sort — because an option to exclude them was checked by default in the background.

Original Data						Sorted Data				
	A	B	C	D	E		A	B	C	D	E
		Sales Team	Q1	Q2	Q3	Q4		Sales Team	Q1	Q2	Q3	Q4
1	Sales Team	Q1	Q2	Q3	Q4	1	Sales Team	Q1	Q2	Q3	Q4
2	Purple	6	10	14	12	2	Blue	5	12	12	10
3	Blue	5	12	12	10	3	Orange	4	15	11	8
4	Yellow	7	8	9	11	4	Purple	6	10	14	12
5	Orange	4	15	11	8	5	Yellow	7	8	9	11

Try It!

- Create a simple spreadsheet comparing the scoring results of four sports teams or four other criteria.
- Enter data similar to the examples above, then perform a simple sort.

Did your sort work?

Sort Using Criteria

More fully-featured sort options are available. Use these choices to select the column[s] you want to sort, plus choose other criteria such as font or cell colors.

- Select a single cell anywhere in the range that you want to sort.
- On the **Data** tab, in the **Sort & Filter** group, click **Sort**.

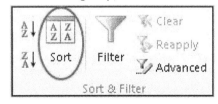

- In the Sort dialog, in the **Sort by** list, select the first column on which you want to sort. [For example, Q1 or Q2.]
- In the **Sort On** list, select either Values, Cell Color, Font Color, or Cell Icon.
- In the **Order** list, select the order that you want to apply to the sort operation — alphabetically or numerically ascending or descending. [A to Z or Z to A for text, or lower to higher or higher to lower for numbers].
- Click **OK**.

- The results of the sort replace your original data. Therefore, as you experiment with sorting, you may want to work with a copy of your data in another visible area of the spreadsheet so that you can compare results.
- In our example, we sorted by the column containing Q1, the data values, and Z to A order, meaning that we wanted the largest results for the first quarter to appear at the top of our sorted list.

	A	B	C	D	E
1	Sales Team	Q1	Q2	Q3	Q4
2	Yellow	7	8	9	11
3	Purple	6	10	14	12
4	Blue	5	12	12	10
5	Orange	4	15	11	8

Notes:

The sort criteria of **Column**, **Sort On**, and **Order** are also known as primary, secondary, and tertiary sorts. You can also think of them as first, second, and third level sorts. When performing the sort, Excel will always proceed in this order.

If your data isn't sorting properly, double-check your cell values to make sure you entered them correctly. Even a small typo may cause problems when sorting a large worksheet.

Try It!

- Use the same spreadsheet that you created for the quick sort.
- Now choose sort criteria for Sort By, Sort On, and Sort Order.
- Click OK.

How did you do?

Create, Modify and Format Pie Charts, Line and Bar Graphs

A wide variety of charting and graphing options are available in Excel. Using charts or graphs in your spreadsheet:

- Provides a graphical way of presenting information
- Makes presentations more interesting visually
- Brings numeric comparisons and results alive
- Shows data in a different way than tabular in order to help people absorb information given the fact that people learn in different ways.

What Is a Legend?

A legend, also called a key, is a display of brief information that helps users understand the components of a graphic. Information in a legend includes what data each bar represents, what each column represents — and the meanings of the lines, bars, or pie slices.

Once the data is presented in a chart or a graph, you can add and customize legends that help to explain the values. Below is an example of a legend at its simplest.

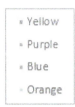

Next we'll explore how to create and modify several types of charts and graphs.

Tip!

There are so many options for changing the appearance of and formatting graphics in Excel. Therefore, expect a period of trial and error when you first begin working with charts and graphs as you experiment with the many options.

Pie Chart

A pie chart gets its name from the fact that it is round – and appears to have slices. Data that is arranged in one column or row on a worksheet can be plotted in a pie chart. Pie charts show the size of items in one data series, proportional to the sum of all of the items. The data points in a pie chart are shown as a percentage of the whole pie. Notice that the pie chart below uses keys to edit the percentages of the whole – largest to smallest order.

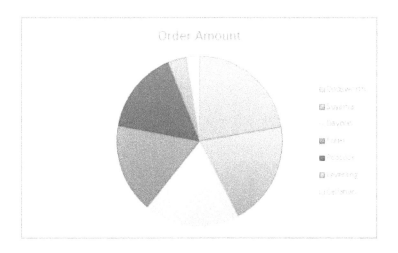

A pie chart is a good choice when the following situations are true:

- All Values in the data range total 100%
- You have only one data series
- None of the values in your data are negative
- Almost none of the values in your data are zero values
- You have no more than seven data categories, all of which represent parts of the whole pie.

To create a pie chart:

- In the spreadsheet, select the range of data for the chart.

- In the **Insert** tab, click the **Pie Chart** icon  in the **Charts** group.

- Click an option such as **2-D** or **3-D** Pie.

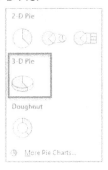

- Excel plots your selected data in a pie chart and applies the category as a title. Click any of the three Chart Elements, Chart Styles, and Chart Filters buttons next to the upper-right corner of the chart to add chart elements like axis titles or data labels, customize the look of your chart, or change the data that's shown in the chart.
- Save the spreadsheet.

Below is a pie chart created in Excel; note the three buttons used to manipulate formatting and overall chart appearance. Here, we have just selected chart elements options.

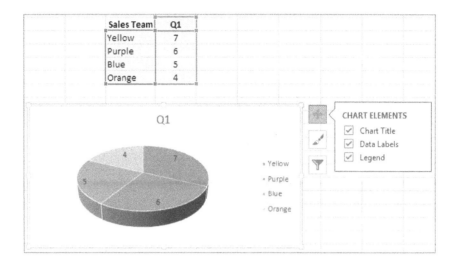

Try It!

- From the Excel data you created for the sorting practice earlier in this unit, select the data in one Quarter [choose from Q1, Q2, Q3, or Q4] to create a pie chart.
- Apply all three types of chart elements by clicking the check boxes, if not already applied.
- Compare results with a neighboring classmate. How did you each do?

Line Chart

In a line chart, category data is distributed evenly along the horizontal axis, and all value data is distributed evenly along the vertical axis. Line charts can show continuous data over time on an evenly scaled axis, and are therefore ideal for showing trends in data at equal intervals, such as months, quarters, or fiscal years. Data that is arranged in columns or rows on a worksheet can be plotted in a line chart.

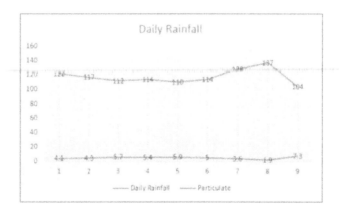

Notes:

- Line charts work best when you have more than one data series in your chart.
- Stacked line charts add the data, which might not be the result you want. It might not be easy to see that the lines are stacked, so consider using a different line chart type or a stacked area chart instead.

To create a line chart:

- Select the range of data for the chart.

196

- In the **Insert** tab, click the **Line Chart** icon 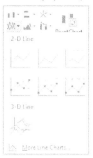 in the **Charts** group, then select a **2-D** [two dimensional] line chart style. [Start simply... :-)...]

- Excel plots your selected data in a line chart.
- Select the chart. Click **Chart Style** and change the style and/or the colour of your chart.
- Click anywhere inside the default chart title; change it to make the title more relevant to your data. Note: The text area expands as you type, if necessary.

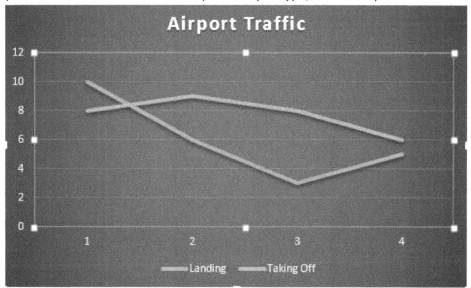

8. Save the spreadsheet.

Try It!

- Think of a favorite team.
- Create a data series that compares the team's scores; you can do this by player, by year, or by whatever other criteria you prefer. You need only 4 or 5 rows to get the effect.
- Create your line chart.
- Change the chart title.
- Change the colour of the lines.
- Compare notes about results with a classmate.

Bar Chart

Bar charts illustrate comparisons among individual items. In a bar chart, the **categories** are typically organized along the vertical axis, and the **values** along the horizontal axis. Data that is arranged in columns or rows on a worksheet can be plotted in a bar chart.

Consider using a bar chart when:

- The axis labels are long.
- The values that are shown represent durations.

To create a bar chart:

- In the **Insert** tab, click the **Bar Chart** icon 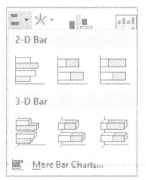 in the **Charts** group.
- Click an option such as the **2-D** or the **3-D** Bar.

- Excel plots your selected data in a bar chart.

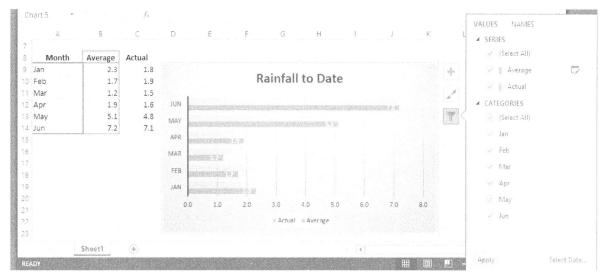

- Change the filters by clicking the filter [funnel] button;   Next to the **Average** series label, click the pencil button. In the Edit Series dialogue, change the value of the first series name to one of your choice. Click **OK.**

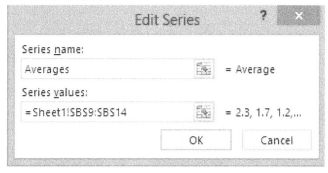

- Save the spreadsheet.

Try It!

- Create a simple set of data comparing two values. Ideas are: temperature, teams, counting coins saved, or any other elements you want to compare.
- Create a bar chart that shows the comparison.
- Edit the title, and change both series names.
- Finally, choose a different chart style, and save your spreadsheet.
- Are your results as you expected? If not, tweak the chart settings as needed.

Unit Summary

In this unit, you have learned about the following topics and concepts:

- Creating a simple spreadsheet on your own
- Formatting cells by applying attributes
- Exploring the IF function to return true or false conditions
- Sorting data through a simple sort, and then by performing a criteria sort
- Creating, modifying, and formatting a graph such as a pie chart and line or bar graphs.

Practice Questions and Activities

1. List in writing and briefly describe three ways in which a spreadsheet application such as Microsoft Excel helps people work with and manipulate information.

2. Think about your life at school and home. How could a spreadsheet make an everyday event or life function easier for you?

3. What steps do you need to follow to format a range of cells as bold – and with an 11-point font?

4. At a simple level, what results does the IF function produce?

5. Use a spreadsheet provided by your teacher to identify cells, cell addresses, ranges, values, labels, rows and columns, and using the mouse/arrow keys to move within the spreadsheet.

6. Create a new spreadsheet with a listing of 5 student names, 5 subjects, and 5 marks for each student. Once your spreadsheet is ready:

   - Create and format a bar chart.
   - Create and format a pie chart to compare the winning results of four student teams, including the team name and the winning amounts. Make it relevant to academics, sports, or any other interest you have. Be creative!

Learning Objectives

This unit is designed to assist students to be able to use database management software to design simple databases. Upon completion, you should be able to:

- Define Database Management Software
- Describe the uses of Database Management software
- Identify and describe parts of a database
- Create tables
- Enter data into tables using appropriate data types.

Note: The procedures and illustrations in Units 11A and 11B are based on Microsoft Access 2013. If you are working with an earlier version, you should find that most features work similarly. You can always press **F1** to get help specific to your product version.

What is Database Management Software?

What is a Database?

A **database** is an organized collection of data with tools used for storing, modifying, extracting, and searching for information. For example, an inventory control specialist in a manufacturing or distribution company would search the inventory or materials database to determine what items need to be reordered. Or a bike shop owner might keep a database of his or her customers for sales tracking marketing purposes.

Relational Database

A **relational database** is a database with a collection of tables of data items, all of which are formally described and organized, or related according to a model. Data in a single table represents a relation, thus the term relational database. Tables may also have additionally defined relationships with each other. The main benefits of using a relational database are:

- Storage of information is more efficient
- Accuracy of information is better because data is entered one time
- With a relational database, you can capture transactions such as all students in a given class.

Database Management Software System

A **Database management software system [DBMSs]** is a specially designed software application that interacts with the user, other applications, and the database itself to capture and analyze data. A general-purpose DBMS is a software system designed to allow the definition, creation, querying, update, and administration of databases.

Examples of DBMSs

Well-known large-scale contemporary DBMSs include Microsoft SQL Server, Oracle, and SAP. Typically these types of systems utilize servers to store the database tables, systems and reports. Users access the database from a desktop or laptop PC — or a mobile device such as a tablet or smartphone. Applications such as Microsoft Access, LibreOffice Base, FoxPro, and FileMaker Pro are not usually developed on such a large scale, but are useful to many individuals and businesses who do not require giant enterprise-wide systems.

Microsoft Access is a good application in which to learn the basics of a database management system. It runs on a desktop or laptop computer, or through the Internet, has learning support tools, and is cost effective.

Why Use Database Management Software?

In Microsoft Excel, you can create and manipulate information tables stored in columns and rows. However Excel does not provide relational capabilities. With a DBMS, you can create and link tables with much greater flexibility and efficiency in terms of how the data is stored, connected, and accessed.

Using a database such as Microsoft access, you can:

- Add new information to a database, such as a new item in an inventory
- Edit data in the database, such as changing the current location of an item
- Delete information, perhaps if an item is sold — or discarded
- Organize and view the data in different ways
- Share the data with others through reports, e-mail messages, an intranet, or the Internet.

Major worldwide retailers such as Amazon.com, Microsoft, and Walmart all perform these tasks and activities with very sophisticated databases, providing certain screens to customers on the "front end" — while also managing their large-scale businesses on the "back end". Other institutions such as government, hospitals, manufacturing companies, accounting firms, and virtually any other type of business of which you can think also depend on database systems to run their businesses.

However a well thought out plan about what data you want to store, how you want to get to it, and what information you want to produce can also be accomplished on a much simpler scale with a database application such as Microsoft Access.

Parts of a Database

In a relational database, several entities – called Objects in access – must work together to form a system. Below are the key terms you should know when learning to use a DBMS.

Table

A database table is similar in appearance to a spreadsheet; data is stored in rows and columns. But for flexibility, the data in a DBMS such as Access must be organized into tables to make sure that no duplication of any information [redundancies] occur.

For example, if you're storing information about employees, each employee's information should only need to be entered once in a table designed just to store employee data. Data about products will be stored in its own table, and data about branch offices will be stored in another table.

Record

Each row in a table is called a record, a place where individual pieces of information are stored. [Think Excel; each row is really a record, too.]

Field

Each record consists of one or more fields. A field holds smallest possible unit of data. Fields correspond to the columns in the table. For example, you might have a table named "Employees" where each record [row] contains information about a different employee. And like Excel, each field [column] contains a different type of information, such as first name, last name, address, email address, and so forth.

Important! In a database, fields must be designated as a certain data type such as text, date, time, number, or some other type of value.

Below we see an example of a customer table with three records — and three fields.

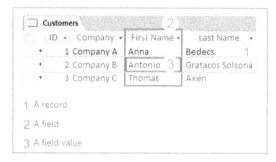

Key

A key is a field with values that are unique throughout a table. Values of the key can be used to refer to entire records, because each record has a different value for the key. Each table can only have one primary key.

Query

A **query** is one or more questions that you ask of your data. To build a query, you ask questions, select a data source, and then use syntax to specify fields which become your criteria, which form a data set. We'll build a query in Unit 12B of the course.

Object

An object is simply a term that describes a component of an Access database; table, query, form, report. In Access, objects are managed in the navigation pane, which we will see shortly.

Access Window Elements

Access — as with other Microsoft office products – features a ribbon that contains tabs. Below, we'll profile the elements of Access that will be using through the rest of this unit to work with databases.

Title Bar

The title bar contains the name of the currently open database. And as with all other Microsoft office applications, on the left is the Quick Access Toolbar.

Ribbon

The Access ribbon contains tabs with groups of feature categories. The ribbon is dynamic; certain tabs on the ribbon will appear or disappear depending upon the task you are performing.

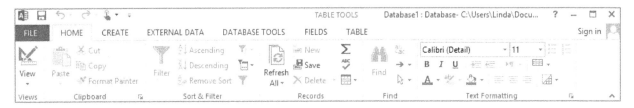

Navigation Pane

The **navigation pane** on the left side of the window displays all Access database objects, listed by object type. These can include tables, queries, reports, or forms.

As the list lengthens, you can filter it by object category. Click the small all Access objects drop-down arrow to expose options for displaying various object types in the navigation pane. For example, as you are working with tables, you might choose only table objects to display.

To work with records and fields in a table, double-click its name in the navigation pane.

The table then opens in the main area of the Access screen. Notice below that there are four tables and one query open. You can distinguish the contents of the tabs by glancing at the icon at the left side of each tab.

Status Bar

The **status bar** at the bottom of the screen displays the view in which you are working. Use the two buttons on the far right to switch between datasheet view — and design view. We'll be learning more about these two views a bit later.

When you have a table open, the status bar tells you how many records there are in the table, and which one is active. You can also click the arrows to move around records in the table, or search for information in a record by entering it in the **Search** window.

Create a Table in a Blank New Database

- You will create a database that tracks customers, employees, and orders. The first table will store information about customers. Later, you'll add to the database, and write a query, and then build a report to identify data from the database.

First, create a new blank database.

- Under **File**, click **New.**
- Click Blank desktop database.
- In the **File Name** box, type a file name for the new database, **BikeShopTracking.** [Access automatically adds the proper file extension.]
- To save the database in a location other than the default folder, click the folder icon noted by the blue arrow below, and navigate to the folder you want as you would with any other Microsoft Windows application.
- Click **Create**.

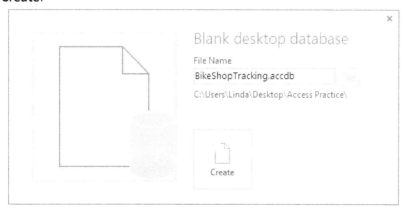

- Notice the new database opens — with a new default table named **Table1** displayed in the navigation pane.

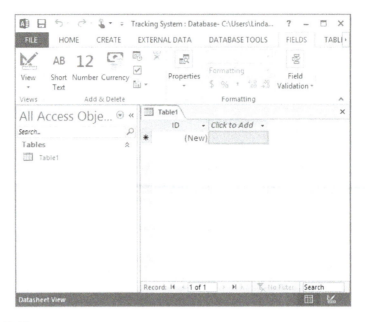

Create Fields for the Table

There are two view options for tables in Access; **Datasheet** – and **Design**.

- **Datasheet**. Datasheet view allows you to display and change data in the table, including field names. This is the default view in Access.

- **Design**. In design view, Access shows the structure of the table so it can be modified. Design view also makes it easier to work with attributes such as field names, field sizes, and data types.

We'll use the **design** view to set up our field names, data types, and field descriptions.

On the **Fields** tab in the **View** group, click **Design View.**

Because we haven't saved anything yet, Access will prompt us to name the table. Type **Customers**, then click **OK**.

Access displays the table in design view, ready for input.

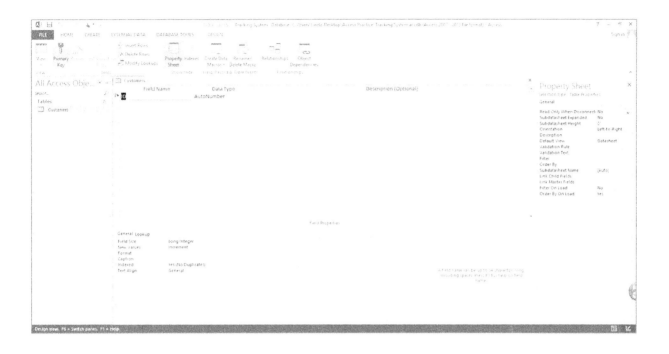

Field Names

We want to track several fields in the Customers table; they are listed below. [Note that three of the fields which contained two words have been put together without any spaces. This is standard practice for naming database fields that contain more than one word.]

LastName

FirstName

Street

City

Jurisdiction [Modify the name if necessary for the way this should be in your country.]

PostalCode

Country.

- In the design view that appears, click in the first field below **ID** and type **LastName.** Note: We will allow Access to set a default data type of short text for the fields.
- Click in the field below LastName, and enter **FirstName**.
- Click in the field below FirstName, and enter **Street**. Click in the **Description** field, and enter **Number and street address** the description.
- Enter the remaining fields: City, Jurisdiction, Country, and PostalCode.

Make sure that your fields in the design view look like this:

Customers		
Field Name	Data Type	Description (Optional)
ID	AutoNumber	
LastName	Short Text	
FirstName	Short Text	
Street	Short Text	Number and street address
City	Short Text	
Jurisdiction	Short Text	
Country	Short Text	
PostalCode	Short Text	

- Notice that Access has placed a small key icon in the selection column to the left of the field name **ID**. We will return to this topic in Unit **12B**.

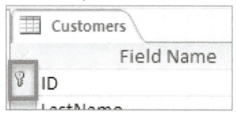

- Click **File > Save**.

    Congratulations! You've set up the fields for your first table!

Adding Records

With your fields defined, now you're ready to add records to your new database.

- Open the **Customers** database.
- On the **Fields** tab in the **View** group, click the **Datasheet** view.
- Click in the field below **LastName**, and enter **Smith**.
- Press **Tab**, then enter **Sally** in the FirstName field.
- Continue pressing **Tab**, making up information and entering it for Street, City, Jurisdiction, County, and PostalCode.

- Click in the [New] row and enter **Zoya**, and then **Zachary**. Add the remaining record data.
- Enter three more records, Thomas, Beaulieu, and Piper.

- Save the table by clicking the **Save** button in the **Records** group in the **Home** tab.

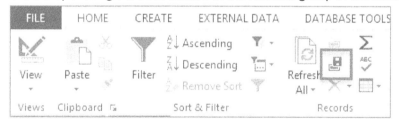

- Close the table by clicking the **X** on the right of the **Document Tabs** bar.

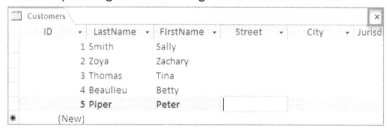

Notice that in datasheet view, Access allows you to work similarly to how you work in a spreadsheet.
Tip! When entering record information, you can also press the left, right, and up and down arrows to move around the data, especially if you need to make a correction to any of your data.

Add a New Field

There may be situations where you need to add a new field. If so, return to the Design view, click below your last field — in this case **PostalCode** — and add the new field.

We'll add two new fields to Customers.

- Open **Customers** in design view.
- Click in the cell below the **PostalCode** field.
- Type **Phone**. Accept the default field type of Short Text.
- Below Phone, type **Email**, and again accept Short Text.
- Save the table. In design view, it should now look like this:

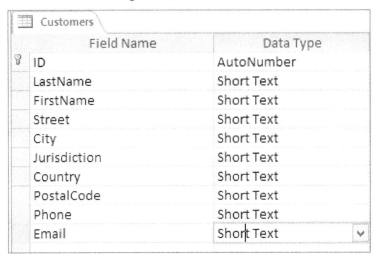

Editing Field Names

To edit a field name:

- Open the table in design view.
- Double-click the field name you want to edit.
- Type over the selection to rename the field.
- Close the table. Access prompts you to save your changes. Click **Yes**.

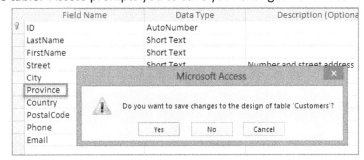

Note: You can also change a field name in datasheet view, however by using design view, you have more options for and information about the field.

Working with Field Data Types

The default data type when you enter a field in datasheet view is **text**.

To change the name of the field — or its data type, open the table in design view, make your changes in the appropriate places, and then save the database.

Caution! If at all possible, change data types and field names **before** you begin entering data records. Otherwise, unpredictable results might occur as you manipulate data, generate queries, or develop reports. [Note: And if you add fields, you must be careful to go back and populate those for earlier records that existed before adding any new fields.]

The following data types, usages, and sizes in the table below are listed in the Microsoft Access 2013 help files. Note: Several of the data types below shown in *italics* represent advanced functionality in Access that are beyond the scope of this learning unit. Help is available by pressing F1.

Data Type	Use	Size
Short Text [formerly known as "Text"]	Alphanumeric data [names, titles, etc.]	Up to 255 characters.
Long Text [formerly known as "Memo"]	Large amounts of alphanumeric data: sentences and paragraphs.	Up to about 1 gigabyte [GB], but controls to display a long text are limited to the first 64,000 characters.
Number	Numeric data.	1, 2, 4, 8, or 16 bytes.
Date/Time	Dates and times.	8 bytes.
Currency	Monetary data, stored with 4 decimal places of precision.	8 bytes.
AutoNumber	Unique value generated by Access for each new record.	4 bytes [16 bytes for ReplicationID].
Yes/No	Boolean [true/false] data; Access stores the numeric value zero [0] for false, and -1 for true.	1 byte.
OLE Object	Pictures, graphs, or other ActiveX objects from another Windows-based application.	Up to about 2 GB.
Hyperlink	A link address to a document or file on the Internet, on an intranet, on a local area network [LAN], or on your local computer	Up to 8,192 [each part of a Hyperlink data type can contain up to 2048 characters].
Attachment	You can attach files such as pictures, documents, spreadsheets, or charts; each Attachment field can contain an unlimited number of attachments per record, up to the storage limit of the size of a database file.	Up to about 2 GB.
Calculated	You can create an expression that uses data from one or more fields. You can designate different result data types from the expression.	Dependent on the data type of the Result Type property. Short Text data type result can have up to 243 characters. Long Text, Number, Yes/No, and Date/Time should match their respective data types.
Lookup Wizard	The Lookup Wizard entry in the Data Type column in Design view is not actually a data type. When you choose this entry, a wizard starts to help you define either a simple or complex lookup field. A	Dependent on the data type of the lookup field.

	simple lookup field uses the contents of another table or a value list to validate the contents of a single value per row. A complex lookup field allows you to store multiple values of the same data type in each row.	

Sizing Field Column and Row Widths

Regardless of the actual field width, Access will store the data you enter, even if you can't see it all in the field on your screen. But you may wish to resize a field column for better readability.

- Click on the **border between the field you want to widen and the following field**. Drag the cursor to the right to widen the boundary line.
- Or, double-click the right border of a column to adjust the column automatically to fit the widest value of the field's contents.
  - Be sure to re-save your database file each time you make any type of change.

Below, we are widening the City **field** by dragging the border cursor to the right.

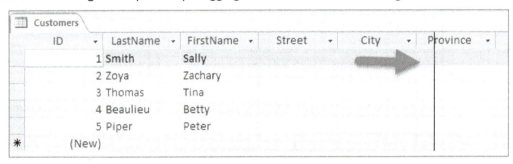

Although not commonly done, you can also enlarge the height of record rows if necessary by dragging the border between any two records downward.

Try It! Using **datasheet** view, choose a field, and make it wider. Since we don't need to save this, close the table, and do not resave it when prompted.

Tips for Working with Tables

When working with tables, you can collapse the navigation pane in order to make more room to display the fields in an open table by clicking the **Shutter Bar Open/Close** button.

Also, make sure to maximize the Access screen if you have many fields for which to enter records.

Unit Summary

In this unit, you have learned about the following topics and concepts:

- The functionality of database management software
- Ways in which database management software can be used
- The components of a database management software application
- Creating fields using the design view for tables.
- Tools for changing field names and modifying field column sizes.
- Procedures for entering data into tables.

Practice Questions and Activities

1. Provide a brief written description of a database.

2. What is the purpose of the Navigation Pane in Access?

3. In addition to the design view, what is the other view for a table, used for entering records?

4. What data type does Access assign as a default when you enter data into a field in a new table?

5. Think of and list several applications at school – or in your local community — in which a database can be helpful. Describe two or three benefits.

6. If you were tracking customers, what are two data types you could use in a simple table?

7. What steps do you follow to change the data type of the field?

8. In the customer table we entered earlier, what other data might one want to track in addition to the fields we covered earlier in the unit?

6. Break into small teams. Create an imaginary business, something that captures the interest of the group. [Try to think of something fun :-)] Design one table with fields, data types, and then populate the fields with four or five records of data. Compare results with the other teams; how did your team do?

Learning Objectives

This unit is designed to help you use database management software to design simple databases. Upon completion, you should be able to:

- Identify and describe a primary key for a database table
- Create relationships between tables
- Query a database using a single condition
- Generate simple reports about your data

More about Database Keys

Fields that are part of a table relationship are called **keys**. A key usually consists of one field, but may consist of more than one field. Values of the key can be used to refer to entire records, because each record has a different value for the key.

Primary Key

A **primary key** consists of one or more fields that uniquely identify each record that you store in the table. Often, there is a unique identification number, such as an ID number, a serial number, or a code that serves as a primary key.

Important! Each table can have only one primary key. For example, in the Customers table we created earlier, each customer has a unique customer ID number. When a primary key contains more than one field, it is usually composed of preexisting fields that, taken together, provide unique values. For example, because of your plans for obtaining information from the database in a certain way, you might use a combination of last name, first name, and birth date as the primary key for a table that tracks information about people.

Foreign Key

Most Access databases also use a **foreign key**, a column or group of columns in one table that points to the primary key of another table. Said another way, the original table you build will contain the primary key; other tables will contain one or more foreign keys that correspond to the primary key in the original table. [Note: In earlier versions of Access, you may have noticed that foreign keys were instead called secondary keys, and possibly also tertiary keys. Microsoft has replaced these two terms with the one term "foreign".]

In Access, to associate data such as suspects with other data important to the investigation, you add a **foreign key field** to a second table that corresponds to the ID field of your first table, and then creates a relationship between the two keys.

Set a Key

Surprise! This already happened in unit 12A when we entered our first field name in the **Customers** table. That's because by default, Access set the ID field as the primary key. This is probably the easiest and most efficient way to deal with keys, especially as you are learning about Access.

But you can also set a key manually in **design view**. Select the field that you want to designate, and then on the ribbon, in the **Design** tab, click **Primary Key** in the **Tools** group.

Tip! When working with keys, it's a good idea to stay away from things such as personal names, phone numbers, email address, postal code, made up facts and numbers, and government identification numbers. Sequential numeric keys – preferably allowing Access to auto assign them – are always a safe bet.

Opening and Closing Database Objects

Let's review to make sure you know how to open and close database objects. This is important when working with relationships and queries, both coming up soon.

Open a Database Object

- In the **Navigation pane**, locate and double-click the desired object.
- Notice that the object appears with a **tab** in the **Document Tabs bar**.

Close a Database Object

9. Select the object you wish to close, then click the **X** on the right of the **Document Tabs bar**.

10. If there are any unsaved changes to the object, you will be prompted to save it. Select **Yes** to save, **No** to close it without saving your changes, or **Cancel** to leave the object open.

11. The active object will close if you opted to close it.

Note: You can also close an object by right-clicking the object's tab on the Document Tabs bar and selecting **Close**. Select **Close All** to close all open objects.

Creating Database Relationships

About Relationships

In Access, a relationship is an association that links the primary key field in one table to a field that contains the same information in another table, known as the foreign key. For example, if customer accounts are assigned to certain sales employees, you can establish a relationship by linking the primary key EmployeeID field in the employees table with the foreign key EmployeeID field in the **Customers** table. This means that each customer account is assigned to only one employee, but each employee can manage many customer accounts, creating what is known as a **one to many relationship**. [This logic is how organizations track results for sales associates, track assignment of sales accounts to them.] The diagram below illustrates a simple relationship between fields in two tables.

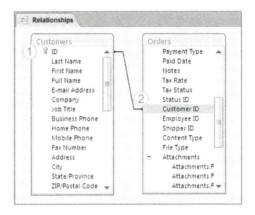

A table relationship, shown in the Relationships window.

1 A primary key, identified by the key icon next to the field name.

2 A foreign key; note there is no key icon.

Build Tables for the Relationships

With our new access database and its ability to pull information based on relationships, we want to track customers who order specific items sold at the bike shop. To do this, we need three tables; Customers, Orders, and Items. We'll build specific relationships among them.

We already have our Customers table, so now we'll create the other two tables.

- Build and save an **Orders** table with the following fields and data types.

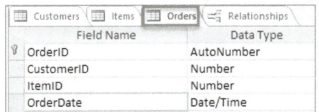

Field Name	Data Type
OrderID	AutoNumber
CustomerID	Number
ItemID	Number
OrderDate	Date/Time

- Now and save an **Items** table with the following fields and data types.

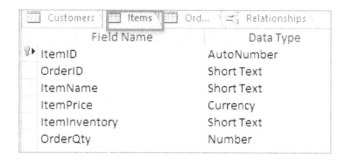

- Add several records with data as shown below for **ItemName** and **ItemPrice.** Remember, Access will automatically assign the **ItemID** as a sequential number, so you don't need to enter anything in the ItemID field.

Create the Relationships

Access has a nifty tool that allows you to add tables to a visual display, and then link fields, creating a type of roadmap that governs how relationships behave in your database.

- On the **Database Tools** tab, in the **Relationships** group, click the Relationships button, and click **Show Table.**

- With Customers selected, click **Add**.

- Now select **Orders,** and click **Add.** Notice that two tables have been placed in the **Relationships** tab. Both tables have a field named **CustomerID**.

- In the **Customers** field list, click **CustomerID**, and then drag it down and over to **CustomerID** in the **Orders** field list.

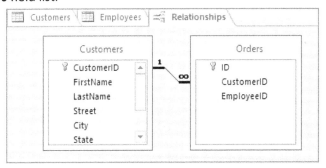

- When you release your mouse button, the **Edit Relationships** dialogue opens. Access has found the CustomerID field in each table.

- In **Edit Relationships**, click the checkbox next to **Enforce Referential Integrity**, then click **Create**. [Note: If you are repeating the relationship step, or opened the edit relations dialog manually, the Create button is replaced by an OK button.]

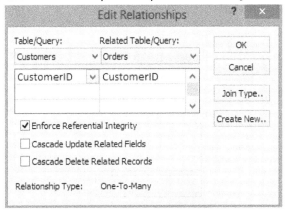

- Notice that a line between the two fields has appeared, linking the primary key in the **Customers** table with the foreign key in the **Orders** table. The number **1** and the **infinity** symbol illustrate the one to many relationship.

We are saying here that one customer may place more than one order. Each order will have the unique order ID; we'll get to that shortly.

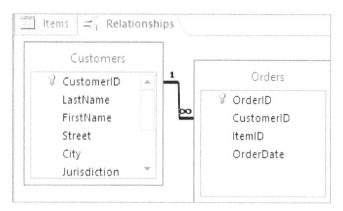

- Add the **Items** table to the relationships following the same steps you used for the previous two tables. **Tip!** You can also drag the table from the navigation pane onto the **Relationships** page.

- In the **Items** table list, click the **ItemID** field, and drag it down and over the **EmployeeID** field in the **Orders** field list. Make sure to turn on **Enforce Referential Integrity** by clicking the check box.
  Notice that Access has now added the relationship between the **Orders** and the **Items** tables.

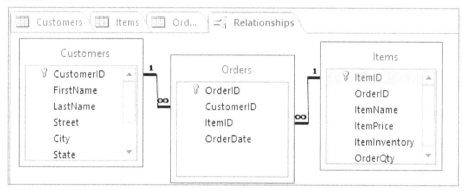

- Click the **X** on the right of the **Document Tabs bar** to close the Relationships page. Click **Yes** to save the relationship layout.

Querying a Database for a Single Conditions

Why Use Queries?

As mentioned earlier, a query in its simplest form is a question you wish to ask about the database. You are creating a statement describing conditions that must be met by one or more matching records. Here are several examples of how queries can be useful.

- Find all products in a specific category that cost more than a certain money amount in order to promote them for a sale.
- Find all customers who have spent more than a specific amount.
- Check inventory levels of items for sale.

At a more advanced level, using a query makes it easier to view, add, delete, or change data in your database. You can:

- Find specific quickly data by filtering on specific criteria, or conditions
- Calculate or summarize data
- Automate data management tasks, such as reviewing the most current data on a recurring basis.

A basic query in Access is a **select query**. A select query does exactly what it implies; it allows you to write criteria that Access will use to select data matches the criteria. Access produces a datasheet with the query's results.

To write our first query, we'll use the Query Wizard.

- Open the table from which you want to query data.
- On the **Create** tab, select **Query Wizard** from the **Queries** group.
- In the **New Query** dialog, accept the default of **Simple Query Wizard**, and click **OK**.

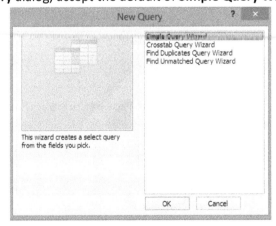

- In the **Simple Query Wizard**, notice the default table, **Customers**. That is fine.
- From the available fields on the left, click **LastName**, then click the top right-pointing arrow to add it to **Selected Fields**.
- Repeat this step to select **FirstName** and **Email** as shown below in **Selected Fields** as shown below.

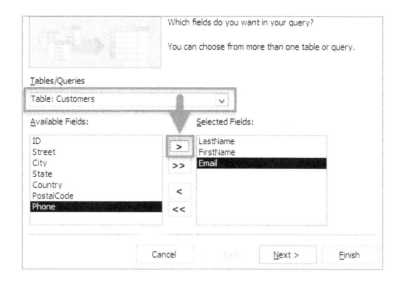

- Click **Next**.
- Accept the title suggested by Access, or replace it with another name. Then click **Finish**.

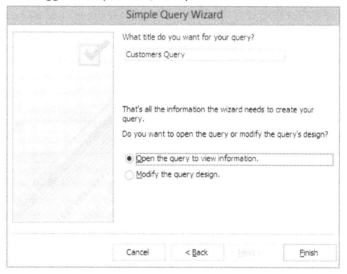

Query results are presented in a datasheet, showing only records that match your search criteria.

Notice that the **Customers** *table* tab is displayed, and then the Customers *query* tab showing the query results. [The small icons on the left of the tab note the difference between a table and a query.]

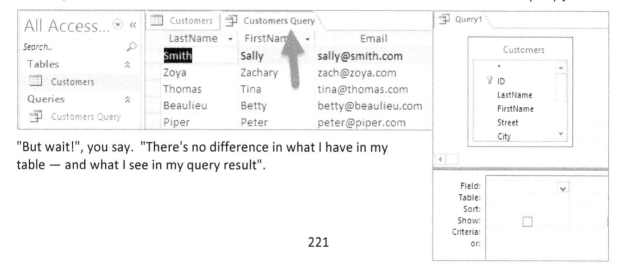

"But wait!", you say. "There's no difference in what I have in my table — and what I see in my query result".

221

Very smart! Here's the reason. We haven't provided the query any criteria yet. So let's do that now. Instead of the Query Wizard, we'll need to generate this query manually using the **Query Designer**.

- On the **Create** tab, in the **Queries** group, click **Query Design**.
- As you did before, click **Add** to select the query designer. **Customers** table and open it in the

Next we'll explore how to create this query in the Query Designer.

The Query Designer

The query designer provides tools for building queries for one or more tables, as well as providing a place to add criteria to select only data that meets your stated conditions.

The **top pane** shows field lists for tables you have selected to include in the query. The key icon indicates the primary field for a table.

In the **bottom pane**, Access performs its heavier lifting. It's a simple place to provide simple answers and choices.

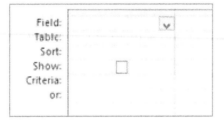

Each row performs a different task, as described below.

Row	Function
Field	Displays the names of the fields that you choose to include in the query
Table	Shows to which table each field belongs
Sort	Indicates upon which fields queries will be sorted, if you include sorting
Show	If **Show** is checked, it means that this field will be displayed in the results. Note: If not checked, the field still be used to determine the results.

Criteria	Conditions or statements that determine which records will be displayed
Or	Establishes any alternative criteria

Query for a Specific Criteria

In the **Customers** table, we want to see only those customers who live in the state of **New York**. We can add the criteria **NY** in the jurisdiction field to limit the query results to this criteria, the value in the database in the jurisdiction field. Here's how we set up this query.

- On the **Create** tab, in the **Queries** group, click **Query Design**.
- Click **Add** to select the **Customers** table and open it in the query designer.

- Drag **LastName** from the table down to the field name in the query.

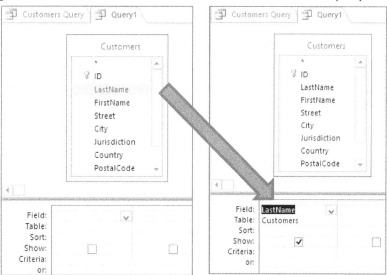

- Do the same for each other field, adding them in order. Notice that by default, Access checks the **Show** field, so the results will appear in the resulting dataset.

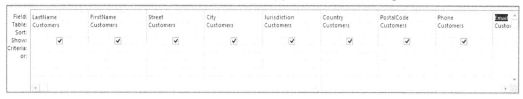

Now we must filter this query by specifying one or more criteria.

- On the **criteria row** in the jurisdiction field, add the abbreviation **NY**.
- Press **Tab**. Access surrounds your text with quotation marks.
- Save the query by right clicking the query tab name and choosing **Save**. Access will assign a default query name and display the query object in the navigation pane.

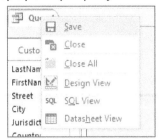

- Run the query by clicking the **Run** button in the **Results** group.

Try it! Did you get three records as your result, all of whom reside in New York?

Query Using a Text Operator

An operator is a sign or symbol that specifies the type of calculation to perform within an expression. There are mathematical, comparison, logical, and reference operators. Access supports a variety of operators, including arithmetic operators, comparison operators for comparing values, text operators for concatenating text, and logical operators for determining true or false values.

In Access, an operator is placed in the criteria row of a field.

Now let's add the operator **NOT** before "NY" so we can query for customers who do *not* live in New York State. Here's how the criteria looks when we add the **NOT** filter.

Looking over your **Customers** database, you can you anticipate the result?

Try It! What happens if you replace NOT with AND? Try this with NY and PA. How many results did you get?

Querying Using Logical Mathematical Operators

Access calls symbols that allow comparisons **comparison operators**, sometimes also called logical mathematical operators. These operators are used in expressions in the criteria row of an Access query to look for conditions that satisfy the criteria. Below are some common comparison operators.

Operator Symbol	Meaning
<	Less than

>	Greater than
<=	Less than or equal to
>=	Greater than or equal to
<>	Less than or greater than
≠	Not equal to

Here are examples of how logical operators can be used to produce specific query results.

Expression	Result Intended
> 20	Find conditions where the value in a record is more than 20.
≠ 0	Find customers who have spent more or less than zero dollars. [Could be less than zero if a credit was given to the customer.]
< 5	Find items in inventory that need re-ordering because the quantity on hand is low.

Create a Logical Operator Query

We have a spring promotion coming up. So we'll query the **Items** table to find all items we sell that cost **less than $20**. In this query, we want to see results for three fields; ItemID, ItemName, and ItemPrice.

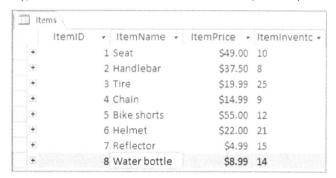

- On the **Create** tab, in the **Queries** group, click **Query Design**.
- Click **Add** to select the **Items** table and open it in the query designer.
- **Drag** the field **ItemID** from the table down to the field name row in the query.

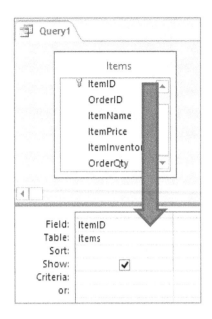

- Next, drag the field **ItemName** from the table down to the next field name column in the query.
- Then also drag the field **ItemPrice** from the table down to the field name in the query.
- In the **ItemPrice** field, on the **Criteria** row, enter **< 20.**

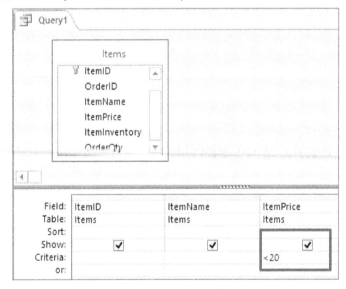

- Click **Run**. You should see all records that meet the logical operator criteria of less than $20 as shown below. If you don't, please revisit the query.

Rename a Query

Once you've built a query, you'll want to rename it to reflect its purpose.

- Save the query by right clicking its tab and choosing **Save**.

- Close the query by again right clicking its tab and clicking **Close**.
- In the navigation pane, right-click the default query name, then click **Rename**. Type the new query name.

Try It!

Create three separate queries for the **Items** table that meet the following conditions. Compare results with a classmate. Did you get predictable datasets?

    <= 5

    >=10

    ≠ 30

Generate Simple Reports

Use a Query to Generate a Report

There are several ways to create reports in Access.

For your first report, it's easiest to use an existing query that provides the data results. Then you can then dress it up using built-in reporting tools using the Report Wizard – or individual tools from the ribbon.

For this learning experience, we'll use the **Less Than 20** query we created in the previous section.

- In the **Create** tab, click **Report Wizard**.
- In the **Tables/Queries** section, click the drop-down arrow and select the query Items for Less Than $20.
- Select **ItemID** and click > to place it in the **Selected Fields** list.
- Do the same for **ItemName** and **ItemPrice**.
- Click **Next**.

- In the next wizard screen, click **Next**. [We don't want to add any grouping levels.]
- Though optional, we can choose a sort order; it makes readability easier for the user. Click the drop-down arrow for sort order 1, and select **ItemPrice**. [Leave the default order as Ascending.]

- Next, consider report layout options. View the options by selecting one and viewing the layout sample to the left. Click **Tabular,** lead the Orientation defaulted to portrait, and the Adjust Field option checked. Click **Next**.

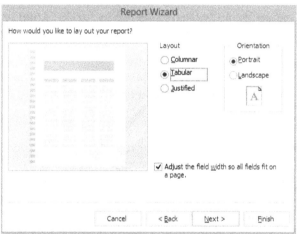

- Finally, Access asks for a title. Enter **Items Less Than $20**. Leave **Preview the Report** selected, and click **Finish**.

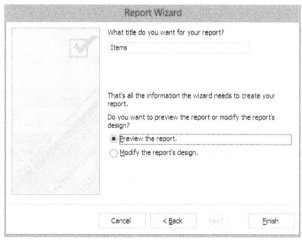

Access provides you a formatted report with the data assembled from your query. Leave the report open on your screen; we will use it further in the next section.

Try It!

First, create a new query to select from the items table items sold for greater than $40 — or less than $10. You do this by placing >40 on the Criteria line, and <10 on the OR line. Save the query with a relevant name.

Then follow the procedure above to create a report based on this query. Save the report with a name that reflects its purpose. Do your results look as expected?

About Report Views

Access 2013 provides four different ways to view your reports.

Report Display Type	Type of Result
Report View	Allows scrolling through report results without page breaks added for printing
Print Preview	Displays the report exactly as it will look when printed
Layout View	Similar to Print Preview, however you can edit the layout
Design View	Allows manipulation of the design of a report

To switch among the views, right-click the report name tab and select a view.

Try it! With the report you just created, right-click its tab, and take a look at each different view.

In preparation for the next section, make sure your report is saved, but leave it open.

Format the Appearance of the Report

Using **Design View**, you can polish up the appearance of your report. Switch to **Design View** by right clicking the report tab and selecting it. The default design layout that Access applied appears.

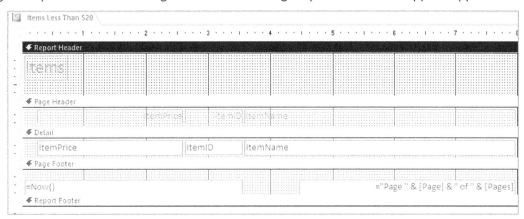

Each entity within the various sections of a report is considered to be an object. Working with objects makes perfect sense when working with report layouts, because you can visually drag objects to reposition or size them, and also change their attributes, such as font or background color.

Important note: To work with any object in the report design view, simply click to select it.

Modify the Header

First, make some formatting changes to the **Report Header**. On the ribbon, there are four tabs of tools in **Report Design Tools**. We'll begin with **Format Tools**.

- Make sure that your report is still open. In the report header, click **Items**.

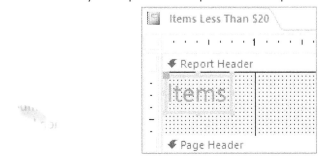

- On the ribbon, click the format tab, then click **Shape Fill**. Select a color from the theme or standard colors in the palette.

231

- Right-click the report tab, and choose **Print Preview**. Is the text readable?
- Close the Preview by clicking **Close Print Preview** on the preview ribbon.

- Back in the report designer, we'll modify the text color, just in case. Click inside the **Items** object and select the four letters of text, just as you would in Word or Excel.
- In the font group, click **Font Color**, and select a darker color, such as **Automatic**, for the default of black.
- View the change again using **Print Preview**. Better? Return to design view.
- If so, save the report.
- Then, lengthen the text box for the word **Items** by clicking its handle on the right side and dragging it across the screen. Preview the results, then return to design view.

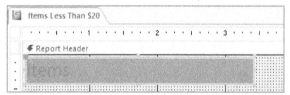

- Save the report.

Try it! Open your copy of the report. Make several changes to the text and attributes in the report header. Experiment with color, and attributes such as bold or italics, and the size of the bounding box. It's pretty easy, right?

Suggestion! Make one change at a time, then preview, and then return to the designer to make adjustments if necessary.

Modify the Page Footer

When Access created the report, it automatically created a footer to appear on each page.

It placed expressions designed to print the current date on the left – and the page number on the right at the bottom of each page of the report. Below you see the report design, and then how the result appears in the report.

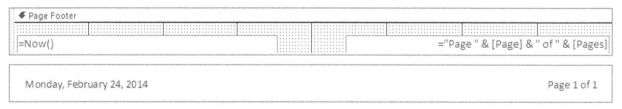

But no worries! Because the date and page number are contained within objects, you can change these, just as you did with objects in the report header.

By now, you can probably guess how to do this... :-).

We'll remove the date, and center the page number.

- Select the object in which you see the page number expression =Now().

- Press **Delete**.
- Select the page object and drag it to the center of the Page Footer area. Preview the results, and return to design view to adjust its location if necessary.
- Save the report.

Try It! Open your report, and make a few changes to the footer. You can change the tools, or the tools in the **Control Formatting** group.

For further thought... The page footer might be an excellent place to put a copyright statement, or even a small company logo. Although these are more advanced options, if Access catches your fancy, experiment with the many options in the report design tools to make your report shine!

Unit Summary

In this unit, you have learned about the following topics and concepts:

- Identifying and describing a primary key
- Creating relationships between tables
- Querying a database using single conditions
- Generating simple reports.

Practice Questions and Activities

1. Write a brief description of the purpose of the primary key in a database table.

2. What is the difference between a primary key — and a foreign key?

3. How do you set a key for a table manually, if it were to be necessary?

4. Working with tables:

   a. How do you open an existing table in a database?

   b. Save a table?

   c. Close a table?

5. For what basic reason does one query a database?

6. What type of query represents the most basic question you can ask of database tables?

7. What is a query operator? Provide two examples and explain the types of data each will produce.

8. What are the two main views for working with queries?

9. Demonstrate your ability to add a field from an existing table to the query designer.

10. What tab on the ribbon allows you to change the appearance of objects in a report using the query designer?

11. Small team exercise.

    a. Build two tables for a favorite made-up business such as a candy store or a gadgets shop. [Hint! Put your heads together and do a bit of design work up front for a better result... What fields, relationships, query, and report.]

    b. Create a customer table, and an items table.

    c. Build relationships between the two tables.

    d. Develop a query to pull information from one of the tables using a mathematical operator or text criteria.

    e. Build a report from your query, using it within the query designer.

    f. Modify the header visually.

    g. Tweak the footer.

    h. Compare results with fellow teams. How did your team do?

Learning Objectives

This unit is designed to help you build competence using desktop publishing software. Upon completion, you should be able to:

- Explain the purposes of desktop publishing software and its features and benefits
- Provide examples of desktop publishing software applications
- Create, format, edit and save and print publications
- Design and print publications using layout, formatting, page, and image tools.

What is Desktop Publishing Software?

Desktop publishing [DTP] is the creation of documents using page layout skills on a computer. Desktop publishing is frame-based; you create a page of content by putting text, images, titles, headings, and so forth into frames. Then you can easily move, resize and overlap each frame; the software will adjust the contents based on your actions. This approach provides much better control as opposed to a word processor, which places everything in one large box on a page basis.

Using desktop publishing software, you can generate layouts and produce typographic quality text and images comparable to traditional typography and printing. This technology allows individuals, businesses, and other organizations to self-publish a wide range of printed matter including newsletters, magazines, flyers, and even books – without the expense of a layout or graphic artist in a commercial production shop.

DTP Software Products and Platforms

Several DTP software products are available. Each software product listed below is graphically based, meaning that what you see on the screen is what you get when viewed or printed. Only FrameMaker addresses the larger layout-based realm using XML, extended markup language.

Product/Platform	Features/Benefits
InDesign CC Adobe Windows/Mac	• Available in 2014 only as InDesign Creative Cloud, a subscription-based model. Provides integration with other Adobe products and web services • Subscription for a year is several hundred dollars for a single user
FrameMaker 12 Adobe Windows/Mac	• Solution for visually authoring, enriching, managing, and publishing technical documentation, visually and or using XML • High-end platform for technical writers, usually in large organizations • Expensive
Publisher Microsoft Windows/Mac	• Part of the Microsoft office 2013 suite, or sold separately • Excellent choice for learning desktop publishing, for end-users in an office environment, and for home and small business use • Moderately priced, similar to Swift publisher, below

QuarkXPress 10	• Favorite of longtime Mac users
Quark	• Alternative to Adobe products such as InDesign and Illustrator
Windows/Mac	• Expensive
PagePlus X7	• Simple desktop publishing; integrated word processor, logo designer and photo editing lab
Serif	• Moderately priced
Swift Publisher	• Simple visual products that can be purchased separately including
Belight Software, Ltd	• Standalone products such as publishing, 3-D, business cards, each sold separately
Mac	• Inexpensive

Note: The procedures and illustrations in this unit are based on Microsoft Publisher 2013. If you are working with an earlier version of Publisher, you should find that most features once inside the product work similarly. Remember, can always press **F1** to get help specific to your product version.

About Microsoft Publisher

Microsoft Publisher 2013 lets you produce visually attractive publications without investing lots of money and time. You can make things as simple as greeting cards and labels, or as complex as brochures, pamphlets, and professional newsletters. In Publisher, all publications begin with a template. There are built-in templates, with many more free templates at Office.com, giving you a wide choice of looks with which to begin your own publication

Working with Desktop Publishing Software

Opening Publisher

To open Publisher, click the **Publisher** icon on your Microsoft Windows desktop, or in the Windows 8 Metro app. Or in Windows 7, click **Start** and type **Publisher** in the search box.

The Backstage view displays tabs at the left of your screen, with options for working with files.

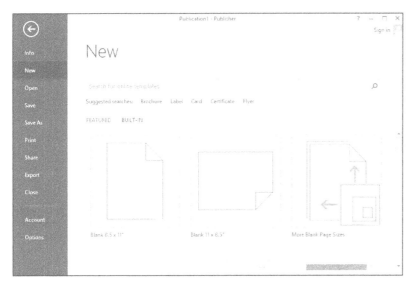

Click a tab to select an option; each is described below.

Tab	Functions
Info	Edit business information, run design Checker, and manage fonts
New	Create a new publication
Open	Access an existing publication page layout
Save	Save your work
Save As	Save your publication with a different name, or in a different location.
Print	Print your publication
Share	Share your file with other people
Export	Output your publication as a PDF/XPS document, in HTML format, change the file type, or use Pack and Go to package your publication for use on another computer.
Close	Close a publication without saving it
Account	Modify the appearance theme or publisher, or sign into your Microsoft account
Options	Adjust defaults and settings for the Publisher product

 Note: If you no longer need to use any of the options in Backstage, click the small arrow at the upper left of your screen return to your publication.

If you're already working with a publication, you can always click the **File** tab to return to Backstage.

Try It! Launch Publisher, and view the file options displayed in Backstage. Then close Publisher.

Using a Template to Create a Publication

The best way to begin a publication is to choose a pre-designed template from the start page when you first open Publisher. You can also return to the Start page at any time by clicking **File** and selecting **New** while working with a publication.

Click **Built-In** to find categories of templates such as flyers, brochures, or greeting cards.

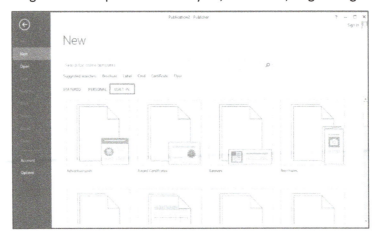

You can also click **Featured** to find individual templates. Or, use the search box to find online templates at Office.com which you can customize after downloading.

Important! While working with a publication, you can change the template using the **Page Design** tab, however this is not a best practice. It is far better to choose your template up front as part of your design process — and then to stay with it.

To open the template, double-click it so you can begin adding content and customizing it.

Try It!

Open Publisher. Search for a Built-In **Newsletter** template, and open it.

The Page Navigation Pane

The **Page Navigation Pane** appears on the left side of your screen, providing thumbnails of each page in your publication.

Click **Page Navigation** in the **Show** group on the **View** tab keep the pane visible.

Click any thumbnail image in the pane to move from one page to another as you are working.

To collapse the page navigation pane, click the small arrow at the upper right corner of the pane.

Try It!

- Review the navigation pane for your chosen **newsletter** template.
- How many pages does it contain?
- Collapse the navigation pane — then expand it.

The Ribbon

The ribbon appears at the top of the Publisher screen. As with all of the other Microsoft Office 2013 products, it is designed to help you quickly find the commands you need to complete a task.

Commands are organized in **groups** located under **tabs**. Each tab relates to a type of activity — such as page design or formatting.

To reduce clutter, some tabs are displayed only when needed; then they will disappear automatically if the software senses that you are finished using them.

Buttons are organized into groups according to the functions they perform. To access a feature, click its button. As you hover your mouse pointer over a button, a Screen Tip appears to provide information about the button.

When you hover your mouse pointer over a button, a **tooltip** pops up to explain the purpose of the tool.

Some groups on the ribbon also contain a small arrow in the lower right hand corner so you can use additional tools related to that group.

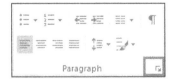

Try It!

- What tab of the ribbon is displayed when you first opened your new template?

- Hover your mouse pointer over the Styles button. What does it tell you about Styles?
- Which groups on this ribbon provide more information?

The File Tab

Use the **File** tab while working in a publication if you want to access any of the options in Backstage.

The Home Tab: Edit and Format Text

On the **Home** tab, you can edit text, format paragraphs, manage styles, insert objects, and arrange text.

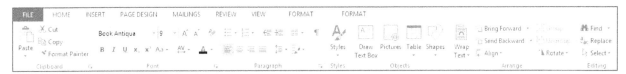

Home Task	Instructions
Clipboard	The **Format Painter** allows you to apply the format of text – or an object – to another text or object. To use format painter, select the text or object, click Format Painter, and then drag and release your mouse over the text or object you wish to make alike. 
	In addition to keyboard shortcuts and tasks you perform by right clicking your mouse, you can also click the buttons on the clipboard to cut, copy, or paste objects or text.
Font	With tools in the **Font** group, you can select text then change the font and point size – and apply appearance attributes. Just as in Word or Excel, click the drop-down arrow next to font or point size to make a change. 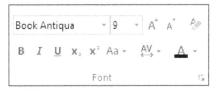
Paragraphs	Just as with text in Microsoft Word, the **Paragraph** group provides tools for applying bullets, numbering, alignment, line and paragraph spacing and multiple columns. If your text is already in the document, be sure to select it before clicking a tool button.

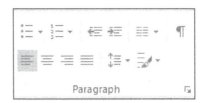

Paragraph

Styles

To apply any of the styles in the styles group, you want to style, and then click the **Styles** button and selecting the style you want to apply.

With **Styles**, you can also import a style from elsewhere on your computer, if available, or create your own new style.

Objects

The four tools in the **Options** group are also available in other tabs in Publisher; they are repeated in this group for convenience. See the **Page Design** and **Insert** tab information in this unit.

Arrange   The **Arrange** group allows you to select and modify text in a frame.

Use the **Wrap Text** options to control how text or graphics flow throughout the frame. Be sure to select your text or objects first.

The remaining buttons in this group are used to control image objects. Click **Bring Forward** to make an object of your in the forefront. Click **Send Backward** to demote an object one level back, essentially hiding it.

Editing   Click **Find** to locate text.

Click **Replace** to replace text.

Click **Select** to select all objects, or to select all text in a text box.

Try It!

- Select a line or two of text in and change the **font** and **point size**.
- Select a paragraph and center its text. Then left-justify the text.
- Apply **bullets** to the selection using the appropriate button in the Paragraph group.
- Change the style of your selection to **body text**.
- Discuss and compare results with a classmate. Leave the publication open for now.

Saving Your Publication

To save a new publication, click the **File** tab, and then choose **Save.** Backstage opens a Save As dialogue. Select a location on your computer – or a storage drive.

Type the name of your publication in the file name field, **then** click **Save**.

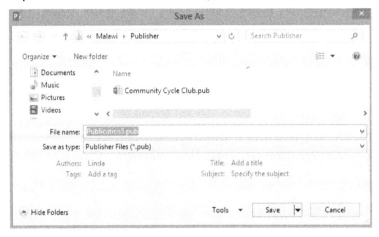

Tip! You can set a default in Publisher where you always want to save your templates and work.

Go to **File > Options > Save** and enter the path to the folder you want to contain all your templates in Default personal templates location. If you do this a new tab, named Custom, will also be available when you are creating a new publication and this tab will contain all your personal templates.

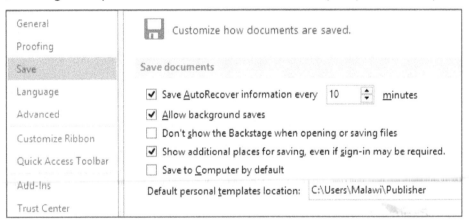

Closing Publisher

When you know you have saved your work, click the **File** tab, and choose **Close**.

Publisher leaves the New screen open in case you decide to do other work. To Exit Publisher completely, click the **X** in the upper right corner of your screen.

Try It!

- Save the publication as **My First Newsletter.**
- Close your publication.
- **Exit** Publisher.

244

The Insert Tab

Using the features in the insert tab, you can add pages and page parts, images, borders and accents, headers, footers, and page numbers.

Insert Task	Instructions	

Pages

Click **Page** to insert a blank or a duplicate page into the publication after the currently selected page.

Or, choose **Insert Page** and make selections; click **OK**.

Note: Catalog Pages is an advanced option, used for inserting fields from an external source in order to create a catalog using Publisher.

Tables

Quickly add a table by clicking **Tables**.

In the table grid, drag the over and then down to select the number of columns and rows, then release the mouse. The table is placed in the publication.

Note: You will want to place the table in an existing or new frame.

Illustrations

Click **Pictures.**

In the **Select Picture** dialogue, locate and select your image, then click **Insert**.

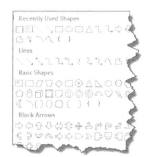

Note: If you choose **Online Pictures** instead, the insert picture dialogue will allow you to select royalty-free pictures from Office.com clip art.

Click **Shapes**. In the **Shapes Palette**, click any shape. In the publication, drag until the shape reaches a size you want, then release the mouse button.

Or, click **Picture Placeholder** to add an empty picture frame as a placeholder for a picture you want to insert later.

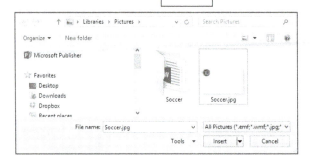

Building Blocks   The **Building Blocks** group contains nifty reusable pieces of content such as business information, headings, calendars, borders, and advertisements that are stored in galleries that you can access and reuse later.

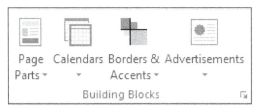

Click **Page Parts.** Select from headings, pull quotes [quotations that are called out in the publication], sidebars [small blocks of text typically set on one side or the other of a page], as well as a host of other preset starters.

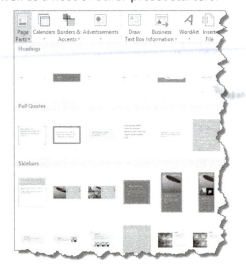

Inserting **Calendars, Borders and Accents,** and **Advertisements** all work similarly, providing numerous reusable content pieces that you can quickly drop into your publication.

246

Text

Draw Text Box allows you to drag the mouse to create a box into which you can place text.

For **Business Information**, Publisher displays your contact information and allows you to add it to a publication. This is handy output such as newsletters or sales brochures.

Using **Word Art**, you can insert visually interesting letter and word effects by clicking to add the effect you want. Style choices appear.

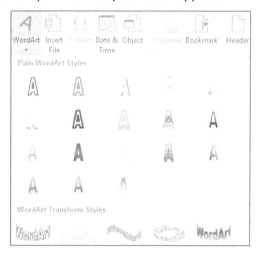

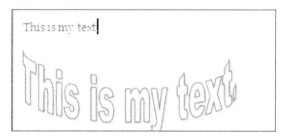

If you first select the text you want to format with Word Art, Publisher will insert it in the Edit Word/Art text dialogue box – along with the option to change the font, point size, or to apply bold or italics. Or, you can use the feature with no text selected, instead inserting your text when the dialogue box opens.

Four other options in the Insert Text group include the ability to insert a file, a symbol, the date, and/or the time, or an object. All function similarly to these tools in Microsoft Word.

Links

Using tools in the **Links** group, you can add a hyperlink to a another document on your computer — or to a website by adding the URL.

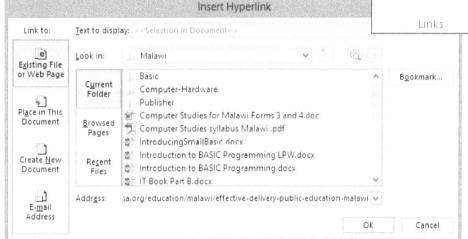

If you're not ready to insert the hyperlink just yet, no worries. Instead, choose to insert a **Bookmark** as a graphical place marker until later. :-)

Header & Footer

To insert a **header** or a **footer**, click either button in the **Header & Footer** group.

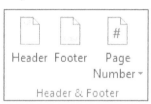

Notice that a text box for a header is added at the top of your publication. You can add text and customize the text just as you customize any other text in frames.

Then click **Close Master Page.**

Don't forget to save your publication after each significant change! :-)

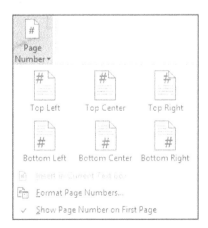

To add page numbering, click **Page Number**.

Publisher adds page numbering in your chosen location on each page. It will number pages automatically. You can also format the appearance of your page numbers.

Try It!

- Open Publisher and select a **flyer** from the Office.com templates. Note: If you're not connected to the Internet, choose a flyer from the built-in templates. It doesn't matter which for practice.
- Insert a new page below the existing page.
- Insert a table anywhere on the second page.
- Insert a third page.
- Insert a pull quote using the Building Blocks group.
- Draw a text box and in it, type or paste in several lines of text.
- Save the publication as MyFirstFlyer, keeping Publisher open.
- Add a footer to all pages.
- Save the publication again, keeping Publisher open.

The Page Design Tab

The **Page Design** tab contains groups for customizing the appearance of your publication.

Page Design Task	Instructions
Margins	On the **Page Design** tab in the **Page Setup** group, click **Margins**.

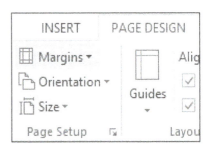

In the **Layout Guides** dialogue, click the selection arrows below **Margin Guides** to increase or decrease the **margin size** for each area of the page. Click **OK**.

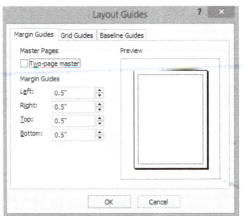

Important! Any changes you make will affect the entire publication.

| Schemes | With a publication open on your screen and a frame selected, hover your mouse over a selection in the **Schemes** group. Notice that your publication is modified to reflect that scheme.   To select the scheme and apply it to your publication, left-click your mouse. |

Also in the **Schemes** group, click **Fonts** to preview and change the font for your design.

Page Background   Click **Background**, then hover your mouse over the selections to view and select a different page background. Choices include no background, solid background, and gradient background. Or you can click **More Choices** and custom-create your own background.

Pages   In the **Pages** group, you can delete, move, or rename pages.

To delete a page, select it, then click **OK**.

To **move** a page, select the page, then in the Move Page dialogue, indicate whether before or after, and click to select the page in **This Page**. Click **OK**.

You can rename a page. This name does not appear in your publication; it only applies when you hover over a page in the navigation pane. For example, you may wish to apply a specific page name if you are working with a very long publication, such as "**Committee News** ". Click **OK** to complete the rename task.

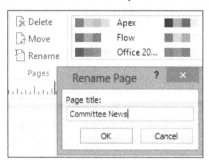

Try It!

- In your flyer, click the **Page Design** tab.
- Change the **scheme** of your flyer.
- Use a different page background; any color, either solid or gradient.
- Move the last page up to become the first page. [Hint: Use the navigation pane.]
- Save the publication, then keep it open on your screen.

The Review Tab

Using the **Proofing** group In the **Review** tab, you can check the spelling for your publication, perform research to support the development of your publication using the **Research** task pane, or use the **Thesaurus** task pane to look up synonyms.

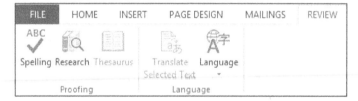

To check spelling, click the **Spelling** button in the proofing group. If **Publisher** finds any potential spelling issues, it will present the check spelling dialogue so you can take action.

The View Tab

In the **View** tab, you can choose a see a different view of your publication, show or hide various aspects of your publication, and change zoom settings.

View Task	Instructions
Views	You can apply a master page to the publication, or edit existing master pages. [Master Pages contain the elements that you want to repeat on multiple pages in a publication.]
Layout	Choose to view a single page, or a two-page spread. [In a two-page spread, you view facing pages of the publication at the same time. This is used mainly when working with a publication that will be printed with leading and trailing pages, either bound or folded.]

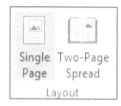

Show	The **Show** group includes options to turn on or off numerous support tools. Click the checkbox next to a tool to invoke an option, or click the checkbox again to dismiss it.

Boundaries show you where your frames begin and end.

Guides are lines added to the screen to help you place frames and objects.

Fields are used if you are adding information to your publication from an outside source.

Rulers provide a visual display with the dimensions of your publication.

Page Navigation exposes or hides thumbnails in the navigation pane.

Scratch Area is a blank workspace on your screen, outside of your publication where you can place images before dragging them to a frame.

Graphics Manager opens a task pane on the right side of your screen to help you manage your graphic images.

Baseline Guides help you precisely align text lines across multiple columns.

Zoom	Click any of the buttons to change how much of the publication you want to see on your screen; 100%, whole page, or only objects that you first select.

Tip! You can also drag the zoom slider at the bottom right of your screen to change the zoom percentage.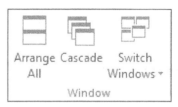

Window   The **Window** group allows you to organize windows to suit how you work. Unless you have two publications open at once, this isn't necessary, especially as you are learning publisher.

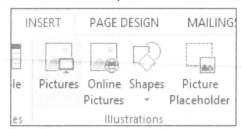

Try It!

- Check the spelling for your publication.
- View two pages at once.
- Turn on all of the options in the Show group. What has changed on your screen? How do you think these options will be helpful?
- Zoom your publication to 150%. Then zoom it down to 75%, and finally back to 100%.
- Save your publication, and leave it open on the screen.

Inserting Graphic Objects

Insert an image into Publisher from your computer as follows:

- Open or create the publication to which you want to add the picture.
- From either the **Home** or the **Insert** tab, select **Pictures**.

INSERT	PAGE DESIGN	MAILING

le   Pictures   Online   Shapes   Picture
                 Pictures   ▾   Placeholder
es   Illustrations

- In the **Insert Picture** dialogue box, locate the folder that contains the picture you want to insert, and select the picture file.

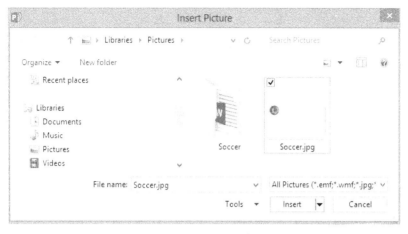

12. Click **Insert**. The picture is placed in the scratch area.

Insert an image into Publisher from an online source as follows:

- In an open publication, from either the **Home** or the **Insert** tab, select **Online Pictures**.
- In **Insert Pictures**, type and image category in the search box and click the search button.

- Scroll through the choices and click to select the image you want to insert. Click **Insert**.

- Notice that image is placed the scratch area.

Tip! When selecting multiple images for each option above, press **Shift** and click each image you want to add before clicking insert.

Try It!

- Ask your teacher to provide an image that you can insert if you don't have one on your computer.
- In your open publication, insert an image from the computer. Where do you put it until you're ready to place it in the publication?
- Create a new frame anywhere in the publication, and then drag the image to place it into a new frame.
- If you have access to office.com, search for a category and add an image to the scratch area. If you don't, ask your teacher to demonstrate.
- What is your impression about the process of adding images to the scratch area in publisher?

Designing Publications

As we learned earlier, in Publisher it's best to always begin the design by selecting a template. Chances are you'll be making your own customizations, but a template gives you a head start on your work. And previewing templates is a good way to gather design ideas as you are learning Publisher.

Types of Publications

Microsoft Office Publisher allows you to design many types of publication materials. You can produce posters, flyers, pamphlets, newsletters or labels using many built-in tools. You can also personalize your creations by adding your company logo, team emblem – or photos relevant to your content topic.

Try It! Open Backstage and explore the template options for brochures. For what different types of brochures are templates available?

Orientation and Page Size

Publisher supports portrait and landscape orientation – and a number of different page sizes.

Orientation

To change the **orientation** for a publication, click **Orientation** in the **Page Setup** group of the **Page Design** tab, then select Portrait or Landscape.

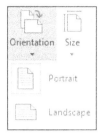

Paper Size

Many paper sizes are available in Publisher. To change the size, click **Paper Size** in the **Page Setup** group of the **Page Design** tab, then select a paper size.

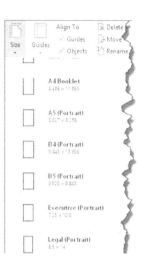

Click **Page Setup** to customize the page width, height, individual margin guides, layout type or target paper size. Notice that the preview will change depending on the selections you make. Click **OK** to save your selections.

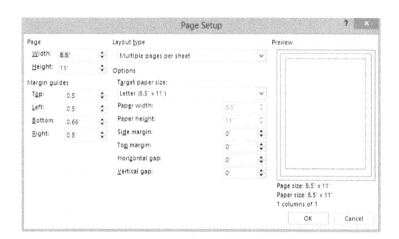

Try It!

- For the open publication on your screen, change the **orientation** from portrait to landscape – or from landscape to portrait.
- In **Page Setup**, reduce the height and width of your publication by 1 inch.
- Then adjust the **right margin guide** by changing it to one inch.
- What's happened to the appearance of your publication?
- Reverse **all** the settings so your publication is back to its original appearance.

Since you reversed your changes, there should be no need to save the publication again. But this brings up a best practice! :-)

If you are happy with the appearance of your publication so far and you're ready to make more than little tweaks, it's always best to save what you have before making more changes! :-)

- So, save and close the current publication. In a and in a way to copy your eye decided I needed to try to slow so it may midsection was leaning up against

Layout Guides

We've already seen **Layout Guides** in the **Show** group on the **View** tab. However they also appear on the **Page Design** tab in abbreviated form when needed.

On the **Page Design** tab, in the **Layout** group, click **Guides**, then select any or all of the guide types.

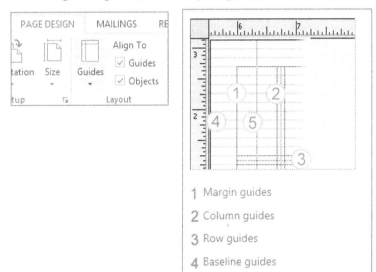

1 Margin guides

2 Column guides

3 Row guides

4 Baseline guides

5 Ruler guides

Once you have chosen your alignment guides, use the **Align To** options to instruct Publisher how you wish to use them, for guides and or for objects.

Text Boxes

In Publisher, text is contained in text boxes — frames, really — which are blocks of text that you can place on the page. When you create or select a text box, the **Text Box Tools** tab appears on the Ribbon, with commands to adjust and format your text box – and the text it contains.

- On the **Insert** tab in the Text group, click **Draw Text Box**.

- The cursor changes to a crosshatch. Click anywhere on your publication and drag to create the text box, releasing the mouse button when the text box reaches a size you want.
- Type or paste existing text into the text box. Notice that the **Format** tab appears once you draw the text box. Note: You can also display at any time your cursor is active in a text box by clicking the **Format** tab under **Text Box Tools**.

You've already learned about how to use some groups in the Format tab, but with a text box open, there are several additional groups of tools we haven't yet explored. These are described below.

Format Task	Instructions
Text	When you select text in a frame, there are three options in the Text Group for how it appears in flows. 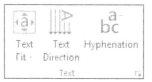
	Click **Text Fit** to change how text is fitted into a text box. Select one of the four options. 
	Click **Text Direction** to flip your text from a horizontal orientation to a vertical orientation.
	If you need precise control, click **Hyphenation** to control how hyphenation is performed for text in a frame. The hyphenation zone is the amount of space to leave between the end of the last word in a line – and the right margin.
	If you check **Automatically hyphenate this story**, the text will be automatically hyphenated based on grammatical rules and the distance of the hyphenation zone.

To reduce the number of hyphens, make the hyphenation zone wider.

To reduce the raggedness of the right margin, make the hyphenation zone narrower. If you have words that are long, you may want to control where the hyphens occur in the word by indicating manually how many letters of a word should appear before a hyphen is added.

Alignment   For a selected frame, you can control the alignment of text, column alignment, and the text margins.

Click one of the 9 **Alignment** buttons to align the text in a combination of horizontal and

vertical settings.

Click **Columns** to select from 1 to 3 or more columns that will appear in the selected frame.

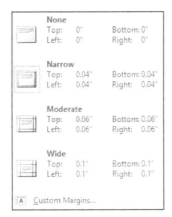

Click **Margins** to select preset controls of the margins for the text within a selected frame.

To customize the controls, click **Custom Margins** to adjust them for the selected text box.

Typography

Typography [from the Greek words typos, or form, and graphe, or writing] is the art and technique of arranging type in order to make the words most appealing.

Drop Cap options let you create a large capital letter at the beginning of a paragraph.

Number Style provides a default and for preset methods for displaying numbers.

Ligatures are combinations of two or more characters put together to create more attractive or readable text. Some fonts include the capability to create ligatures.

Stylistic sets provide alternative character shapes.

Swashes add flourishes for a decorative effect

Stylistic Alternates provide three ways to modify spacing between words.

Try It!

- On an empty page of your publication, add a **text box**. Type or paste some text into the text box; a short paragraph. Save the publication.
- Change the text fit. What is different?
- Change the text direction? What happened? [Return it to normal by reversing the text direction.]
- Experiment with the hyphenation settings, especially the Manual Settings. What changed?
- Now, try out the alignment settings. Which of the settings do you think you might use most often?
- Finally, apply a **Drop Cap** to the first letter of a new paragraph. How do you like the effect?
- Just for grins, save the file exactly as it is. Remember this is just practice; it's okay to have a little fun as you're learning!

Manipulating Images

An important term to understand when working with graphic images is **handle**. Handles are small shapes displayed around the boundary of the object when you select it. Clicking a handle allows you to make a change to the object.

When you add or manipulate images, publisher provides a **scratch area** — and open space to the right of your publication — so you can manipulate the image if necessary before placing it.

As with other portions of Publisher, new tabs on the ribbon will open and close dynamically as needed based on what you are doing.

Resizing an Image

There are several ways to resize an object such as, picture, shape, or text box.

Dragging an object to resize it:

- Select the object.
- Move your mouse pointer over one of the handles.
- Click and drag the object.

Dragging an object while keeping the center in the same place:

13. Select the object.

14. Press and hold **Ctrl**.

15. Move the mouse pointer over one of the handles, and then click and drag the object.

16. Release the mouse button before you release Ctrl.

Dragging while maintaining the object's proportions:

17. Select the object.

7. Press and hold **SHIFT**.

8. Move the mouse pointer over one of the corner, and then click and drag the object.

9. Release the mouse button before you release SHIFT.

Note: You can override the settings to snap to ruler marks, guides, and objects by holding down ALT while you drag the mouse.

You can also manually set an object to a specific height and width as follows:

- Right-click the object.
- On the shortcut menu, click **Format <object type>**.
- In **Format Picture**, click the **Size** tab.
- Under **Size,** enter measurements for the height and width of the object.
- Click **OK**.

Cropping

Use the editing features in Publisher to crop an image. We will use a picture as an example.

- Select the picture, and on the **Picture Tools** tab click **Crop**.
- Position the **cropping handle** over a point.

1 Cropping handle

- Do one of the following:
- To crop one side, drag the center handle on that side.
- To crop evenly on two sides at once, hold down **Ctrl** as you drag a handle.
- To crop all four sides at once while maintaining the proportions of your picture, hold down **Ctrl+Shift** as you drag a corner handle.

Moving an Image

To move an image, select it, and then drag it, releasing the mouse left button to place it.

Flipping and Rotating

Rotating an Image

You may decide to rotate a photo or image such as clipart to add visual interest through asymmetric positioning. For example, the wooden shoes on the left below appear fairly predictable. But when rotated slightly, the shoes now suggest the impression of movement.

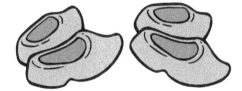

To rotate an image:

- Select the image by clicking the object.
- On the **Arrange** menu, click **Rotate or Flip**, and then do one of the following:
- Click **Rotate Left 90°** or **Rotate Right 90°** to rotate the clip in 90-degree increments. Click once to rotate the clip 90 degrees. Continue to click until the clip is in the position that you want.
- Click **Free Rotate**, and then place the pointer over the round green handle at the top of the object. When you see a circle around the green handle, drag until the object is at the angle that you want.
- Release the mouse.

Flipping an Image

You may add a piece of clipart that would present a better balance to the page if you flip it. Or perhaps you want to create a pair of images that seem to surround some text in your content, perhaps serving as "bookends".

18. Select the image.

10. On the **Arrange** menu, click **Rotate or Flip**, and then click **Flip Horizontal** – or **Flip Vertical**. [Here we see a flipped image next to the original image.]

Changing Contrast and Brightness

You can change the appearance of an image by adjusting its contrast and brightness.

- Select the image.
- On the **Picture** toolbar, do any of the following:

  To increase the brightness, click **More Brightness** .

  To reduce the brightness, click **Less Brightness** .

  To increase the contrast, click **More Contrast** .

  To reduce the contrast, click **Less Contrast** .

- Adjust the levels and compare the differences. For example, you can make a clip darker by decreasing the brightness, or you can subdue it by reducing the contrast.

If you want to place the image behind text, you can wash it out by clicking **Color** on the **Picture** toolbar – and then selecting the **Washout** option.

Practice Working with Images

Try It!

Now that you've had an opportunity to look at various ways to manipulate images, try the following:

- Add an image of your choice from the built-in templates or office.com to any blank page on one of your publications. Be sure to place it in scratch area.
- Move the image inside a new text frame in the publication.
- Resize it; make it larger.
- Now, crop the image slightly.
- Flip it, and then rotate it.
- Finally, crop the image slightly.
- What do you think about working with images? Do you find it fairly straightforward?

Tip! Don't forget to save frequently as you are making changes. It can save you a lot of lost time later, especially if you've had made several changes – but hadn't saved them.

Now, take a moment to pat yourself on the back. You've done a lot of hard work learning how to work with Publisher. We're almost done!

Exporting a Publication

Publisher provides numerous options for exporting your publication to another source.

From inside your publication, click **File**, and then in Backstage, choose **Export**.

So you don't have to memorize, as you click an Export option, Publisher explains its purpose – and provides a button to execute the option.

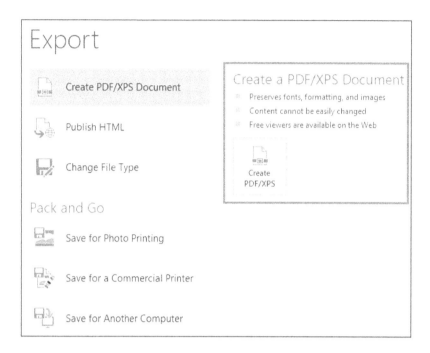

Here's a summary of the purposes of the first three export options.

Export Option	Purpose
Create PDF/XPS Document	An **XML Paper Specification [XPS] document** is a document format you can use to view, save, share, digitally sign, and protect your document's content. An XPS document is like an electronic sheet of paper: You can't change the content on a piece of paper after you print it, and you can't edit the contents of an XPS document after you save it in the XPS format. You can create an XPS document in any program you can print from, but you can only view, sign, and set permissions for XPS documents in an XPS Viewer. A PDF file is a file output in Portable Document Format [PDF] – an open standard for electronic document exchange. With both formats, your appearance is preserved, content cannot be easily changed, and viewers are available free on the Internet.
Publish HTML	With HTML output, you can publish a document on a webpage.
Change File Type	Publisher 2013 supports a number of file types for saving publications. Several support earlier versions of publisher, and there are some options to create graphics files with extensions such as .PNG and .JPG.

What is Pack and Go?

Pack and Go is a feature in Microsoft Publisher that allows you to package your publication and move it to another computer, or prepare and package your files to take to a commercial printing service. The **Pack and Go Wizard** names and numbers packed files and adds a .puz file extension. A Readme.txt file and an Unpack.exe program are also included with the packed files. Pack and Go is an easy way to simplify the process of preparing, packing, and unpacking your publication files. There are three **Pack and Go** options.

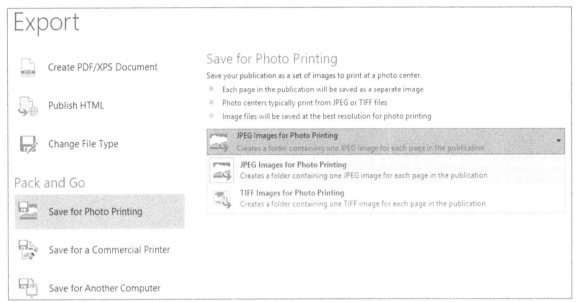

Below are the steps the wizard and will follow using the option **Save for Another Computer**.

The wizard confirms what it will do. Click **Next**.

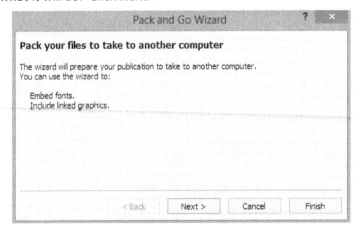

Next it asks where to save the files. Indicate your selection. Tip: if you place it in another location on the computer, you can always output it to external storage later. Click **Next**.

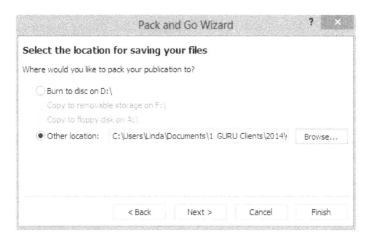

Then the wizard offers options for commercial printing. If you're not sure, select all three. Click **Next**.

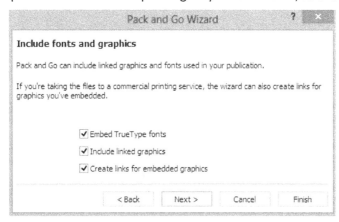

Finally, the Wizard confirms your selections and file locations. Click **Finish** to write the files.

Below is a brief summary of each of the three **Pack and Go** options.

Pack and Go Option	Purpose
Save for Photo Printing	Saves each page of the publication as a separate image with the best possible resolution for printing

Save for a Commercial Printer	Provides options for selecting the best quality and file type suitable for professional printing
Save for Another Computer	Uses a wizard to assemble the necessary files, compress them, and then decompress them as you place them on another computer

Try It!

- Open a publication with which you been working. Export it in **PDF** format to a folder of your choice.
- Now export the same file in a graphics format such as with a .JPG extension. Locate and open the file by double-clicking it. With what software application does it open? [Depending on what applications are installed on your computer, you may need to ask your teacher to demonstrate this instead.]
- Try the pack and go feature **Save for Another Computer**. How did the wizard work for you?

Printing Publications

Sometimes you may want to print a copy of your publication so you can proof it on paper — or have others look it over.

From inside your publication, click **File**, and then in Backstage, choose **Print**. The default printer associated with your computer appears in the printer section.

[Or, in the publication, press the keyboard shortcut, **Ctrl + P.**]

Select from the following print settings: number of pages to print, how many pages per sheet, paper size, one or two-sided printing, and whether to print as an RGB [red-green-blue] publication.

Notice you can also click the checkbox at the bottom to save the settings for this specific publication so you won't have to repeat this process as you continue working with. This is a nice timesaver!

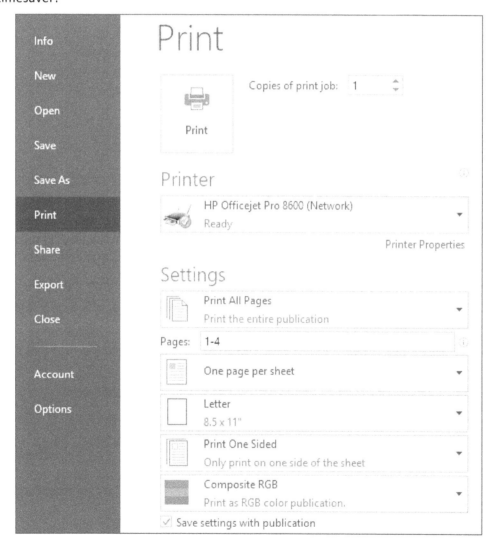

Try It!

If your computer is connected to a printer in your classroom or lab, print one page of your choice.

Unit Summary

In this unit, you have learned about the following topics and concepts:

- The purposes of desktop publishing software and its features and benefits
- Examples of desktop publishing software applications
- How to create, format, edit, save and print publications
- Tools for designing publications; layout, formatting, page, and image tools.

Practice Questions and Activities

1. Briefly describe the purposes of desktop publishing.

2. What are two DTP products in addition to Microsoft Publisher?

3. List six tasks that you can perform In Backstage using Publisher.

4. Why do tabs sometimes appear on the ribbon — and then disappear?

5. Describe the purpose of a frame as used in desktop publishing.

6. What is meant by a handle?

7. What is the purpose of the Scratch Area?

Individual or Small Group Practice Exercise

8. Think of a topic. Ideas can be something team related, a school project, a small business such as a bike shop, or even family news.

9. Using a newsletter template, create a new two-page newsletter. After entering some real text to replace the placeholder text, use the editing and formatting tools in the **Home**, **Insert**, **Page Design**, and **View** ribbon tabs to make the text really support your topic.

10. Save the publication on your hard drive with a name appropriate to the topic.

11. Replace any included images with those on your computer or at office.com. Make sure to choose relevant images.

12. Use the various image tools [resizing, cropping, moving, and flipping/rotating] to place the images in frames to visually support your newsletter.

13. Print your newsletter to make sure you're happy with the results so far.

14. Make any adjustments based on your review of the printed copy.

15. Save the publication again.

16. Export a copy as a PDF file.

17. Compare your results with classmates, or other teams, then share them with the whole class.

Learning Objectives

This unit is designed to help you learn to use software to create and make a presentation. Upon completion, you should be able to:

- Explain the purposes of presentation software and list several examples of presentation software products
- Create a simple presentation using the ribbon, and task panes
- Use options in various tabs and groups to edit and format elements of the slides
- Save and print a presentation
- Insert images, tables, shapes, SmartArt and symbols
- Use shortcuts such as Key Tips to reduce the time taken to type or use the mouse
- Close and exit a presentation
- insert, manipulate, and format slides using themes, and the slide master
- Save a presentation as a template
- Apply slide transitions, and slide information
- Present a slideshow
- Export a presentation

Definition of Presentation Software

Presentation software is a computer application software program that provides visual information placed on "slides" – to accompany the oral delivery of information to an audience.

Harvard Graphics, released in 1986, was a pioneering presentation program developed for DOS and Microsoft Windows by Software Publishing Corporation [SPC]. Harvard Graphics, Inc. released the first version in 1986 as Harvard Presentation Graphics.

Microsoft PowerPoint first began as a product named Presentation, but was renamed PowerPoint due to copyright issues. Microsoft PowerPoint launched on May 22, 1990, as a part of the Microsoft Office suite, the same day that Microsoft released Windows 3.0.

Word Perfect Presentations as well as lesser known programs such as Astound and Key Presenter.

As of 2012, various versions of PowerPoint claimed approximately 95% of the presentation software market share, with installations on at least 1 billion computers world-wide.

In 2014, PowerPoint 2013 is the most recent edition, part of the office 2013 software suite, running on Windows

Features and Benefits of Presentation Software

A presentation program is a software package used to display information in the form of a slide show. It has three major functions: an editor that allows text to be inserted and formatted, a method for inserting and manipulating graphic images, and a slide-show system to display the content. Some presentation software also has the capability to create custom animations and slide transitions.

Types of Presentation Software

Although Microsoft PowerPoint has around 90% of the presentation software market worldwide, there are other products available.

Product/Platform	Features/Benefits
PowerPoint Microsoft Windows and Mac	Slide-based presentation program developed by Microsoft, officially launched on May 22, 1990, as a part of the Microsoft Office suite, the same day Microsoft released Windows 3.0. **Benefits:** • Used worldwide; abundant support tools, books, e-books • Integrates with Office, leading to ease-of-use due to similarity with other Office products [Ribbons, tools] • Moderately priced, either bundled with office or purchased separately **Disadvantages:** • Users can overcrowd and overuse bulleted slides, leading to audience boredom, sometimes termed "death by PowerPoint"
Keynote **Apple** Mac	Keynote for Mac makes it simple to create and deliver beautiful presentations. It allows you to work seamlessly between Mac and iOS devices, and its file format is portable to PowerPoint. **Benefits:** • Takes advantage of Mac architecture and features • File compatibility with PowerPoint for exchange with colleagues • Runs on Mac and iOS iPad and SmartPhone • Very inexpensive **Disadvantages:** • The master file does not support animations • The toolbar is not customizable
Prezi Windows, Mac, iPad	Introduced in 2009, Prezi is a cloud-based [SaaS] presentation software and storytelling tool for presenting ideas on a virtual canvas. The product allows users to zoom in and out of their presentation media, and to display and navigate through information. Prezi allows you to create eye-catching custom animations. **Benefits:** • Cloud-based subscription model, with free entry level version • Intense zoom effects **Disadvantages:** • Some have claimed zoom effects can promote dizziness • Not widespread use as with Office/PowerPoint

OpenOffice Impress Apache	Open office is a tool for creating effective multimedia presentations. Your presentations will stand out with 2D and 3D clip art, special effects, animation, and high-impact drawing tools. Impress is part of the OpenOffice suite. **Benefits:** • Free for individuals; easy download • Excellent no-cost tool for home use • File export capability to PowerPoint **Disadvantages:** • None
Haiku Deck Giant Thinkwell, Inc. iPad/iOS devices	Haiku Deck is an easy to use app for quickly building short, simple, and attractive slides. **Benefits:** • Built-In access to a wealth of free art **Disadvantages:** • No sound, transitions, or animations • Cannot manually place text or change the background color for charts
Presentations Corel Windows	Corel Presentations is part of the Corel WordPerfect office suite. It includes full multimedia support an ample customization options. **Benefits:** • Excellent variety of help and support options • Software layout similar to other products such as PowerPoint • Full PowerPoint compatibility **Disadvantages:** • Expensive; must purchase the full Corel WordPerfect Office suite whereas PowerPoint can be purchased separately

Note: The procedures and illustrations in this unit are based on Microsoft PowerPoint 2013. If you are working with an earlier version of PowerPoint, you should find that most features once inside the product work similarly. Remember, you can always press **F1** to get help specific to your product version.

Working with Presentation Software

When learning PowerPoint, it's best to work from simple to complex. First, you learn to create slides, then how to perform formatting and editing. Learning about themes helps you add visual interest. Then you can create custom animations; controls for entrance, emphasis, and exit of elements on a slide. Transitions allow you to animate and control movements between slides. Finally, you'll need to know how to present, print and export presentations.

Opening PowerPoint

To open PowerPoint, click the PowerPoint icon on your Microsoft Windows desktop, or in the Windows 8 Metro app. Or in Windows 7, click **Start** and type **Publisher** in the search box.

A blank presentation appears, called **Presentation1** by default.

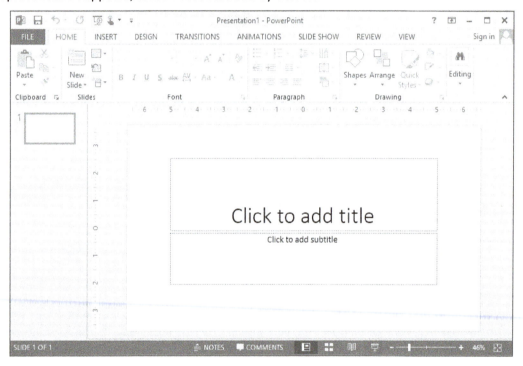

Creating a Presentation

When you open PowerPoint, a screen appears so you can begin with a blank presentation – **or** a theme. For now, double-click **Blank Presentation**. [Later, we will learn how to use Themes to make your work easier.]

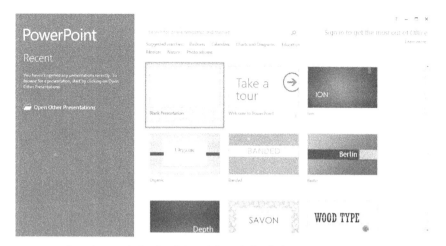

The work screen opens, showing a default slide with a default layout.

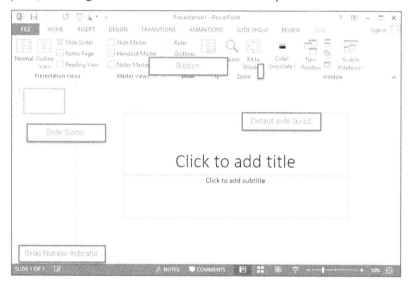

The Ribbon

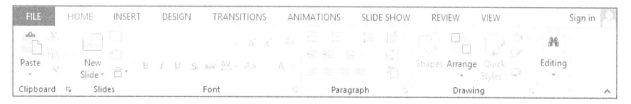

The ribbon appears at the top of the PowerPoint screen. As with all of the other Microsoft Office 2013 products, it is designed to help you quickly find the commands you need to complete a task.

Commands are organized in **groups** located under **tabs**. Each tab relates to a type of activity — such as page design or formatting.

To reduce clutter, some tabs are displayed only when needed; then they will disappear automatically if the software senses that you are finished using them.

Buttons are organized into groups according to the functions they perform. To access a feature, click its button. As you hover your mouse pointer over a button, a Screen Tip appears to provide information about the button.

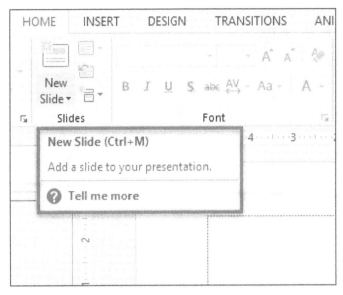

Some groups on the ribbon also contain a small arrow in the lower right hand corner so you can use additional tools related to that group.

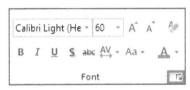

In the default slide that appears in the new presentation, type **My Title.** Notice that as soon as you begin typing, groups on the ribbon begin to light up, available for use.

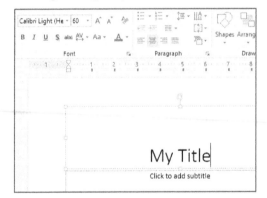

Try It!

- Hover your mouse pointer over the **Shapes** button in the **Drawing** group. What does it tell you about **Shapes**?
- What tab of the ribbon is highlighted when you first open your new presentation?
- Which groups on ribbon provide in your new presentation provide more options?
- What does this screen tip for **Arrange** in the **Drawing** group tell you?

Working with File Options

Click **File** on the ribbon to access all options available regarding working with a file. Backstage opens.

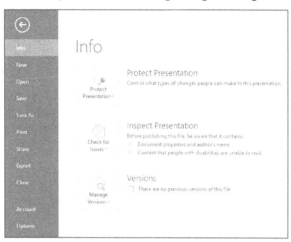

Here are the functions of the File tabs.

File Tab	Functions
Info	Protect your presentation, inspect your presentation, or manage versions
New	Create a new presentation
Open	Access an existing presentation
Save	Save your work
Save As	Save your presentation with a different name, or in a different location
Print	Print your presentation
Share	Share your file with other people
Export	Output your publication as a PDF/XPS document, in HTML format, change the file type, or use Pack and Go to package your publication for use on another computer
Close	Close a publication without saving it
Account	Modify the appearance theme or publisher, or sign into your Microsoft account
Options	Adjust defaults and settings for the Publisher product

Note: When you're working in Backstage, click the small arrow at the upper left of your screen to return to your publication. If you're already working with a presentation, you can always click the **File** tab again.

Try It!

- Launch Publisher, and view the file options displayed in Backstage. Then exit to your presentation.
- What is the benefit of organizing tools this way in separate screen?

A Note about Practice Exercises

Later in the course will be learning how to work with slide layouts. But in order to practice for the next several topics, you will need a blank slide. To create one from the default slide in a presentation, click the text box surrounding "Click to add title" and press **Del** to delete it. Do the same for the text box surrounding "Click to add subtitle". You should now have a blank presentation for practice purposes. [Ask a classmate or your teacher for help if necessary.]

Try It!

- Open a new blank presentation.
- Save your new blank slide as **My Practice Presentation**. Leave the presentation open.

Editing and Formatting Text

Typically, you enter text and then edit it. We'll learn about some tools for working with formatting and editing text.

Using Task Panes

As you select text formatting features, task panes will appear, docked to the right of the screen.

To access a task pane, right-click an object such as a shape, and choose **Format Shape** to see the available options for a shape in the task pane. Right-click a picture, and the task pane changes to show picture formatting options. This this gives you another way to perform tasks in addition to using the groups on the Ribbon.

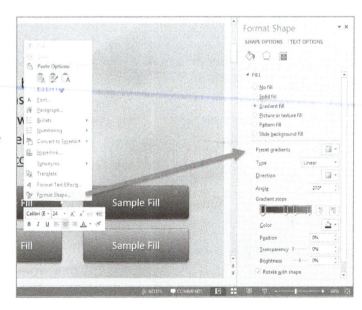

The **Home** tab contains groups with tools for editing and formatting text.

Inserting Text

- Click **Insert**.
- In the **Text** group, click **Text Box.**
- Drag your mouse, and then release the left button to create a text box.

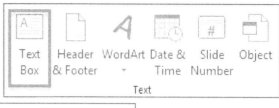

- In the text box and type the text.

The Font Group

You can select text and use tools in the **Font** group to change the font and font size – and apply appearance attributes. Click the drop-down arrow next to font or font size to make a change.

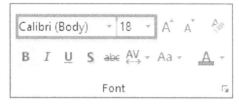

The tools in the upper right of the Font group allow you to increase or decrease the font size, and to clear all formatting that you have applied to the font.

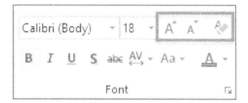

You can also apply bold, italics, text shadow, and superscript, adjust character spacing, change case, and change the font color.

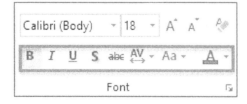

The Clipboard Group

The **Format Painter** allows you to apply the format of a block of text or an object to a different text or to an object. To use Format Painter, select the text or object you want to mimic, click **Format Painter**, and then drag and release your mouse over the text or object you wish to paint to make it alike.

You can also click the buttons on the Clipboard to perform cut, copy, or paste tasks.

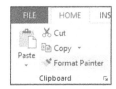

Try It!

- Insert a text box, and add a few lines of text.
- Change the font to one of your choice.
- Make the font size larger.
- Select and copy the text using the clipboard tool.
- Create a new text box, and paste the text, again using the clipboard tool
- Bold the text in the text box, and change the font to a color of your choice.
- Leave the presentation open.

Format Paragraphs

The **Paragraph** group provides tools for applying bullets, numbering, alignment, line spacing and multiple columns to paragraphs in your presentation. Select the text you want to format, and then choose an option by clicking its button.

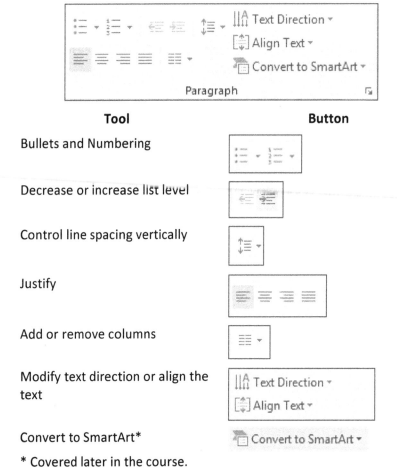

Tool	Button
Bullets and Numbering	
Decrease or increase list level	
Control line spacing vertically	
Justify	
Add or remove columns	
Modify text direction or align the text	
Convert to SmartArt*	

* Covered later in the course.

An editing tool is located on the far right of the format tab.

- Click **Find** to locate text.
- Click **Replace** to replace text.
- Click **Select** to select All, Objects, or to open the Selection task pane.

Note: Some groups on the home tab will also appear on other tabs, depending on the task you are performing.

Saving a Presentation

- Click **File**.
- Click Save As.
- Type a File name.
- Click **Save**.

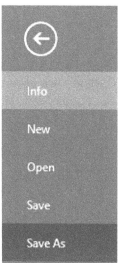

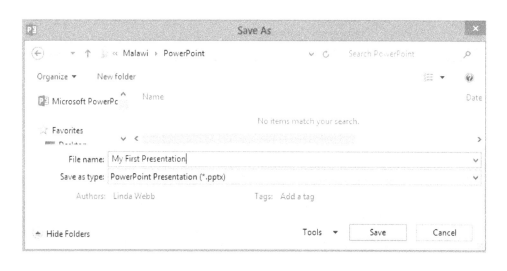

Try It!

- Using the open presentation from the previous exercise, select some text.
- Apply bullets.
- Right justify the text.
- Widen the line spacing between two sentences.
- Save the presentation as **My Paragraph Practice**.
- Leave the presentation open.

Using Views

You can view your PowerPoint slides in a variety of ways by using the **Presentation Views** group in the **View** tab on the ribbon. Some view choices are best for creating your presentation — while others are useful for delivering your presentation.

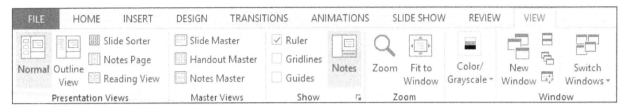

Below, we explore the most commonly-used groups on the ribbon.

Normal view displays one slide at a time on your screen. You can advance to the next slide at any time.

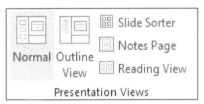

Outline View allows you to jump between slides and select them for editing from the **Outline Pane**. To exit outline view, select a different view.

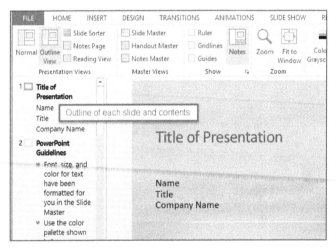

Slide Sorter displays thumbnails of all of your slides with the current slide selected. Double-click any slide to display it on the screen.

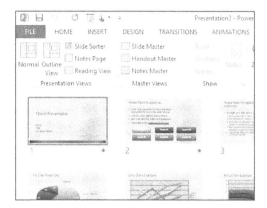

The **Notes Page** shows the slide on top, with an area for speaker notes below.

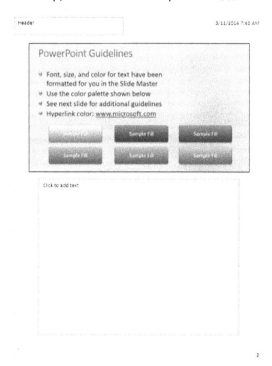

Reading View provides a full-screen display, slide by slide, as if you were making the presentation.

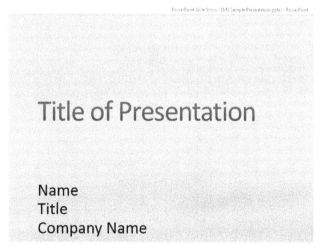

To exit reading view, press **Esc**.

Using Zoom

Click any of the zoom buttons to change how much of a slide or slides you want to see on your screen. 100%, whole page, or only objects that you first select.

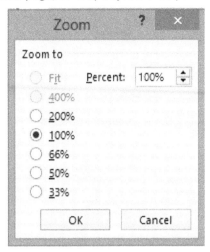

Tip! You can also drag the zoom slider at the bottom right of your screen to change the zoom percentage.

Printing

To print your presentation, click **File**, then click **Print**. Select your settings, and click **Print**.

Using the Insert Tab

The Insert tab contains tools for inserting tables, images, illustrations, text and other objects.

Inserting Images

Use tools in the **Images** group on the **Insert** tab to insert pictures, a screenshot, or a photo album.

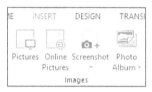

To insert a picture:

1. Click Pictures.

2. In the **Select Picture** dialogue, locate and select your image, then click **Insert**.

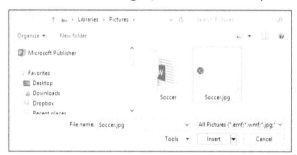

Note: If you choose **Online Pictures** instead, the insert picture dialogue will allow you to select royalty-free pictures from Office.com clip art or through an Internet search.

Insert a Screenshot

The **Insert Screenshot** feature allows you to insert a screenshot of an open application or browser window into PowerPoint.

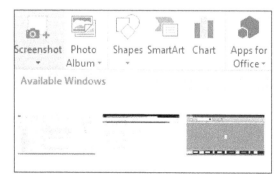

Clicking the screenshot will automatically open a browser and take you to the webpage, image, data source, document, or other content. Embedding a link into a screenshot stores the link with the slide that contains the screenshot, but hoped that it doesn't send information to Microsoft.

To remove a link from a screenshot, right-click the screenshot, and click **Remove Hyperlink**.

Try It!

- Insert an online image from office.com if you have Internet access. Or, ask your teacher to provide an image to save on your computer's hard drive.
- Open your web browser and visit a site such as Microsoft.com. Then insert this window into your presentation as a screenshot.

Inserting a Table

Using a table, you can quickly add data — and then apply a style.

- Click **Table** in the **Tables** group.
- Drag your mouse over and then down to select the number of columns and rows, then release the mouse. The table is placed in the presentation.
- To add information, click in the cell and then type your text or numbers.

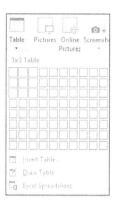

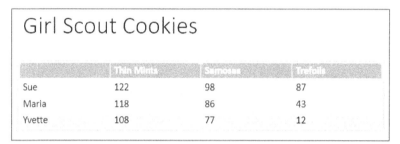

Working with Rows and Columns

When you click anywhere inside an existing table, the **Layout** tab for **Table Tools** displays.

Add a Column or Row

- Select a column or row in the table.
- Under **Table Tools**, on the **Layout** tab, in the **Rows & Columns** group, do one of the following:

  To add a row above the selected cell, click **Insert Above**.

  To add a row below the selected cell, click **Insert Below.**

  To add a column to the left of the selected cell, click **Insert Left**.

  To add a column to the right of the selected cell, click **Insert Right**.

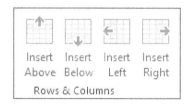

Delete a Column or a Row

- Select the column or row you want to delete.
- Under **Table Tools**, on the **Layout** tab, in the Rows & Columns group, click **Delete**.

Modify the Appearance of the Table

To change how your table appears, click anywhere in the table. The **Table Tools Design** tab appears.

Select options by clicking the checkboxes in the **Table Style Options** group to indicate to which components of the table you want to apply style effects. Click a style in the **styles** group to apply a preset style. Customize the style further by applying shading, borders, and other effects.

Try It!

- Open a blank presentation.
- Add a table with four columns – and four rows.
- Enter information of your choosing.
- Add a fifth row.
- Choose a different style for the table, and apply it to all table style option choices.
- Add borders by clicking the borders button in choosing a border option in.
- Save the presentation as MyFirstTable.
- Close the presentation.

Inserting a Shape

- Click **Insert**. The Insert tab displays.
- Click **Shapes** from the **Illustrations** group.
- Click any shape from the shapes palette, such as a flow symbol.
- Click in the text area, then drag your mouse. Your chosen shape appears.
- Release the mouse button when the shape reaches the you want.

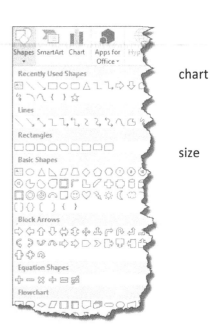

chart

size

Inserting a Picture

- Click **Insert**, then click **Pictures** in the **Images** group.

- In the **Insert Picture** dialogue, locate the picture that you want to insert. For example, you might have a picture file in My Documents or in Libraries.
- Double-click the picture that you want to insert.

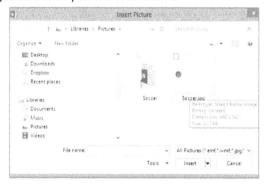

3. Click **Insert**. The picture is placed in the document at the cursor location.

Insert SmartArt

SmartArt is a library of graphic information organized by category. It allows you to communicate information with graphics instead of just text.

- Click **Insert**.
- Click **SmartArt** from the **Illustrations** group.

- Browse **SmartArt** categories on the left, then select an image from the list in the center.
- Click **OK.** [You can also add a chart in the same way by clicking Chart.]

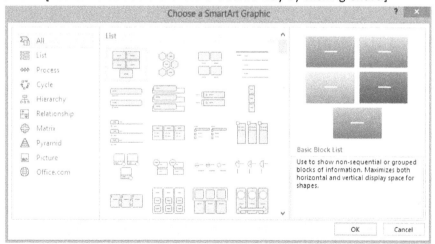

Inserting WordArt

Using **Word Art**, you can insert visually interesting text effects by selecting the effect you want.

- Click **Insert**.
- Click **WordArt** from the **Text** group.
- Click to select a WordArt style for text.

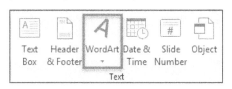

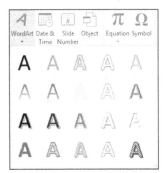

- PowerPoint adds a text box formatted in the WordArt style you selected. Delete the default text, and type the text you want.

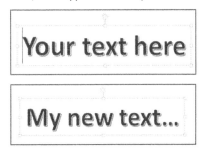

If you click any letter of text already formatted with WordArt, the **Format** tab under **Drawing Tools** will appear. You can choose other **WordArt** styles, use **Text Fill**, apply a **Text Outline**, or apply other **Text Effects**.

Three other options in the Insert Text group include the ability to insert a file, the date, and/or the time, or an object. All function similarly to these tools in Microsoft Word.

Try It!

- Open a blank new presentation.
- Add several lines of text.
- Experiment with SmartArt.
- Leave the presentation open.

Inserting Media

You can add a video to your presentation by clicking **Video**. PowerPoint prompts you to provide the folder location of the video file. You can also add an audio clip in the same way by clicking **Audio**.

Inserting a Symbol

- To insert a symbol, first create a Text Box. The cursor in the text box awaits text entry.
- Click **Symbol** in the **Symbols** group on the **Insert** tab.
- Select a symbol, and click **Insert**.

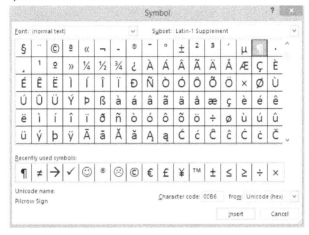

- Click **Close**.

Try It!

- In a blank presentation, insert a text box, and add a symbol.

Using Shortcuts and Commands

The PowerPoint 2013 ribbon comes with new shortcuts — called **Key Tips –** that allow you to execute commands by pressing one letter or number. To show the Key Tip labels in the ribbon, press **Alt**. The text will appear as small black letters or numbers located near the applicable function.

To invoke a shortcut, simply press the number or letter that represents the Key Tip you want to use.

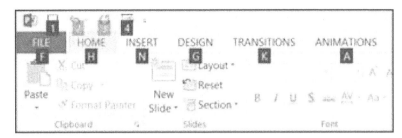

You can also use keyboard shortcuts to move between panes such as the outline pane or an open task pane.

To accomplish this:	Press:
Move clockwise among panes in Normal view	F6
Move counterclockwise amongst panes in Normal view.	SHIFT+F6
Switch between the Thumbnail pane and the Outline View pane.	CTRL+SHIFT+TAB

Note: if you're not happy with the result of a shortcut or a Key Tip command, you can always back out of your most recent task by clicking **Undo** on the **Quick Access Toolbar** in the upper left corner of your screen.

Try It!

- In any open PowerPoint presentation, click on the slide area of the screen and press **Alt.**
- Examine the results of the Key Tips. How do these shortcut keys make your work easier?

Closing a Presentation

- Make sure you save your most recent work in the presentation, especially if it is a new file.
- Click **File.**
- Click **Close** in Backstage.

Exiting PowerPoint

- To fully exit PowerPoint, if prompted, save the file.

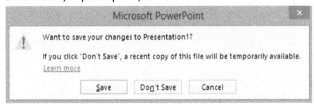

- Add a file name, and click **Save.**

Try It!

- Close and save the presentation on your screen.
- Close any other presentations with which you have worked up until now.
- Exit PowerPoint.

Formatting a Presentation

PowerPoint has many tools for working with slides and formatting your presentation.

Inserting Slides

Insert a new slide by clicking **New Slide** in the **Slides** group on the **Home** tab. PowerPoint inserts a slide below the current slide. You can see it in the thumbnail pane on the left of your screen.

If you want instead to select a layout for the new slide, click the drop-down arrow in the New Slide button, and select a layout. The new slide is inserted with your selected layout.

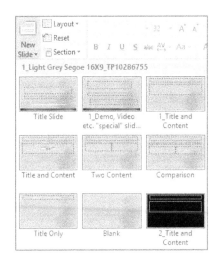

Copying, Moving, and Deleting Slides

Copy a Slide

- In the Thumbnail pane, select the slide you want to copy.
- Click **Copy** in the **Clipboard** group.

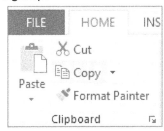

- Click in the white area where you want to paste the slide. Notice the cursor becomes a horizontal line below the current slide. This is the insertion point.

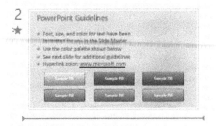

- Click Paste in the **Clipboard Group.**
- Notice the slide is copied at the location of the insertion point.

Move a Slide

To move a slide, select it and drag it up or down in the thumbnail pane.

Delete a Slide

To delete a slide, and press **Del.**

Try It!

- Open PowerPoint and select a recent presentation you created earlier in the course...

- Insert a new slide below the first slide in your presentation.
- Copy the first slide, and paste it immediately below it.
- Delete the slide you just pasted.
- Leave the presentation open.

Working with Slide Layouts to Format Slides

Each slide contains the formatting for the slide, such as theme colors, fonts, and effects. In PowerPoint, this is called **layout**. Layout is one of the biggest changes you can make in terms of the overall appearance and purposes of your slide. When you are arranging the content in your slides, you can pick the slide layout that best suit your content.

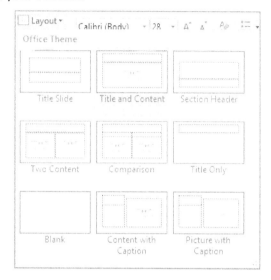

The diagram below illustrates the various components of a layout that you can include on a PowerPoint slide.

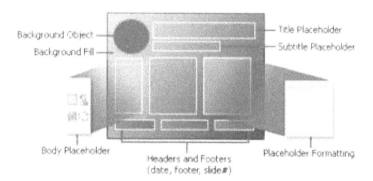

Change the Layout of the Slide

- On the **View** tab, click **Normal**.
- In Normal View, in the thumbnail pane on the left, click the slide to which you want to apply a layout.
- On the **Home** tab, click **Layout**, and then select the layout that you want.

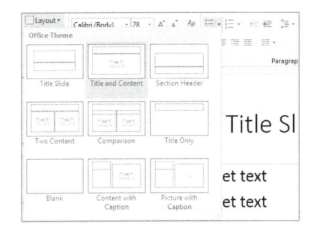

Typically, you will have at least one title slide – and slides with title and content. Beyond that, it's all about what you want to convey in your presentation. For text, you might choose **Title and Content** which is preset to apply bullets. If you are adding an image, you'll want a simple slide not designed for bullets.

Let's say you decide to switch a slide with a layout of *Title and Content* for a *Two Content* Slide.

Click **Layout** in the **Slides** group in the **Home** tab to change the layout of the slide. PowerPoint does its best to adjust your text and images, however you'll probably need to make some adjustments to the slide content in its new layout.

To return a slide's layout to its default settings, click **Reset.**

Tip! The best way to learn about layouts is to experiment; select a layout, and then preview the result.

Try It!

- Change the layout of one of the slides with content in your current presentation for example, change a Title slide to a layout of Title and Content.
- Preview the result. Do you need to tweak the contents because of the layout change?
- Experiment with two or three other layouts.

Using Themes

PowerPoint Themes are predesigned slide selections that do the design work for you. Each theme has a small subset of Variants, variations in color – and some design elements for that theme.

You can access Themes both from the Start screen when you first enter PowerPoint — and also in the Design tab.

- Create a new file. On the **Start** screen, click a Theme to preview its variants.

- Scroll through previews of the Theme Title, Title and Content, Smart Chart and Photo layouts before making your selection.

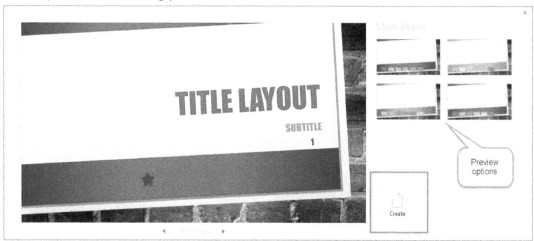

- If you like the theme, click **Create**. Otherwise, click the X in the upper right corner of the panel, returning to things on the start screen.

Modifying a Theme

It's best to make changes to themes before you begin working. But you can easily make a change up front by clicking the Design tab inside your presentation and selecting a different theme. Notice that here you can also preview variants and perform customizations.

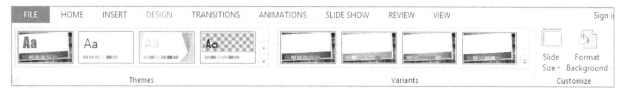

Slide Design Task	Sample Options
Themes	Click a theme to apply it. Click another one if desired. Click the bearing

Variants	Click a variant to experiment with different colors suitable for the style.

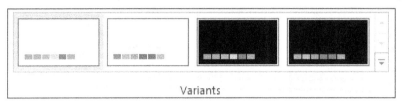

Variants

Customize	Change the size of the slide – or format the background of the slide.

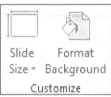

Try It!

- Create a new presentation by clicking **New**.
- Scroll through the themes, taking some time to preview the attributes of several.
- Select a theme.
- Explore the layout options for the theme.
- Select a different theme using the design panel.
- Save the presentation as My Theme.

Using the Slide Master

Slide masters are designed to help you create great looking presentations in less time, without a lot of effort. When you want all your slides to contain the same fonts and images [such as logos] make those changes to the Slide Master.

Every theme consisting of a palette of colors, fonts, and special effects] you use in your presentation includes one slide master – and a set of related layouts.

You change the slide layouts that are built in to PowerPoint in **Slide Master** View. The image below shows the slide master – and two of the ten layouts within the Basis theme in Slide Master View.

Change a Slide Layout in Slide Master View

- On the **View** tab, click **Slide Master**.

- In Slide Master View, in the thumbnail pane on the left, click a slide layout that you want to change.

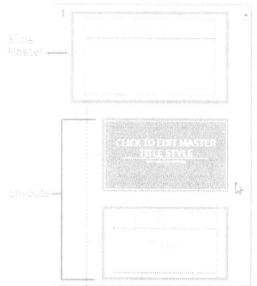

- On the **Slide Master** tab, to change the layout, do one or more of the following:

   To add a placeholder, click **Insert Placeholder**, and then pick a type of placeholder from the list.

   To rearrange a placeholder, click the edge of the placeholder until you see a four-headed arrow, and the drag the placeholder to the new location on the slide.

   To delete a placeholder, select the placeholder, and then press **Delete** on your keyboard.

   To add a new layout, click **Insert Layout**.

   To rename a layout, in the thumbnail pane on the left, right-click the layout that you want to rename, click **Rename Layout**, type the new name of the layout and then click **Rename**.

Extremely Important! If you apply a slide layout to a slide in your presentation, and then go into Slide Master View and change that layout, you must go into Normal View and reapply the layout to the slides that follow the layout so the slides adopt the changes you made to that layout.

Tip! Working with slide Masters takes some patience. As you begin learning, make one change at a time, then preview it. If you're satisfied, great... keep going. Or, return to the slide master, undo your change, and try again.

Try It!

- Open a practice file of your choice.
- Choose a slide, and then in slide master view, change the layout of one slide.

- Preview it.
- Return to normal view and update the layout of any other similar slides, if applicable.

Saving a File as a Template

Just as with other Microsoft office applications, you can save a presentation as a template so you can use it again later. PowerPoint saves templates with a file extension of .potx .

To save a file as a template:

- On the **File tab**, click **Save As**.
- Under **Save**, click **Browse**.
- In the **Save As** dialog box, in the **File name** box, type a file name, or do nothing to accept the suggested file name.
- In the **Save As** type list, click **PowerPoint Template** [.potx], and then click **Save**.

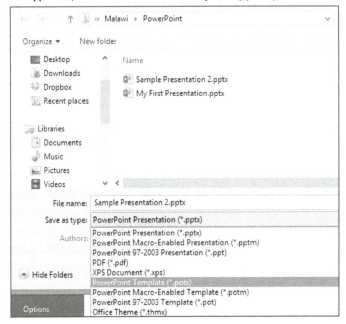

Tip! Save your templates to the Templates folder at **C:\Program Files\Microsoft Office\Templates** to make them easier to locate.

Another Tip! You should not need to create a template from scratch. There are a multitude of free PowerPoint templates on Office.com that you can use or revise to meet your needs.

Applying Slide Transitions

Slides that snap or jerk from one to the next can be annoying to an audience. If you want the pace of your presentation to feel more controlled and flowing, add transitions between slides. All of the transitions tools are on the **Transitions** tab.

Add a Transition to a Slide

The transition setting dictates how that slide enters — and how the preceding slide exits.

- In the **Thumbnail Pane**, click the slide to which you want to apply a transition. [Below, if you add a transition to slide 3, it controls how slide 2 leaves, and how slide 3 enters.]

- On the **Transitions** tab, find the effect that you want in the **Transition gallery**. Click the **More** button ⏷ to see the entire gallery. Click the effect that you want for that slide — and to see a preview. For example, **Fade**.

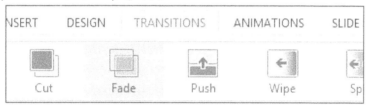

- Click **Effect Options** to change how the transition occurs – for example, what direction the slide enters from.

- Enter a time at **Duration** to set how fast the transition goes. Set the number higher to make the transition go slower.

- Click **Preview** to see what the transition looks like with all the settings.

Preview

Preview

PowerPoint can automatically advance your slides. In the **Timing** group, to advance each slide when you click your mouse, select **On Mouse Click**. Or, instead check **After** and set a time after which each slide will advance automatically.

Tip! If you want all slides in the presentation to transition the same way, click **Apply to All** in the **Timing** group.

Remove a Transition

Remember that a transition applies to a slide's *entrance*, not how it exits. So if you want to remove the exit effects for slide 2, remove the transition from slide 3. To remove a transition:

- Click the slide for which you want no transition.
- Then on the **Transitions** tab, in the Transitions gallery, click **None**.

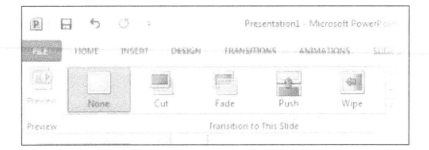

As mentioned above, if slide 3 has no transition, it appears instantly as slide 2 disappears.

A word about transitions... As with themes, expect to experiment with transitions in order to more fully learn how to use them. Also, don't overdo it because too much can exasperate your audience.

Try It!

- Open a presentation you created earlier in this course.
- Choose two slides from the thumbnail pane, and set a transition effect from the transitions tab.
- Preview your transition. Then select a different transition effect.

- Set the slides to advance after 10 seconds each.
- Save the presentation as **My Transitions**, and keep it open on your screen.

Adding Slide Animation

Animating bullets or objects such as pictures, shapes, or SmartArt on your slide can be a great way to grab your audience's attention.

There are four different types of animation effects in PowerPoint 2013:

- **Entrance** effects. For example, you can make an object fade gradually into focus, fly onto the slide from an edge, or bounce into view.
- **Exit** effects. These effects include making an object fly off of the slide, disappear from view, or spiral off of the slide.
- **Emphasis** effects. Examples include making an object shrink or grow in size, change color, or spin on its center.
- **Motion Paths.** A motion path is the path that a specified object or text will follow as part of an animation sequence for a slide. You can use these effects to make an object move up or down, left or right, or in a star or circular pattern [among other effects]. You can also draw your own motion path.

Remember that in PowerPoint, animations are not the same as transitions. *A transition animates the way one slide changes to the next.*

To apply an animation effect to text or objects:

- Select the object or text on the slide that you want to animate. [It's best to try and object first.]
- On the **Animations** tab, click **Add Animation**, and pick an animation effect.
- Accept the duration setting of Auto, or click to change it.

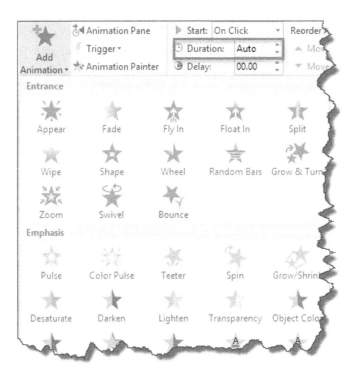

- Click Preview.

As with slide transitions, if you don't like the results you previewed, simply return to the Add Animation panel and choose a different animation effect and/or timing..

Tip! The gallery of animation effects on the **Animations** tab shows only the most popular effects. See more options by clicking **Add Animation**, scrolling down, and clicking **More Entrance Effects**, **More Emphasis Effects**, **More Exit Effects**, or **More Motion Paths**.

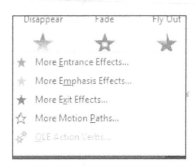

Note: If you want to make your animations fancier, you can combine multiple animation effects together. For instance, to make a line of text fly in while it grows, apply a **Fly In** entrance effect and a **Grow/Shrink** emphasis effect to it. Click **Add Animation** to add effects, and use the Animation Pane to set the emphasis effect to occur **With Previous**.

Try It!

- Add two objects to your My Transitions presentation.
- Animate the first object with a motion effect of your choice, then preview it.
- Change the duration.
- Animate the second object with a different effect.
- Apply a mouse click to each animation, and compare. Which effect you prefer?

Presenting Slideshows

When it's time to give your presentation, you use Slide Show mode.

- On the **Slide Show** tab, do one of the following:

  To start the presentation at the first slide, in the **Start Slide Show** group, click **From Beginning**.

  If you're not at the first slide and want to start from where you are, click **From Current Slide**.

- Press **Page Down** or left-click your mouse to advance to the next slide.
- Press Page Up to move back one slide.

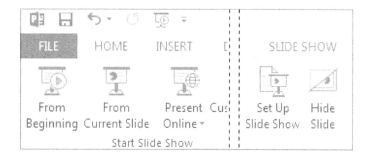

- To exit the slideshow, press **Esc**.

Try It!

- Display your My Transitions presentation in presentation mode.
- At any slide, move back one slide.
- Exit the presentation. How did it go?

Exporting a Presentation

PowerPoint provides for options for exporting your publication to another source.

From inside your publication, click **File**, and then in Backstage, choose **Export**.

As you click an Export option, PowerPoint explains its purpose – and provides a button to click to execute the option.

Here's a summary of the purposes of the export options.

Export Option	Purpose
Create PDF/XPS Document	An **XML Paper Specification [XPS] document** is a document format you can use to view, save, share, digitally sign, and protect your document's content. An XPS document is like an electronic sheet of paper: You can't change the content on a piece of paper after you print it, and you can't edit the contents of an XPS document after you save it in the XPS format. You can create an XPS document in any program you can print from, but you can only view, sign, and set permissions for XPS documents in an XPS Viewer.
	A PDF file is a file output in Portable Document Format [PDF] – an open standard for electronic document exchange.
	With both formats, your appearance is preserved, content cannot be easily changed, and viewers are available free on the Internet.
Q&A video	With HTML output, you can publish a document on a webpage.
Package Presentation for CD	Create a package on a CD so that others can watch the presentation. The packaging will include links to outside or embedded items and any other files that may have been added to the presentation.
Create Handouts	Create handouts places a copy of your files and presentation notes in Microsoft Word document. It automatically creates a link to the PowerPoint presentation. Therefore, if you make changes to your presentation, they are also updated in your Microsoft Word document. Saving you time and reducing chances for error, this is an excellent example of the power of a software suite of applications such as Microsoft Office.
Change File Type	Publisher 2013 supports a number of file types for saving publications. Several support earlier versions of publisher, and there are some options to create graphics files with extensions such as .PNG and .JPG.

Below is an illustration of the Package dialogue where you can name the CD, add files, and also make a copy to a folder.

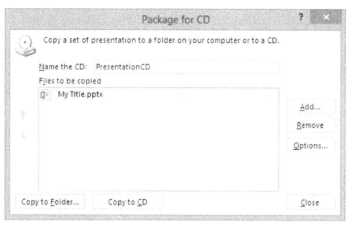

Try It!

- Export one of your presentations to PDF format. Open the newly export file and preview the results. Are they accurate?
- Try exporting using package for CD, however choose copy to folder instead. Open the newly exported presentation in the folder and preview it. Are the results what you expected?

Share a Presentation

PowerPoint has tools that allow you to extend your presentation to others in several ways.

Click **File** and then click **Share**.

Invite people to view your presentation, by uploading it to OneDrive.

Send the presentation as a Microsoft outlook email attachment, as a PDF attachment, or as an XPS attachment. There's also a fax option, if you have access to a fax service provider on the Internet.

Present it online. This assumes SharePoint account.

Publish your slides. This assumes you have access to an existing slide library, or SharePoint account.

Follow the prompts for your chosen option depending on services and account excesses you have at your school.

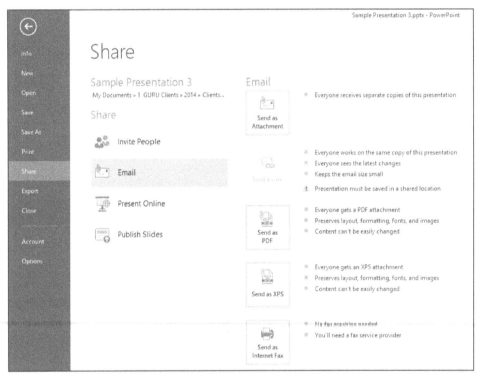

Unit Summary

In this unit, you have learned about the following topics and concepts:

- The purposes of presentation software and list several examples of presentation software products
- How to create a simple presentation using the ribbon, and task panes
- Using options in various tabs and groups to edit and format elements of the slides
- Saving and printing a presentation
- Inserting images, tables, shapes, SmartArt and symbols

- Using shortcuts such as Key Tips to reduce the time taken to type or use the mouse
- Closing and exit a presentation
- Inserting, manipulating, and formatting, slides using themes, and the slide master
- Saving a presentation as a template
- Applying slide transitions, and slide information
- Presenting a slideshow
- Exporting a presentation.

Practice Activity

You have learned about many tools and features in PowerPoint that allow you to create attractive presentations. In this practice exercise, you will apply what you learned as you build a complete presentation.

You are the owner of a small business. It could be a bike shop, a candy store, or any other business that interests you. You will create a presentation to be used to market your services to neighboring businesses in the community.

Keep the presentation short; perhaps no more than 10 slides. Even five might do.

Notes:

- Your teacher might elect to have you work in pairs or small groups.
- He or she will also advise you how much time you have to complete the assignment.

Here are the elements to include in your presentation.

- A theme, selected from the design tab
- A text slide, formatted with bullets
- Other text that you have inserted, formatted and edited
- An image such as a shape whose appearance you have edited
- A table, with a theme applied
- slide master
- Applying slide transitions, and slide information
- Presenting your work as a slideshow
- Behind the scenes, you should have made one modification to your slide master that you are prepared to show your classmates.
- Also, save the presentation as a template

Be prepared to demonstrate to your classmates and your teacher. Now go forth and present! :-)

Learning Objectives

This unit is designed to help you make and edit movies. Upon completion, you should be able to:

- Describe the purposes of multimedia management software
- Create and run a movie based on imported photos or an existing movie
- Add special effects including transitions, titling, sound, and animation
- Save and publish the movie to a number of destinations.

Why Use Multimedia Management Software?

Multimedia management software is software that allows you to create movies that incorporate sound, graphics, text and special effects. With this type of software, you can:

Import photos or videos

Create movies using various multimedia elements

Add effects to movies such as transitions, titles, and narration to fine tune the movie

Publish the movie.

Microsoft Moviemaker

Windows Movie Maker is free software you can download from Microsoft.com to create multimedia. With Movie Maker, you can experiment with the best ways to arrange your photos to tell a story. As you do, you learn which elements hold the viewer's attention — and make for good storytelling. After saving your movie, you can share it with your classmates and teachers, families, and friends.

Add Photos

To begin, you'll need to import some photos. Place them on your computer in the **Pictures** folder below the **My Documents** folder. That's where Movie Maker will look for import them. [Note: Depending on the Version of Windows that is installed on your computer, the folder names and locations may differ slightly.]

To insert photos, also called clips:

- Open Movie Maker.
- On the **Home** tab, click **Add videos and p**hotos.
- Select the pictures that you want in your movie.
  Tip! Press and hold down the **Ctrl** key to select multiple images.
- Click **Open**. The pictures are added to the storyboard.
- Notice the main parts of Movie Maker; the storyboard area, the player, and the ribbon with tabs.

You can also import photos from your digital camera, a flash memory card, DVDs, or your mobile phone. They are imported into Microsoft Photo Gallery, free software that comes downloaded along with Movie Maker.

To import from a camera:

- Connect the camera to your computer by using a USB cable, and then turn on the camera.
- Click the **Movie Maker** button.
- Click **Import from device**. If the Photos and videos will be imported into Photo Gallery message appears, click OK.
- Click the camera device image.
- Click **Import**.
- On the **New photos and videos were fou**nd page, you can choose to review and select the photos – or click **Import all new items now.**

- Type a name for all the photos and videos. [Optional]
- Click **Next.**
- In Photo Gallery, select the check box in the upper-left corner for each photo or video you want to use in your movie.

311

- On the **Create** tab, in the **Share** group, click **Movie**. When the photos and/or videos appear in Movie Maker, you're ready to start working with your movie.

Play the Movie as Imported

Even though you haven't done any editing yet, you can still play the movie as-is.

Click the **Play** button in the **Player**. The cursor moves across the rows of pictures as the movie plays. By default, each picture shows for five seconds. You can monitor the time below the images.

Try It!

- Import photos of your own, or use some supplied by your teacher.
- Play your movie as-is in Movie Maker. Did you see what you expected?
- Add a Video

- You can also import a video.

Add a Video

You can also bring in a video and then edit it just as if you had added individual photos. [That's how film is edited in the movie industry; frame by frame, or clip by clip.]

On the **Home** tab, in the **Add** group, click **Add videos and photos**.

Select the video you want to add, and then click **Open**. The separate clips that make up the video are added.

Make Edits and Enhancements

Work With Clips

Do any of the following:

To **move** a picture, drag it to a new position.

To **delete** a picture, select it and click **Del**.

To **add** a picture, click **Add videos and photos** on the **Home** tab.

To change how long a clip displays, select the picture, and then, on the **Video Tools Edit** tab, change the duration.

Add a Title

To add a title, click the first clip in the storyboard.

On the **Home** tab, click **Title** and type the title.

Click the **Text Tools Format** tab to change the formatting — or to add a background color.

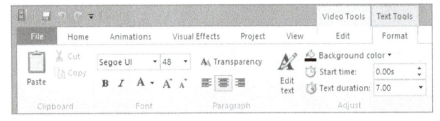

Formatting options are:

Change the font and/or the font size

Apply attributes such as bold, italics, font color or size tweaks

Drag the transparency slider to increase or decrease the transparency level of the text

Justify the title left center or right

Edit the text

Change the background color

Adjust the start time and or text duration.

Save the Movie

Now that we've done a good bit of work, it's time to save our first movie. To save:

On the **Home** tab, in the Share group, click the arrow next to **Save Movie**.

Choose **Recommended for this project**.

In the save movie dialogue, and a file name, then click **Save**.

314

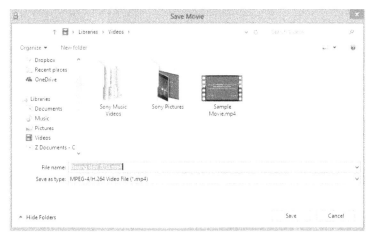

Notice that Movie Maker returns, with your movie open, ready for more work.

Try It!

- Add a title.
- Using formatting options, experiment with tweaks to the title; font color, justification, and anything else you like.
- Save your first movie in a folder on your hard drive.

Add Captions

To add a caption:

- Select a clip.
- Then on the **Home** tab, click **Caption** and type the caption.
- Change the formatting as you did with the title by using tools in the Format tab.
- Notice that the caption appears below your selected clip.

If you don't like the location of the caption, you can drag it to reposition it as it plays with the clip.

Add Text

Besides adding a title, you can add other types of text relevant to movies by selecting features in the **Add** group on the **Home** tab. Options include adding credits, the name of the director, starring actors, location, and the soundtrack producer.

Credits are the names of people involved in making of the movie. We'll add movie credits as an example.

In the **Add** group, click **Credits.**

Type the credits text. On preview, you will notice that they are added at the end of the movie, rolling up the slide the same way as would the credits in a major motion picture film.

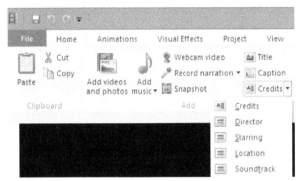 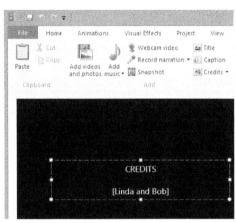

Notice that using the credits drop-down arrow, this is the same place to add director, starring, location, and the name of the person responsible for the soundtrack.

Add Animations

You can add animation effects, movement, using the **Animations** tab on the ribbon.

The two options are to add **transitions**, and to apply **Pan and Zoom** effects.

Transitions are the method in which one slide exits — and the next slide enters.

In photography, the term **pan** refers to the rotation in a horizontal plane of a still camera or video camera. Panning a camera results in a motion similar to that of someone slowly shaking their head from side to side.

Zoom in film is a shot using a lens whose focal length is adjusted to focus in during the shot, or to pull out.

To use either Transitions or Pan and zoom, click any clip and then:

>   Click a button in the **Transitions** group to apply a transition effect.

>   Or, Click a button in the **Pan and Zoom** group to pan and/or zoom.

Note that for both animation options, you can click **More** to see more possibilities.

If you like the effect[s], click  so that you have uniform effects throughout the whole movie. Or, you can limit the effects to just one or several slides.

Tip! It is a good idea to try one animation effect and preview it before adding a second one; you may find that applying both effects to all clips makes the movie too busy.

Note: To remove a transition or pan and zoom, click the **No transition** button in the Transition group – or **No Pan and zoom** in the Pan and zoom group.

Try It!

- Add a caption to your movie, then preview. Make adjustments using text features if necessary
- Add one or more credits at the end of the movie. Preview them as they roll upward.
- Add a transition. If you're not sure, apply different one. Then preview the movie.
- Add a Pan and Zoom effect. Do you want both animations? If no, remove one.
- Save the movie and leave it open.

Add Sound

There are two options for adding sound; **music**, or a **recorded narration**.

Add Music

To add music that will play with the movie:

- Select the clip where you want to add the music.
- On the **Home** tab, click **Add music**, and then click **Add music** or **Add music at the current point**.

- Browse for the music file that you want to use, and then click **Open**.

Now preview your movie and enjoy the added music!

Add Recorded Narration

If you prefer to provide more of a "travelogue" experience for your viewer, you can record a personalized movie narration.

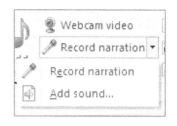

- Select the clip where you want to add the narration.
- In the **Add** group, click **Record narration.**
- The recording tool opens. Plug in your microphone, and then click **Record.** When finished, click **Stop.**

- Movie Maker prompts you to name and save the file in **My Music**, and your narrative is added to the movie.

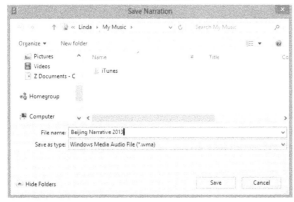

You can remove the music or narrative as follows:

- Right-click the brown sound indicator below the clip where it was added.
- Select **Remove.** You can always add it again. :-)

Try It!

- If you have a music clip, copy it to My Music on your pc. Otherwise, ask your teacher for a sample.
- At the music clip to your movie and preview.
- If you have a microphone, try adding a narrative. Again, preview the results. What you think?
- Save the movie.

Finalize and Publish

After you're done editing your project in Movie Maker, you can share it with family, friends, and other people by choosing one of the options in the **Share** group. [Remember that you'll need an account in order to log into these online sites.]

Upload to Share

Click one of the sites in the Share group; Microsoft OneDrive, Facebook, YouTube, Vimeo, or Flickr.

Choose a **resolution** for your movie. Remember, the higher the resolution, the larger the file size.

You'll be prompted to log into your selected sharing site. Follow the prompts for the site you selected.

Save in a Format for Email

You can also email your movie to another email user.

Click **Save Movie**, and choose **For Email**.

You are prompted to save the movie in a folder on the hard drive of your computer. Then you can send it as an email attachment. Consider the file size; many email systems will not handle attachments with over the large file sizes.

Unit Summary

In this unit, you have learned about the following topics and concepts:

- The purposes of multimedia management software
- Creating and running a movie based on imported photos or an existing movie

- Adding special effects including transitions, titling, sound, and animation
- Saving and publishing the movie to a number of destinations.

Practice Questions and Activities

11. What is multimedia management software?

12. Create a simple movie/video-clip from another subject area such as biology or physics or environmental issues. Incorporate what you have learned in this course; sound effects animation, and text formatting. Share your results the class.

13. Make a movie about a day in your life. Pick an interesting day, and bring your camera with you wherever you go. Plan on taking more pictures than you will need for your movie. That way, you'll have plenty of pictures from which to choose. For example, if you want to make a one-minute movie and show each picture for about five seconds, you will need at least 12 pictures for the movie. So, shoot at least 30 pictures to make sure you have enough choices. Apply editing, finalize the movie and share it.

Appendix A: Glossary of ICT Terms

Term	Definition
Abacus	An early calculating device using beads moving on strings.
Address	The identification of a particular location in memory where a data item or instruction is stored.
Algorithm	A set of well-defined rules for solving a problem in a finite number of operations.
Aligning	A data item residing in a cell usually be aligned in one of three positions within the cell, namely left-align, right-align or centered.
Antiglare screen	A polarized screen attached to the front of the monitor, which reduces eye strain.
Assembler	A program which converts text in ASSEMBLY LANGUAGE into MACHINE CODE to be used by a computer.
ALU	Arithmetic and Logic Unit. The part of the Central Processing Unit that handles all mathematical calculations, addition, subtraction and multiplication; and logic operations, such as comparisons for greater than, less than, and equal to an identified number.
Automation	Computer control of machines and process.
Backing store	A relatively permanent storage location for large quantities of data outside the processor of the computer system.
Backup copy	A copy of a disk onto a second disk that is for everyday use, protecting the original disk in case of damage.
Bandwidth	A characteristic of a communication channel that determines the speed at which data can be transmitted over the channel
Bar code	A series of thick and thin black bars separated by spaces of varying widths representing data.
Baud	A unit of speed in data transmission system which now represents one data signal per second.
BCD	BCD is an abbreviation for Binary-Coded-Decimal. In this number system, each digit of a number is written as a BINARY number, rather than converting the whole number. For example, 47 would be coded as 01000111, the binary codes for 4 and 7. Contrast this with 101111, which is the true binary code of 47.
Binary	Base two numbering system. A binary digit can be a 0 or a 1 [bit].
Bit	The smallest unit of memory or information. A bit is represented by a 0 or 1.
Bistable device	A device which can exist in two discrete stable states.
Boot	To get the computer started. [Switched on] warm boot and cold boot
Border	In printing a spreadsheet certain groups of column or rows may be designated as left or top borders to ensure that the information they contain will appear

	on all pages of the print out.
Bulletin	An electronic equivalent of a conventional bulletin board. It is used as part of a communication network where users can post messages, read messages posted by others users, communicate with the system operator and upload or download programs.
Byte	Represents 8 bits or a character e.g.?, . , /, 1-9, a-z, *, &, %, #, @ and so on.
CADD	Acronym for computer-aided design and drafting. The use of computers and graphics in design and drafting process.
CAM	Acronym for computer-aided manufacturing. The use of computers to control machines in the manufacturing process.
CD	Compact Disk. There are two types of CDs: [I] CD writer - a peripheral device that can write once to a CD-R disk to create an audio or a CD-ROM. [ii] CD-R - [Compact Disk Recordable] The medium on which CD writers create CDs and CD-ROMs.
CD-ROM disk	Compact-Disk-Read-Only-Memory disk. A type of optical laser storage medium.
Central processing unit	The logical component of a computer system that interprets and Unit [CPU/Processor] executes program instructions.
Character	Any keyboard character: letter number or symbol which can be input, stored, processed, and/or output by a computer system. [Eight bits of memory]
Character codes	Binary patters used to represent characters in a computer system.
Character string	A string of alphanumeric characters.
Chip	An integrated circuit made of a semiconductor [silicon] and containing electronic components. It can be as little as ¼ inch square.
Communication	Acts of transmitting or exchanging information, ideas or opinions over a communication channel.
Compiler	A program that translates the sources program into executable machine code, and saves the code to a file [the object program] for later execution.
CPU	Central Processing Unit
Computer	An electronic device that is controlled by a stored program which accepts data, processes it and stores the results of processing, to provide an output in the form of information.
Computer system	A collective reference to all interconnected computing hardware, including processors, storage devices, input/output devices, and communications equipment. In short it's the computer and its peripheral devices.
Control Unit [CU]	Controls the entire computer system, as well as the central processing unit; responsible for coordinating all devices connected to the system, determines which activity to perform, as well as how and when to perform it.
Cursor	A flashing symbol on the monitor's screen, which indicates the position of user activity.
Cyberphobia	The irrational fear of and aversion to computers.

Data	Unorganized facts or material including numbers and words that are processed by the computer.
Data corruption	The introduction of errors into data stored in a computer system.
Data flow diagram	A pictorial representation of network of process linked by data flows illustrating the flow of data to and from process in a system.
Database	A collection of data files that may be used by number of applications with storage and access to the data controlled by a set of programs known as Database Management System. [DBMS]
Database Management System	Programs and database files that allow timely and easy controlled access to data by a number of users.
Decode	To reverse the encoding process.
Decision table	A pictorial representation of program logic illustrating, in the form of a table, the appropriate actions to be taken for each combination of conditions.
Decision tree	A pictorial representation of program logic illustration, in form of a mathematical tree, the actions to be taken for each combination of conditions.
De facto standard	A usage which has become a standard, although not officially or legally authorized.
Desktop	The screen in windows upon which icons, windows, a background are displayed.
Device	A machine with a specific function.
DTP	Desk Top Publishing.
Direct mode	The passing of COMMANDS to the OPERATING SYSTEM without the use of a program. Certain commands such a RUN, SAVE, and LOAD are nearly always used in direct mode by typing the command words on the keyboard then pressing the return key. Interpreted language like BASIC permits a much wider range of direct mode commands.
Download	Process whereby programs or data are transferred via communications channels, from a computer and stored on media located at the user's computer
Dry-run	A manual traversal of the logic of a program.
Dumb terminal	A standalone keyboard and display screen that can send or receive data but can do no processing of that data.
Duplex	A transmission system that allows data to be transmitted in both directions at the same time. This system is sometimes called Full Duplex.
DVD	Digital Video Disk or Digital Versatile Disk. A high-density compact disk for storing large amounts of data, especially high-resolution audio-visual material.
EBCDIC	An acronym for Extended Binary Coded Decimal Interchange Code. The code uses eight binary positions for each character thus allowing a character set of 256 characters.

Electronic mail	A computer application whereby messages are transmitted via data communications to "electronic mailboxes" also called e-mail.
EPROM	Erasable programmable read-only memory. A type of memory chip that can be erased by moving it from the circuit and exposing it to ultraviolet light. The chip can then be programmed.
E-Time	Execution time. The elapsed time it takes to execute [carry out] a computer instruction and store the results.
Expert system	A software package that acts as a consultant or expert to the user. It is "expert" in a specialized application or area and provides assistance to the user in solving problems in that area.
Feasibility study	In-depth study of an application area for the purpose of establishing whether automation would be cost effective. In general, the expected benefits should exceed the combined cost of installing the computer and developing the system.
Field	[1] A section of a record containing data relating to one attribute of an entry. [2] Part of a machine instruction containing an operation or address.
File	A collection of related records. Transforms secondary storage into an electronic filing cabinet. Any data or set of instructions that have been given a name and stored on disk.
Floppy disk	A flexible magnetic coated disk, commonly used with microcomputers, on which data can be stored magnetically.
Flowchart	A diagram that illustrates data, information, and workflow by means of specialized symbols which, when connected by flow lines, portray the logic of a system or program.
Folder	Similar to the file jackets you use for your research assignments or those used in a filing cabinet to store documents [files]. A holding or storage area for data files on a disk.
Font	A family or collection of characters [letters, punctuation marks, numbers and special characters] of a particular size and style.
Formatting	Initialize the disk i.e. we prepare the disk for use.
Fourth generation	A computer programming language which allows the program to Language [4GL] specifics "what" is to be achieved rather than "how" it is to be achieved.
Gigabyte	The equivalent of one billion bytes.
Global Village	Refers to the society in which computers and people are linked within companies and between countries. It can also be regarded as an outgrowth of computer networks.
Half duplex	A transmission system that allows data to be transmitted in one direction at a time. That is the system can transmit and receive data but not at the same time.
Hard disk	A permanently installed, continuously spinning magnetic storage medium made

	up of one or more rigid disk platters. [Same as fixed disk or Winchester disk].
Hardware	The physical tangible parts that make up a computer system.
Home page	The file available for access at a World Wide Web site intended chiefly to greet visitors, provide information about the site, and direct them to other sites with more related information.
HTML	Hyper Text Markup Language. A mark-up language used to structure text and multimedia documents used extensively on the World Wide Web.
HTTP	Hyper Text Transfer Protocol. A protocol used to request and transmit files, especially Web pages and Web page components, over the Internet or other computer network.
Icon	Pictures used in place of words on a screen display.
Immediate access	The memory within the central processor. Also referred to as Storage internal use or main store.
Indexing	Creating a secondary file which contains pointers items in an associated database file and allows rapid location of records in the file.
Information	Data that have been collected and processed into meaningful form.
Information Retrieval	The process of retrieving specific information from data files.
Inherent addressing	The address mode in which the address fields are implied in the operation code.
Input	Data entered into a computer system for processing.
Integrated package	This package combines several applications in a suite of programs. Most of these packages combine a word processor; spreadsheet and database program. Data are shared easily between these integrated programs.
Intelligent terminal	A terminal that has built in memory and microprocessor which enables it to perform some processing in addition to the usual input and output functions.
Interactive processing	A processing system that allows "dialogue" between computer and user.
Internet	A global network that connects thousands of networks, multi-user computers and users in many countries.
I-Time	Instruction time. The elapsed time it takes to fetch and decode a computer instruction being executed.
Interpreter	A computer program which interactively translates and executes a source program without permanently storing any executable code.
Invoke	Process of starting up a program by using its name [or selecting its icon.
Joystick	An input device that uses a lever to control movement of the cursor or graphic images.
Justification	This is the adjustment of alignment of one or more lines of text with a

	particular margin e.g. alignment with the left margin, the right margin or both. The term justification often is used to refer to full justification of the alignment of text along both margins.
Keyboard	A device used for keying [typing] in data entry.
Key-to-disk	Keyboard of rapidly and accurately entering data into a computer via the keyboard as an input device.
Kilobyte	One thousand bytes.
LAN	Acronym for Local Area Network. A type of computer network where two or more computers are directly linked within a small area such as a room or building site. A common characteristic of this system is that computers are linked by direct cables rather than by telecommunication lines.
Light pen	A light-sensitive input device which when it touches the screen detects the presence or absence of light. It is used to select an entry or indicate a position.
Load	To transfer data or programs from secondary to primary storage.
Magnetic disk	A mylar [floppy disk] or metallic [hard disk] circular plate on which electronic data can be stored magnetically. Suitable for direct or random access data storage and retrieval.
Magnetic tape	A storage medium consisting of a flexible plastic strip of tape covered with magnetic material on one side, used to store date. It is available in spools or cassettes.
Mainframe	A large computer that can service many users simultaneously.
Mail-merge	A facility found in full-fledged word processing programs that draws information from a database, usually a mailing list, to print multiple copies of a document. Each copy contains some common text but each bearing different address.
Media	Materials on which data and instructions are stored as electromagnetic signals e.g. magnetic tapes, diskettes, CDs
Menu	A display with a list of processing choices from which a user may select.
Menu driven	The characteristics of a software program that provides the user with a menu.
Merge	The combination of two or more files on the basis of common field [key field]
MICR	Magnetic Ink Character Recognition
MIDI	Musical Instrument Digital Interface. A standard for representing musical information in a digital format.
Microsoft Disk Operating System	MS-DOS. A microcomputer operating system. An operating system is the software that controls the execution of all applications and system software.
Microcomputer	A small computer designed for use by an individual. [Also called a Micro or PC-Personal Computer].
Microfiche	An output medium consisting of microfilm sheets. Very high density storage can be attained using this method of storage.

Microfloppy disk	Refers to 3.5 inch floppy disks. They are housed in rigid plastic casting having a sliding shutter which automatically closes when the disk is removed from the disk drive.
Microprocessor	The processing component of a microcomputer.
Minicomputer	Mini. A mid-sized computer.
Modem	Acronym for modulator-demodulator. A device that converts signals from analogue to digital and vice versa. A model allows computers to exchange information through telephone lines.
Monitor	A television-like display for soft copy output in a computer system.
Mouse	A point-and-draw device, that when moved across a desktop pad a particular distance and direction, causes the same movement of the cursor on a screen.
Natural Language Processing	The use of the computer to understand and translate a natural language, like English, into commands to perform a given operation
Network	Two or more communicating devices that are connected electronically to form a system which shares information and resources.
Object code	Machine language program produced by a compiler.
On-line	A processing technique whereby terminals and other peripherals are connected to and controlled by the central processor. It provides the means for using computers on the basis of time sharing, on- line data input, interactive conversational-mode processing, random enquiries and for real-time processing.
Operating system	A set of programs that controls and supervise the resources of a computer system. It also acts as an interface between the user and the computer.
Output	Data transferred from RAM to an output device for processing.
Peripheral device	Any hardware other than the processor.
Plotter	An output device specially designed to produce a hard copy of graphical data.
Point of sale Terminal	A device that reads data at the source of a transaction [e.g. a supermarket checkout] and stores it for subsequent transmission directly to the computer system for processing.
Printer	A device specially designed to produce a hard copy of computer output.
Processing	Manipulating or handling data to produce information.
Processor	A logical component of the computer system that interprets and executes program instructions.
Protocol	A set of rules and procedures controlling the transmitting and receiving of data so that different devices can communicate with each other.
Pseudo code	A language consisting of English-like statements used to define algorithm.
Program	Computer instructions structured and ordered in a manner that, when executed, causes a computer to perform a particular function.
RAM	Random Access Memory. The memory area in which all programs and

	data must reside before programs can be executed or data manipulated. [Provides temporary storage for programs and data]. Also called primary memory/storage.
Record	A collection of fields on data related to one entity.
Register	A permanent location in the internal memory of a processor used for the temporary storage of data during processing operations.
Real-time	A processing mode in which the passage of real-time is critical to the application.
Resolution	A characteristic of a monitor's screen, determined by the number of pixels that can be displayed by it.
Retrieve	The process of recalling stored information for use.
ROM	Read Only Memory. Memory or storage area that can be read only, not written to. [Used to hold permanent instructions that your computer needs to get started].
Save/Store	The process of storing information for future uses.
Software	The programs/instructions used to direct the functions of a computer system.
Scrolling	The act of shifting the contents of the screen up or down. In upward scrolling the lines formerly appearing at the top of the screen are "scrolled away", those below are moved up and new lines of data which exist below those formerly on screen now come into view. In downward scrolling the reverse takes place. Scrolling usually proceeds a line at a time, [may be facilitated on some computers by use of a scroll-on/off key] in combination with up and down cursor movements. Scrolling may also be performed sideways to the left using left and right cursor movements.
Search	Process of locating data in a database file by reference to a key field[s] in the records.
Sector	A pie-shaped division of each disk track.
Simplex	A transmission system that allows data transfer in one direction only.
Sort	Redistribution of data into an order on the basis of the contents of a key item [sort-key]
Source-code	Program written in a given computer language.
Source document	A document used for the initial recording of data relating to business transactions. Very often source data needs to be converted into machine-readable form e.g. punched cards or paper tape, before it can be processed by a computer.
Spell-check	A directory feature associated with a word processor which allows the user to easily detect and correct errors in spelling. One can add new words to the directory so that the latter may grow with usage e.g. in WordPerfect, WordStar and Microsoft Word.
Structure chart	A pictorial representation of a system depicting the interrelationships between

	the modules of the system.
Structured walkthrough	Manual traversal of a model of a system
Super computer	The category that includes the largest and most powerful computers.
System	A set of arranged parts acting together to perform a function.
Syntax	A set of rules defining the structures of a computer program.
Telecommunication	The process of transmitting data between devices using transmission facilities such as telephone lines or microwave links.
TCP/IP	TCP/IP stands for Transmission Control Protocol. This is a common language used by computers on the Internet to communicate.
Telecommuting	A method of working where an off-site employ uses computer and a communication channel to communicate with the office computer.
Telemarketing	The employment of telephone lines and computers to market products and manage accounts.
Template	A specification of the number of fields and the kinds of data which fields in a database are allowed to hold.
Terminal	The combination of a monitor and keyboard to input and check data and to view output. A terminal does not necessarily include a processor.
Title	In a spreadsheet a group of rows or columns may be designated as a horizontal or vertical title respectively, which ensure that they always appear on the screen irrespective of where the cursor has moved in the spreadsheet.
Touch terminal	Also called a touch screen. A device that allows data to be input touching a screen with the finger or other object. The surface of the screen consists of a number of programmed touch points each of which may trigger a different action when selected by the user.
Track	The path on a tape, disk or drum on which data are stored. On a disk these paths are concentric circles; on a tape there are several tracks parallel to the edge of the tape; on a drum there are bands of equal size along the circumference of the drum.
Turnaround document	A document which, after being output by the computer, can be used to record data.
Two's complement	A method of representing numbers in which the computer does not perform subtraction in the normal way but inverts digits to be subtracted and adds to them.
Up-load document	Process of reading data from a user's computer storage and sending it to another computer via communication channel.
URL	Each page on the Web has a unique address called the Uniform Resource Locator [URL]
Usenet	Short for Users Network is the largest discussion forum in the world. Usenet allows people with common interest to communicate with one another.

Validation	A checking process in a program which is aimed at finding out if data is genuine. Validation should be carried out on any data that is entered from the keyboard, even when this simply a Y or N response.
Volatile memory	Solid-state semiconductor RAM in which the data are lost when the electrical current is turned off or interrupted.
Web page	A document on the World Wide Web, consisting of HTML file and any related files for scripts and graphics and often hyperlinked to other Web pages.
Web site	Set of interconnected Web pages, usually including a home page, generally located on the same server, and prepared and maintained as a collection of information by a person, group, or organization.
Web browser	A web browser is a programme that allows users to view and explore information on the World Wide Web. Examples of popular browsers are: Microsoft Internet Explorer and Netscape Navigator.
World Wide Web [WWW]	The World Wide Web commonly referred to as the 'Web', is a graphical easy-to-use system of inter-linked files on the Internet. Vast amounts of information can be obtained through the use of the 'Web'.
Window	A rectangular section of a display screen that is dedicated to a specific document, activity or application.

INDEX

I-Time · 331

J

Joystick · 331
Justification · 154, 331

K

Keyboard · 6, 0, 0, 20, 22, 67, 68,
85, 150, 151, 152, 332
Key-to-disk · 332
Kilobyte · 80, 332

L

LAN · 115, 116, 215, 332
Light pen · 332
Load · 332

M

Magnetic disk · 332
Magnetic tape · 332
Mail-merge · 332
Mainframe · 332
Media · 10, 17, 109, 110, 111, 296,
332
Menu · 332
Menu driven · 332
Merge · 146, 332
MICR · 332
Microcomputer · 333
Microfiche · 333
Microfloppy disk · 333
Microprocessor · 333
Microsoft Disk Operating System ·
41, 332
MIDI · 332
Minicomputer · 333
Modem · 10, 106, 333
Monitor · 9, 73, 86, 333
Mouse · 5, 6, 19, 25, 70, 85, 151,
152, 307, 333

N

Natural Language Processing · 333
Network · 11, 63, 66, 94, 115, 116,
332, 333, 336

O

Object code · 333
On-line · 333
Operating system · 33, 41, 333
Output · 8, 9, 59, 67, 72, 75, 76,
142, 241, 282, 333

P

Peripheral device · 333
Plotter · 9, 74, 86, 333
Point of sale Terminal · 334
Printer · 9, 73, 85, 272, 334
Processing · 5, 7, 9, 12, 34, 77, 87,
145, 161, 326, 327, 334
Processor · 5, 7, 8, 9, 12, 34, 67, 76,
147, 149, 327, 334
Program · 305, 334, 335
Protocol · 330, 334, 335
Pseudo code · 334

R

RAM · 60, 61, 82, 333, 334, 336
Real-time · 334
Record · 14, 207, 323, 334
Register · 62, 334
Resolution · 73, 334
Retrieve · 57, 334
ROM · 60, 61, 82, 83, 84, 327, 334

S

Save/Store · 334
Scrolling · 6, 26, 334
Search · 52, 93, 209, 243, 335
Sector · 335
Simplex · 335
Software · 5, 7, 11, 14, 15, 16, 17,
18, 33, 34, 62, 63, 64, 65, 66,

115, 124, 205, 206, 239, 240,
275, 276, 277, 278, 315, 334
Sort · 14, 191, 195, 196, 197, 226,
335
Source document · 335
Source-code · 335
Spell-check · 335
Structure chart · 335
Structured walkthrough · 335
Super computer · 335
Syntax · 174, 189, 192, 335
System · 7, 13, 14, 33, 49, 51, 52,
181, 191, 205, 328, 335

T

TCP/IP · 335
Telecommunication · 335
Telecommuting · 335
Telemarketing · 336
Template · 16, 18, 146, 242, 305,
336
Terminal · 9, 71, 336
Title · 14, 18, 148, 175, 207, 281,
301, 302, 318, 336
Touch terminal · 336
Track · 336
Turnaround document · 336

U

Up-load document · 336
URL · 95, 128, 129, 253, 336
Usenet · 336

V

Validation · 336
Volatile memory · 336

W

Web browser · 337
Web page · 99, 330, 336
Web site · 330, 337
Window · 6, 12, 14, 26, 147, 207,
258, 337
World Wide Web [WWW] · 337

www.ingramcontent.com/pod-product-compliance
Lightning Source LLC
Chambersburg PA
CBHW080352060326
40689CB00019B/3975